*"A Train is a Place That's Going Somewhere"*
—*CP Rail promotional brochure for the* Canadian

# THE AMERICAN PASSENGER TRAIN

## MIKE SCHAFER
### WITH JOE WELSH AND KEVIN HOLLAND

MBI Publishing Company

# DEDICATION

I would like to dedicate this book to author/editor and longtime friend Jim Boyd. Few people I have known during my first half-century-plus on this planet have had such a profound affect on me in terms of career direction and my passion for railroading—and the intertwining of both of those aspects of my life.

The railroading interest has been there as long as I can remember, but I had no clear-cut direction on how to manifest that interest other than to join the local model railroad club in my home town of Rockford, Illinois, which I did in 1963 at the age of almost 15. The following year, so did Jim.

That boisterous but affable 22-year-old, just out of photography school and now a newsroom photographer for one of the local TV stations, made quite an impression on all the club members, especially two of us younger punks—me and my best high-school railfan buddy, Parry Donze. The turning point was when, after the usual Friday night club procedures of trying to wire track, paint scenery backdrops (as a budding young artist, that was my job), and keep HO trains on the track, Jim would haul in his projector and begin showing his latest railroad slides to whomever cared to watch.

Parry and I were blown away. There was a real world out there beyond our hometown railroads (Illinois Central, Burlington, North Western, and Milwaukee Road), and quite obviously Jim knew all about it. Although I had taken crude, black & white, snapshot-type photos of trains as early as 1962, the color slide medium was a real eye-opener for me.

More so, I wanted to ditch the model trains and get out to learn about and experience real railroading, close up and first hand. Eventually, early in 1965, Jim lowered himself to the dredges of us know-it-all, smart-alecky 16-year-olds (which some of my friends say I still am) and promised to take us "railfanning" and show us the ropes of photography. He did this many, many times, and his infectious enthusiasm began to rub off on us, and suddenly I couldn't get enough of railroading and photography.

But Jim was more than a great railroad photographer; he was a published photographer and he had a bent for writing. It was Jim who first introduced me to the legendary *Trains* Magazine editor, David P. Morgan, in 1967, and it was Jim who urged me to consider doing writing and photography for the railroad press. Suddenly, I knew where I might find a future career (even though he neglected to mention how miserable it paid in terms of money).

At one point, Jim and I began collaborating on a book project. That particular book never did come to fruition; I went off to college while his career took an abrupt left turn, putting him into the Electro-Motive Division of General Motors as a locomotive field instructor. After that, he went to work for the Illinois Central. Just about the time I got out of college, landing a job in railroad-book publishing (with David P. Morgan as one of my bosses, ironically), he too landed a job in the railroad publishing field. I guess that's where we both belonged, because that's where we both still are.

And now, more than 35 years later, our respective careers have begun to more closely intertwine. Although we have yet to co-author a book per se, we have and do on many occasions help each other with various aspects of our own books, including Jim's companion book to this one, *The American Freight Train*.

Thanks, Jim; I wouldn't have traded this career for anything!

First published in 2001 by MBI Publishing Company, Galtier Plaza, Suite 200, 380 Jackson Street, St. Paul, MN 55101-3885 USA.

© Andover Junction Publications, 2001

Photography by Mike Schafer except as noted

Book design and editing by Mike Schafer, Andover Junction Publications, Lee, Illinois, and Blairstown, New Jersey. Layout assistance by Kevin J. Holland, type&DESIGN, Burlington, Ontario. Technical production by Jim Popson, Andover Junction Publications. Editorial assistant, Wendy Yegoiants.

Cover design by Tom Heffron, MBI Publishing Company.

The information in this book is true and complete to the best of our knowledge. All recommendations are made without any guarantee on the part of the authors or Publisher, who also disclaim any liability incurred in connection with the use of this data or specific details. We recognize that some words, model names, and designations, for example, mentioned herein are the property of the trademark holder. We use them for identification purposes only. This is not an official publication.

MBI Publishing books are also available at discounts in bulk quantity for industrial or sales-promotional use. For details, write to Special Sales Manager at Motorbooks International

Wholesalers & Distributors, Galtier Plaza, Suite 200, 380 Jackson Street, St. Paul, MN 55101-3885 USA.

Library of Congress Cataloging-in-Publication data available

ISBN: 0-7603-0896-9

**Front cover:** Delaware & Hudson Railroad's southbound *Laurentian* sweeps along the New York shoreline of Lake Champlain on a summer day in 1968. For decades, the *Laurentian* provided a scenic link between Montreal, Quebec, and New York City, as a joint operation of D&H and New York Central, the latter forwarding the *Laurentian*'s through cars between Albany and Grand Central Terminal in Manhattan. Powering this day's train is one of D&H's four "new" Alco PA-type passenger diesels—long considered one of the most attractive passenger diesels ever designed. To spruce up its passenger service, in 1967 the D&H acquired surplus PAs (from the Santa Fe) and lightweight coaches and buffet-lounges (from Rio Grande)—a move that raised eyebrows in an era of severe decline in U.S. passenger-train service. JIM SHAUGHNESSY

**Frontispiece:** Children aboard a New York Central train are about to set out on every kid's dream adventure in the 1950s: a train ride. New York Central, courtesy Bob Yanosey, Morning Sun Books.

**Title page:** A sense of pride still emanated from Pennsylvania Railroad's *Broadway Limited* as it made its grand exit from Chicago on a late summer afternoon in 1967. The locomotives and cars had been washed to a shine, and the all-Pullman train for Pittsburgh, Philadelphia, and New York would probably be right on time the following morning into Manhattan. But the pomp and circumstance of this great streamliner clattering across the "diamonds" (crossings) of the Chicago & Western Indiana, Illinois Central, and Santa Fe hid the truth: in just a few short months, the *Broadway* would be combined with its coach-and-Pullman running mate, the *General*, and no longer be an all-private-room train. Fortunately, the *Broadway Limited* would be one of the few lucky liners to survive into Amtrak, lasting for almost another 30 years after this photo was taken.

**Back cover, upper photo:** Chicago & North Western train No. 13, the day local between Chicago and Omaha, Nebraska, charges across the Iowa countryside near Boone on October 10, 1953. Although streamlined trains had become relatively common by this time, steam-powered "heavyweight" trains like this still provided yeoman service on rail routes throughout North America. SANDY GOODRICK

**Back cover, lower photo:** Amtrak's *Southwest Chief* highballs through the desert near Wagon Mound, New Mexico, in September 1999. The new GE Genesis-type locomotives contrast with the 1920s-era semaphore signals on Burlington Northern Santa Fe's main line over Raton Pass. TOM KLINE; CHIEF BAGGAGE DECAL, MIKE MCBRIDE COLLECTION

**End paper:** The Baltimore & Ohio was among the very first American railways to handle passengers, in 1830. Little more than 100 years after the first B&O passenger train rolled between Baltimore and Ellicotts Mills, Maryland, the railroad's esteemed *Capitol Limited* steams across Thomas Viaduct near Baltimore, Maryland, en route from Chicago to Jersey City, New Jersey. H. W. PONTIN, HERBERT H. HARWOOD COLLECTION

Printed in Hong Kong

ILLINOIS CENTRAL
*Main Line of Mid-America*

# Acknowledgments

Writing (and designing) books about passenger trains has long been a dream of mine, and *The American Passenger Train* represents the third time this dream has come true (for the record, the first was *Classic American Streamliners* and the second a small companion book, *Streamliner Memories*). But there is no way I could have done a project of this magnitude by myself. That's why readers will see many different names throughout this volume.

First, I'd like to thank longtime friend and fellow passenger train aficionado Joe Welsh, who authored most of text of chapter 6 and a goodly part of chapter 7, and then helped proofread the entire book (under the usual impossible time constraints); thanks are also due to Joe for sharing his remarkable collection of train brochures and folders. I

first worked with Joe back in the 1980s when I was editor of the late, lamented *Passenger Train Journal*, and I was elated to discover his enthusiastic talents. Not only is Joe an excellent passenger-train historian, but he is also a professional in the field of contemporary rail passenger service.

Next, I would like a round of applause for Kevin Holland for his authorship and layout of chapter 4. For quite awhile, I've been looking for an individual who has the rare combination of being a railway historian, writer, and designer to help with my company's many ongoing book projects. Short of cloning myself—which, even if it were scientifically possible, I (and certainly my friends and relatives) would not at all recommend—Kevin was the perfect choice, and a passenger-train devotee at that. Kevin is another fellow I met while editing *PTJ* in the 1980s, although only recently I discovered he was an artisan, too.

Another longtime friend of mine, Bill Howes, generously provided a splendid selection of historical photos from his archive of Baltimore & Ohio illustrations, as well as much insight on various rail passenger matters and additional assistance with proofreading the book. With Bill's background as a former director of The Pullman Company and Director of Passenger Services for the affiliated Chesapeake & Ohio-Baltimore & Ohio, his insight and assistance was especially meaningful.

To all the photographers represented herein, I want to give special thanks, for without your artistic eye, this book would be considerably less colorful: Forrest Becht, John J. Becht, Ed Birch, Jim Boyd, Alan Bradley, Warren Calloway, Barry A. Carlson, John Dziobko, Sandy Goodrick, Phil Gosney, Joe Greenstein, Scott Hartley, Jim Heuer, Kevin Holland, Glen Icanberry, Tom Kline, John Leopard, Alex Mayes, Al McClelland, Ron McDonald, Joe McMillan, Jim Neubauer, Terry Norton, Bob Schmidt, Jim Shaughnessy, Brian Solomon, and Martin S. Zak.

Similarly, I would also like to thank the following people and organizations who shared items from their photo and illustrative collections: Bernice Argo (for the Preston George photos, through Terry LaFrance), Phil & Bev Birk, Bill Caloroso (Cal's Classics), Ed Crist (for Robert F. Collins photos), Art Danz, Ron Flanary, Dave Ingles, Oliver D. Joseph, Bill Kratville (Union Pacific Museum Collection), Mike McBride, Milwaukee Road Historical Association, C. W. Newton, David P. Oroszi, Bob's Photo, Chuck Porter, William A. Raia, *Railfan & Railroad* Magazine, Steve Smedley, Jay Williams (Big Four Graphics), Robert Yanosey, and Kevin Zollars.

On other fronts, still more people deserve my gratitude. I would like to thank Mitch Markovitz for sharing some of his stellar art-

work (page 52), as he has with earlier book and magazine projects. Thanks also go to Cliff Black at Amtrak, Bob Johnston, Tom Halterman, and Craig Willett for their suggestions and help with matters relating to contemporary rail passenger subjects.

Closer to home, I would like to thank Jim Popson, another longtime friend, railroad aficionado, and our company's production technician. Also, my cousins Paul and Mark Magnuson played a big role in assisting with the production of this book, as did my business partner and good friend (except when I'm running late on a book project), Steve Esposito. More thanks—this time to Tanya Anderson at our Blairstown, New Jersey, office and to Wendy Yegoiants, our new editorial assistant at our Illinois production office. Wendy has been learning fast about railroad lingo and authors obsessed with whether the Choctaw Rocket terminated at Amarillo or Tucumcari (honest, Joe; I could have sworn it was Tucumcari). And thanks, too, go to Erik Rasmussen for help in gathering photos.

To all of you, many, many thanks. One of the best dining-car meals I ever had was aboard the dome dining car of Union Pacific's *City of Los Angeles*, and if that train and its incomparable dome diner were still running, I'd treat you all to dinner. (But, since it's not, would you settle for a cup of that excellent Green Mountain coffee on the *Acela Express*?)

—*Mike Schafer, Andover Junction Publications*

Mike Schafer was born to write this book. He was four years old in 1953 when he rode his first passenger train and remembers to this day having bacon and eggs for breakfast in the diner of the Illinois Central's *Hawkeye* en route from Rockford to Chicago. By age 15 in 1964, he was venturing out to ride and photograph the passenger trains that had become his passion. I was a few years older and got to know Mike about that time when I moved to his hometown of Rockford, Illinois. I had a job, a driver's license, a car, and similar railroad interests, and Mike and I became good friends. Often along with our mutual friends, we made many weekend trips into the Chicago area and elsewhere, photographing trains (photo). My interests ran more toward locomotives and freight trains, but Mike made sure that the passenger trains got equal attention.

Chicago in the mid-1960s was a railroad wonderland, even though I didn't fully appreciate it at the time, lamenting as I did, the almost total loss of steam locomotives. But Chicago's railroads were numerous and colorful, with an incredible variety of motive power. While I tended to be drawn to the roundhouses, engine terminals, and freight yards, Mike would pester me to get lineside for the predictably scheduled passenger trains. Thanks to his persistence, I have a lot of passenger train photos that I would probably not have otherwise.

It would be literally decades before I would appreciate the subtleties of those "window trains." In the 1960s, I could tell a baggage car from a boattail observation car, but that was about the extent of my passenger car appreciation (and to me a "baggage car" could be anything from a storage car to an Railway Post Office, and it would be a long

time before I would appreciate the difference between the Milwaukee Road's parlor versus sleeper versions of its dramatic Skytop observation cars). Mike seemed to have an instinct for that stuff, even as a teenager.

We both managed to turn our railroad interests into careers. I went to work for a locomotive builder (Electro-Motive Division of General Motors), while Mike went to art school and got a job as a book editor and layout artist for Kalmbach Publishing Company in Milwaukee. A short time later I moved to New Jersey and went to work for a publisher myself, Carstens Publications. In 1974 I became editor of *Railfan* Magazine, and in 1980 Mike went to work with Kevin P. Keefe for *Passenger Train Journal*, initially serving as the art director for PTJ Publishing Company and then becoming *Passenger Train Journal*'s editor in 1983.

Mike had ridden and photographed passenger trains in their last glory years, and I felt sorry for someone who had to edit a magazine about passenger trains in the post-1971 Amtrak era. Mike did an excellent job of enthusiastically reporting on Amtrak's struggling years while presenting issue after issue of stories and documentation on the great trains and streamliners of the recently departed past. His distinctive style of magazine layout made the subjects attractive and colorful (and I confess that I simply copied his style in *Railfan* on more than one occasion).

So as you go through this book, you are riding with Mike on the journey that has been his life's dream and reality over the years. All aboard!
—*Jim Boyd*
*Crandon Lakes, New Jersey*
*August 30, 2001*

## STUDENTS AT CLASS: PASSENGER TRAIN OPERATION 101

It's shortly before noon on a miserably damp January day in 1967 at the former Wabash Railroad station in Decatur, Illinois. On hand are five onlookers (including the photographer who is, of course, out of the scene), observing the mechanics of how to split one passenger train—the combined *Blue Bird* and *Wabash Cannon Ball* from St. Louis—into two. Norfolk & Western crews are hustling as they position the locomotives that will continue the separated trains on to Chicago and Detroit, respectively, once they have been refueled. Intently watching the proceedings, from left to right, are future Amtrak engineer and manager Craig Willett, author Schafer, Randy Imfeld, and future editor/author Jim Boyd. MIKE MCBRIDE; PLAYING CARDS AND TICKETS, MIKE SCHAFER COLLECTION

# INTRODUCTION

Why on earth would someone who has dined in the Turquoise Room on Santa Fe's *Super Chief,* watched as a red carpet was rolled out for passengers boarding New York Central's *20th Century Limited,* snoozed away the night between crisp sheets and under a warm blanket in a Pullman on Louisville & Nashville's *Humming Bird,* and absorbed the historic beauty of the Potomac River from the Superliner Lounge of Amtrak's delightful *Capitol Limited* want to christen the unremarked, hand-me-down conveyance at left as his all-time favorite passenger train?

Well, for one thing, Illinois Central's *Hawkeye*—shown at 21st Street Junction on the final approach to Chicago's Central Station in 1966—is, for me, the train that started it all. Having made it known to all family members at a very early age that I was "railroad aware," my mother made it a point to take me on my first train ride as soon as she felt I was old enough to appreciate such an event. And so, in the dark, early morning hours on the day after Thanksgiving 1953, I was awakened by my mother with a surprise: she was taking my sister and me to Chicago on the train. I bolted out of bed and was dressed and ready to go in nano-seconds.

Fast forward an hour or so to the Illinois Central depot on South Main Street in Rockford, Illinois. It's closing in on 5:20 A.M., and it's still very dark outside. We're on the station platforms with quite a crowd of other people anticipating the arrival of IC train 12 from Sioux City, Iowa.

A horn in the distance, and soon after a headlight glow. The gateman in a tiny, elevated shanty next to South Main rings a gong and the black-and-white-striped gates descend. The *Hawkeye* sweeps into the station, horn blasting. I scream with the delicious kind of terror that tykes thrive on when they know everything's really in the name of fun, and then we board the big steel cars.

It's still dark outside—what an adventure to be up this early!—when we enter the crowded dining car for breakfast. Imagine actually eating on a train, bacon and eggs and all. All too soon, the blustery dark gives way to the gray light of a cloudy November morning. Tracks are everywhere outside the window as the *Hawkeye* makes a staccato march across a million other tracks. (Many years later, I would deduce this memory vignette to be No. 12 crossing the Chicago & Western Indiana and Pennsylvania Railroad mains at 21st Street, right about where I took the photo at left.)

Shortly, the *Hawkeye* was wending its way between tall buildings, and then it descended a ramp track into the biggest railroad station I had ever seen. "*Twelfth Street— Central Station—End of the line! This is as far as we go!*" the conductor blurted out as he hurried down the aisles.

A kind of controlled chaos ensued as passengers began standing up, gathering their belongings, and pressing toward the vestibules. Once on the platform, we moved with the crowd toward the front of the train. Passengers with reason to go into the depot climbed stairs, but those of us heading straight to Michigan Avenue were directed to cross the station tracks and head right onto 12th Place. This was another scary venture for me, as there were locomotives—all diesels—moving about.

After a day in the Loop, during which my mom bought me a little wind-up *Train of Tomorrow* floor toy (boy, I wonder what *those* are worth today!), we returned to Rockford on the streamliner *Land O' Corn*. I had been big on railroads before this trip, but now I was hooked more than ever.

Most subsequent rail trips to Chicago involved the *Land O' Corn* (although I recall seeing the line's third passenger train, the *Iowan*, on several occasions, its "reverse" schedule was not conducive to making day trips to Chicago; the *Iowan* was dropped in 1957), but in November 1961 I renewed my acquaintance with the *Hawkeye* when my sister, then 19, and I, then almost 13, went into Chicago the day after Thanksgiving (this post-Thanksgiving day venture into the Loop for Christmas shopping is still a ritual for Midwesterners). Now being more railroad aware than ever, this trip seemed to be a turning point for me, and I became more intensively interested in railroading in general and passenger trains in particular.

By the mid-1960s, a longtime school friend of mine, Parry Donze, who was also into railroads, and I had made it almost a nightly ritual to hike down to the IC tracks at 11th Street on the east side of Rockford to watch either (or both) the *Land O' Corn* or the *Hawkeye* make their grand entrance into town from Chicago around 6:30 and 9:30 P.M. respectively. We found the *Hawkeye*'s late night arrival westbound particularly intriguing, not only for the mystique of watching a night sleeper train, but for the fascinating array of equipment. The *Hawkeye* of 1964 was still very much a holdover from the steam-era: heavyweight baggage cars, a working Railway Post Office (through which, when No. 12 was making its station stop, I used to mail my Christmas cards so they would be postmarked "CHI & SIOUX CITY RPO"), express boxcars, at least two heavyweight coaches, and a streamlined 6-section, 6-roomette, 4-double bedroom Pullman sleeper (usually *Banana Road* or *Petroleum*, both originally built in 1942 for *Panama Limited* service). Powering the train, almost invariably, were a pair of "passengerized" Electro-Motive GP9 freight locomotives, either the 9200 and 9203 or the 9201 and 9202—all four of them constituting IC's fleet of high-speed passenger "geeps" (pronounce that with a "j" sound). Although some readers of this book may consider non-streamlined locomotives pulling passenger trains to be heresy, we thought these functional locomotives had kind of a blue-collar look appropriate to a work-a-day train like the *Hawkeye*. After all, here were totally non-pretentious diesels, painted a somber black, that could quickly accelerate the *Hawkeye* to sustained speeds of nearly 85 MPH—and they would do every bit of this if No. 12 were a bit late leaving Rockford early in the morning for Chicago.

Since the *Hawkeye* was the train most people along IC's Iowa Division utilized to make connections in Chicago with other trains (the *Land O' Corn* being more of a "shoppers' train"), consists swelled markedly during holiday periods, especially Thanksgiving and Christmas. Two RPOs

became the norm as well as extra head-end cars for storage mail and express. The number of coaches grew from the usual two or three to six or seven, and on some occasions I recall seeing two sleepers. Although the dining car I had eaten in during my first trip had disappeared more than a decade earlier, IC occasionally added a buffet-lounge to the train when passenger loadings were particularly heavy, such as the westbound trip the day before Thanksgiving.

By 1965, we were on our own when making rail trips to Chicago, and we often used the *Hawkeye* and the *Land O' Corn* in one direction or the other. Without mothers, grandmothers, or sisters along to plot the day's itinerary, our routine changed from wandering the halls of Marshall Field's department store to strolling the platforms at Chicago Union Station, La Salle Street Station, North Western Terminal, or Grand Central Station (Dearborn being the only depot adamant about not letting tripod-laden teens onto the platforms, but they at least let

us peer through the gates).

Chicago was where the *Hawkeye* and *Land O' Corn* delivered me so that I could satisfy my insatiable thirst for knowledge of passenger trains outside of Rockford. Here in the Windy City we could see great domeliners boarding for the West Coast, the stately *20th Century Limited* awaiting departure for New York City, and a raft of funky trains of which we'd only been vaguely aware: Pennsy's day local—a remnant of the *Red Bird*—to and from Cincinnati; B&O's *Washington Express*; Erie Lackawanna's *Lake Cities*; Grand Trunk Western's *International Limited*; the joint IC-NYC *Indianapolis Special*. After a day of hoofing about Chicago, sometimes venturing out to places like Englewood station, Joliet, Hammond, or closer in at 16th Street tower or famous 21st Street Junction to see arriving and departing trains (title page), the *Hawkeye* would hurry our exhausted bodies home.

As early as 1963 I had begun riding other railroads and other trains. In April of that year, I rode a steam-powered schoolkid special on the Burlington out of Rockford, and that summer I rode my first commuter train: a short jaunt on the Chicago & North Western between Lake Geneva and Williams Bay, Wisconsin.

I loved my old "friends," the *Hawkeye* and the *Land O' Corn*, but I wanted to learn more about other passenger trains. In March 1964, four of us high-schoolers rode Mil-

waukee Road's *Arrow* from Davis Junction (near Rockford) to Chicago and the fabled Rock Island out to Joliet, riding in in 1920s-era, open-window commuter coaches behind a jostling, smoking Alco road-switcher. We returned to Chicago on Rock Island's *Aerotrain*, then serving in suburban service, and then back to Rockford on the *Hawkeye*.

The big trip for me in 1965 was a church-sponsored convention train from Chicago to Miami—one of my ten best rail trips ever. By this time, though, it was becoming alarmingly clear to me that the passenger train was in deep trouble—a point that would become especially poignant when the *Land O' Corn* was discontinued in 1967. I vowed to at least sample anything and everything within my paltry means. Usually traveling with fellow railroad buddies, I soon found myself aboard the likes of GM&O's *Midnight Special*, C&NW's *Flambeau "400"*, Monon's *Thoroughbred*, Burlington's *Black Hawk*, NYC's *Fifth Avenue-Cleveland Limited*, MP's *Missourian*, Milwaukee Road's *Southwest Limited* remnant, New Haven's *Merchants Limited*, Southern's *Royal Palm*, and countless commuter trains. All the while, I grew ever more appreciative of the ambiance of rail travel and all that it encompassed.

My world all came crashing down when, on the evening of April 30, 1971, I boarded Milwaukee Road-UP's final westbound "City of Everywhere" (which is what we were calling the combined *City of Los Angeles/City of San Francisco/Challenger/City of Denver/City of Portland*) at Chicago Union Station for a farewell dinner trip to Savanna, Illinois. The following morning, I rode my beloved *Hawkeye* into Central Station—and history—for the last time. (Almost a year later, through an interesting set of circumstances, I would become the last passenger to detrain from a scheduled intercity passenger train at Central Station.)

Fortunately, the world of passenger trains didn't end with Amtrak's arrival. Rather, it turned out to be a new beginning. In the 30 years since that fateful May 1, 1971, I have enjoyed countless train trips—intercity and commuter—and some of my best times aboard the rails ever. And I would witness things that, on April 30, 1971, I never would have believed could happen: the resurrection of the *California Zephyr*, *Capitol Limited*, and even passenger train service to Rockford in the form of Amtrak's *Black Hawk*; the development, construction, and delivery of brand-new passenger locomotives and rolling stock; and then, finally, 150-MPH "bullet" trains for the U.S.

As a sat in my super-comfortable first-class seat on Amtrak's *Acela Express* on July 6, 2001, cruising at near 150-MPH speeds along the beautiful Connecticut coast, I mulled over my passenger train events of the previous 48 years while making notes for the final work on this book. There's a story to be told about the American passenger train, its history and operations, its trials and tribulations, and even its uncertain future. Though a plenitude of fortunate events, which include the meeting of many lifelong friends and associates, I'm able to help tell that story in *The American Passenger Train*. Climb aboard and enjoy the ride.
—*Mike Schafer*

# The American Passenger Train Is Born and Raised: 1829–1900

Like a lot of things in nineteenth century America, the concept of rail transport was "imported" from England. Since the late 1700s, tramways—small fixed-guideway, horse-powered transport systems dedicated to moving a single commodity short distances—had been used to transport bulk items like coal and rock in the confines of a quarry or mining area.

The inherent efficiency of moving heavy items on vehicles connected together that followed a track did not go unnoticed, and early in the 1800s tramway operations in England began to spread. Now, not only were commodities being moved about within a quarry or mine complex, but also *between* those quarries and mines and nearby waterways, where the commodity could be transloaded into boats. The boats then floated the commodities to populated areas for distribution.

Americans had been independent of England for more than a quarter century as the 1800s got under way, but the influence of England on America remained strong indeed. So, in the 1820s, small rail-related operations began to emerge in isolated areas of the original 13 colonies. One of these operations was large enough to be a concern unto itself: the two-mile Granite Railway of Quincy, Massachusetts, a rock-hauling line opened in 1826 and generally acknowledged to be America's first commercial railroad.

### THE FIRST SCHEDULED PASSENGER TRAIN

ABOVE: Baltimore & Ohio's replica *Tom Thumb* locomotive is shown during a 1977 exhibition. The real *Tom Thumb* pulled the first scheduled passenger train in America in May 1830. JIM BOYD

### CIVIL WAR SURVIVOR

LEFT: Made famous by its role in the Civil War following an 1862 Union raid and subsequent "great locomotive chase" on the Western & Atlantic, the *General* was preserved and operated by the Louisville & Nashville a century later. The locomotive and a "Jim Crow" (segregated) passenger car are shown on tour in the summer of 1963, moving on the New York Central near Springfield, Ohio. During the *General's* commemorative runs early in the 1960s, folks got a rare glimpse of railroading the way it was in the nineteenth century. W. ALLEN MCCLELLAND

## FROM LITTLE ACORNS . . .

The tremendous strides taken in the evolution of the American passenger train during its first 110 years is vividly portrayed in this 1947 view at Baltimore & Ohio's Camden Station in Baltimore, Maryland. A short passenger train typical of the 1830s headed by B&O's *Lafayette* steam locomotive is dwarfed by the new General Motors/Pullman-Standard *Train of Tomorrow* during the latter's nationwide exhibition tour. The two trains are a world apart except for one thing: both feature "high-level" seating. Carriages on the 1837 train featured upper-level seats; so did the 1947 train, in the form of domes. BALTIMORE & OHIO, WILLIAM F. HOWES JR. COLLECTION

But, who was the first rail passenger in America? Probably some anonymous mine or quarry worker who hopped a ride on a moving tramcar to save a few steps—and whose identity has been lost to antiquity. What is known is this: The mule-and-gravity-powered Summit Hill–Mauch Chunk Railroad opened in eastern Pennsylvania in 1827, and the Delaware & Hudson Canal Company—whose canal system included rail segments operated by gravity and cable—opened in 1828. Both lines were built to haul coal, but both lines began to also carry "real" (that is, paying) passengers in 1829, although the passengers might have been riding more for pleasure than to get from Point A to Point B to visit Aunt Kate. (As an interesting aside, the Mauch Chunk operation is considered by some historians to be America's first roller coaster ride.) The Baltimore & Ohio—chartered in 1827 and considered America's first operating common-carrier railroad—carried its first passengers (and freight) in January 1830.

The distinction between "common-carrier" and "other" is important. A common-carrier is a transportation company that has been mandated or authorized, often by a government entity, to operate for public and commerce. Although a common-carrier may be of the private sector, it is obligated to accept passengers and/or goods or commodities to be transported, upon payment of an established fee or tariff.

Not well known is the fact that a relatively comprehensive system of paved roads and canals had already been established in the Eastern U.S. by the time these first railroads and their passenger trains appeared late in the 1820s.

Destined to become the nemesis of the passenger train a century hence, improved roads—often called turnpikes—had quickly evolved in New England, New York, and Pennsylvania following the War of 1812. By the time the first U.S. railroads mentioned earlier were chartered, the State of Pennsylvania already had well over a thousand miles of paved road, while New York sported over 4,000. The Congressionally mandated National Road was in 1806; early passenger trains were still a novelty early in the 1830s when this road reached Ohio.

Canals, too, had acquired a substantial following. The most famous of all U.S. manmade waterways, the 364-mile Erie Canal linking Albany and Buffalo, New York, was begun in 1817 and completed in 1825. But canals often froze over in the winter months, and roads were likewise vulnerable to weather: there was still only so much weight—freight or passenger—that a team of horses pulling wagons could move over these early roads. However, once the steam locomotive appeared on American soil in the late 1820s, unveiling the tremendous potential of rail transport, a sweeping change began.

It began in small steps. In January 1830, when the fledgling B&O completed its first mile and a half of track, it sold one-way tickets for 9 cents to ride the line on horse-drawn cars. In May of that year, B&O operated the first scheduled rail passenger service, between Baltimore and Ellicotts Mills, Maryland. At the end of that year, on the South Carolina Canal & Transportation Company—a future component road of the Southern Railway—the first locomotive-hauled passenger train carried 141 passengers for six miles. On August 9, 1831, a passenger train of New York Central predecessor Mohawk & Hudson steamed along on its first journey between Albany and Schenectady. By 1833, on New Jersey's Camden & Amboy Railroad & Transportation Company—a predecessor line of the Pennsylvania Railroad—passengers could rocket along the 80-odd miles between Jersey City and Philadelphia in seven hours behind the *John Bull* or one of its sister engines. Fare: three dollars—pricey, but well worth the speed and comfort in deference to a careening stagecoach ride.

The frail, new conveyances on the likes of the B&O, M&H, and SCC&T, providing then what were probably almost whimsical trips, were the precursors to today's *Capitol Limited, Crescent, Lake Shore Limited, Acela Express*—and countless other rail-bound liners that would bind the continent for the next 170-plus years. The public and shippers were captivated by the new form of transportation, which quickly ascended to prominence. In 1833, for example, the B&O—now having reached nearly 80 miles to Harpers Ferry, West Virginia, with a branch to Washington, D.C.—carried nearly 100,000 passengers that year. In 1834, the 394-mile, state-sponsored Main Line of Public Works—a combination railway, canal, and incline-plane system that was to pave the way for one of the greatest railroads in American history—opened between Philadelphia and Pittsburgh. This new transportation artery shortened the passenger travel time between those two cities from some 20 days to less than five. Nonetheless, in 1846, the State authorized the charter of the Pennsylvania Railroad, which would soon replace the MLofPW with an all-rail route and ultimately become one of the largest operators of passenger trains in America until its demise in 1968. In a similar vein, the fledgling collection of railroads that formed an all-rail route between Albany and Buffalo finally overcame canal interests and in 1853 consolidated as the New York Central, sealing the fate of the parallel Erie Canal—if not the future of canals in general. Coordinated through-car service between Albany and Buffalo had already commenced a dozen years earlier.

During the infancy of American railroading, the distinction between freight and passenger trains was often blurred, as commodities and passengers often were carried aboard a single train. As business grew—and generally freight traffic grew at a faster pace than passenger—separate freight and passenger trains became the rule, with passenger trains operating on published schedules. The boom in rail transport prompted the formation of several companies in the 1840s whose business was solely devoted to locomotive and railcar construction. Locomotives and passenger cars took on an evolution of their own.

Initially, passenger-carrying trains were such a novelty—and astonishingly speedy—that travelers were willing to put up with the inherent discomforts of early, crude rolling stock and the sometimes cantankerous locomotives that pulled them. However, as railroads flourished, passengers became more discriminating, demanding greater comfort, speed, and service.

By 1840 there were some 3,000 miles of track laid in the U.S., most of it east of the Appalachians. A decade later, this amount had tripled as railroads pushed the frontier west toward the Missouri River, and when the Civil War began, there were nearly 30,000 miles of track! During this period, countless new railroads were born—including some that would become some of the most recognized carriers in American railroad history. Meanwhile, many proposed companies were stillborn while others bounded to life, only to collapse into bankruptcy. Still others were swallowed up by larger companies through merger or outright purchase.

For the prospective passenger, this produced a bonanza of options for getting around an adolescent America that was rapidly heading for the Pacific Coast as civil war erupted between North and South in 1861. But it also meant a barrage of headaches. Schedules between the neophyte companies rarely interlocked with those of connecting carriers, which could mean overnight stays in the squalor of hostelries at cities where various railroads converged. Further, competition between railroads had resulted in a misfit transportation network. Many companies built their railroads to their own track gauges (distance between rails), precluding the operation of through cars handled by even "friendly" connections, and a change of trains at connecting points could result in chaos for the passenger. For example, into the late 1800s, travelers en route from Washington, D.C., to New Jersey had to

## MIXED FREIGHT AND PASSENGER

The afternoon train between Cobleskill and Cherry Valley, New York, on the Delaware & Hudson pauses at the Seward station in 1875. In this era, trains were simply trains, and it was not unusual to find a mixture of freight and passenger cars strung together in one consist, especially on lightly trafficked lines. In time, freight was separated from passenger operations, and passengers got their own train with a schedule more tailored to their travel needs. DELAWARE & HUDSON, JIM SHAUGHNESSY COLLECTION

## WATCH YOUR STEP

Mishaps like this were almost a way of life in the early days of railroading, before safety signal systems and standardized rules. On September 23, 1865, the consist for the Rutland & Washington's night sleeper train to Rutland, Vermont, was being moved from the yards to the Troy, New York, station for boarding when the engineer overlooked the fact that the railway bridge over the Hudson River had been opened to let a steamboat pass. Engine *Jay Gould* and one car hit the drink, but there were no fatalities. COLLECTION OF GERALD M. BEST, COURTESY JIM SHAUGHNESSY

endure an awkward, plodding, horse-powered streetcar trip through Baltimore to bridge the gap between the Baltimore & Ohio and the Philadelphia, Wilmington & Delaware railroads.

The serious implications of not being able to transfer cars—freight or passenger—freely between many of the railroads was driven home by the Civil War (1861–1866), which forced them to cooperate or lose the battle. After the hostilities, 4-feet 8½ inches was adopted as the standard gauge for nearly all U.S. and Canadian railways. In that war, railroads proved to be particularly strategic as they handled another type of "passenger"—soldiers. Railroads played a critical role in deploying troops in the Civil War and would do so again during wars to come.

With the Civil War behind them, American railroads refocused on the goal of reaching the West Coast. On July 1, 1862, President Abraham Lincoln signed the Pacific Railway Bill, authorizing the Union Pacific and Central Pacific railroads to complete a transcontinental line between Omaha, Nebraska, and California. One of the most well-known events of American railroad history, this line was completed at Promontory, Utah, on May 10, 1869. A coast-to-coast trip that had taken months only a few years earlier now was reduced to a few days. Other transcon routes opened soon afterward, and the need for more passenger trains grew rapidly.

As a plethora of new railroads and expanding established carriers built a spiderweb of lines that would become the tapestry of an industrialized America, competition between carriers heated up in the post-Civil War period as each vied for a share of the traffic pie, passenger and freight. Austere, stifling (or freezing), wooden-benched, boxes-on-wheels were out as the accepted conveyance; in their place were new—and increasingly elegant—passenger cars with gas lighting, cushioned seating, and improved heating and ventilation. The sleeping car had made its debut several years before the Civil War, and about the time that war got under way, sleeping-car operating companies began to emerge. After the war, a myriad of companies, including the most famous—the Pullman Palace Car Company (chapter 3)—were dispatching cars full of snoozing patrons all over the country, attached to various carriers' regularly scheduled passenger trains.

The remainder of the nineteenth century was marked by the spectacular growth of a number of railroads—often through questionable business practices involving rate wars, watered stock options, and outright swindling. Such was the "rail baron" era of American railroading, a time when some of railroading's most notorious names—Cornelius "Commodore" Vanderbilt, Jay Gould, and others—were indelibly etched into the history books. The shenanigans of these high-profile players prompted strict governmental controls that would haunt American railroading for the next century, including the 1887 formation of a regulatory body known as the Interstate Commerce Commission (ICC). The fate of many of a passenger train would be determined by the sweeping hand of the ICC in the late 1950s and 1960s.

Despite such new controlling forces, the 1880s were kind to the passenger train. For example, this decade saw the development of railroad dining and lounge cars. Prior to

this, passengers were obliged to carry their own provisions aboard the train or eat at extended "meal stop" stations, tangling with a hundred other passengers at the depot restaurant in a rush to down a sandwich and coffee before the train resumed its journey. Coupled to advances in passenger-train technology, including electric lighting, enclosed vestibules (facilitating car-to-car passage), steam heating (eliminating the dangers of stove heating), automatic air-brake systems, and coil-spring trucks (wheel assemblies), these new cars meant that passenger trains had truly become "a place that was going somewhere," complete with all the comforts of home.

Concurrent to these developments of locomotive and passenger rolling stock, the railroads themselves were revamping their infrastructure. Heavier rails allowed carriers to accommodate larger, heavier cars—and at higher speeds. The manual-block system of train control together with the telegraph, which had become a widely accepted means of dispatching trains by this time, permitted safe, higher-speed movement of trains.

Passenger trains could now be tailored to certain duties in designated markets and began to take on lives of their own. Specific car types were now being assigned to specific runs, and the naming—and marketing—of trains began to catch on, with railroads touting the features of their premier flyers, be they in terms of accommodations or schedules. It is said that in 1876, the Pennsylvania became the first railroad to introduce the term "limited," as applied to fast passenger trains with a minimal number of scheduled stops. "Limited" could also mean limited accommodations, in the sense of first-class only—i.e., no riff-raff, please. Limited and its cousin term, "express," are still used today, usually as part of a train's name.

The Pennsy later used the term as a formal part of a train's name when it inaugurated the *Pennsylvania Limited* between Jersey City and Chicago in 1881. Rival New York Central System, which in the early 1870s had assembled its own New York–Chicago route by pulling the Lake Shore & Michigan Southern under its corporate umbrella, launched the first of a generation of high-speed passenger trains on the route in 1875, with some runs reaching 75 MPH (only 4 MPH less than New York–Chicago passenger trains are permitted today over most of their routes). Among these NYC runs was the *Chicago Limited*, which would be supplemented by a new New York–Buffalo train in 1891 christened the *Empire State Express*. In 1893, this train—wheeling along behind 4-4-0-type locomotive No. 999, now in the custody of Chicago's Museum of Science

and Industry—reached 112.5 MPH. That same year, NYC launched its new *Exposition Flyer* in recognition of the World's Columbian Exposition in Chicago. The *Flyer* was scheduled to make the 960-mile run between New York and Chicago in 20 hours at an average speed of 48 MPH including station and servicing stops—or roughly the same as today's Amtrak *Lake Shore Limited* on the same route.

Elsewhere in the East, dense with new railroad lines, more services were added to accommodate public demand for rail travel. In 1876, the *Centennial Trains* established through service between Boston and Philadelphia, where the Centennial Exposition was being held. The unusual service was operated jointly by the New York & New England, the New York, New Haven & Hartford, and the Pennsylvania railroads. Although the New Haven and PRR both served metropolitan New York City, no direct connection existed between the two due to the water barriers of the Hudson and East rivers. The *Centennial Trains'* through cars were carried by a steam ferry across the rivers to bridge the gap. PRR launched a more-notable train in 1885 with its *Congressional Limited Express* between Jersey City (across the Hudson River from Manhattan) and the nation's capital.

After Henry M. Flagler almost single-handedly began the transformation of Florida from wilderness to vacation paradise, the railroads—including his own Florida East Coast—built deep into the Sunshine State. In 1888, the first-class *Florida Special* ushered in fashionable through service between Jersey City and Jacksonville. The train featured six elegant Pullman Palace cars, a dining car (house speciality: roast antelope), a library-refreshment car, and three standard sleeping cars, all electrically lighted.

## STATE OF THE ART, 1876

Thanks to the California State Railroad Museum in Sacramento, visitors can see firsthand what locomotives and passenger cars of the last half of the nineteenth century were like. Locomotives such as the North Pacific Coast's No. 12, the *Sonoma*, built in 1876, were works of art, with elegant pin-striping and polished brass fixtures. Wood passenger cars were also becoming more ornate, and by the end of that century would—except for the lack of air-conditioning—become rolling palaces. JIM BOYD

## E&WV WOOD COMBINE

This Erie & Wyoming Valley "combine"—a car that is part baggage and part passenger-carrying—illustrates the overall format of passenger equipment circa 1880: clerestory roof (for ventilation), tongue-in-groove car siding, open-end platforms, highly varnished exterior, and intricate pinstriping and lettering.
ANDOVER JUNCTION PUBLICATIONS COLLECTION

## ST. LOUIS UNION STATION

To accommodate the phenomenal growth of rail passenger service, a number of new major-city terminals sprung up throughout North America in the late 1800s. Among the most well known was St. Louis Union Station, opened in 1894. It featured a huge arch train shed over 32 stub-end station tracks. St. Louis Union Station served as a gateway between the East and the West, hosting trains from both coasts as well as the Gulf of Mexico. Patriotically framed, this postcard view of the station shows the front of the depot on what is today Market Street. The last scheduled passenger trains left the rambling station in 1978. The exterior of this landmark structure—today a highly successful retail and hotel complex—remains essentially unchanged. PHIL & BEV BIRK COLLECTION

UNION STATION. ST. LOUIS, MO.

## GAS CAR LIGHTING

Manufacturer advertising from the 1870s promoted the advantages of economical gas lighting in passenger cars.
KEVIN ZOLLARS COLLECTION

In what is now Middle America, Chicago had emerged as America's railroad capital, and new passenger runs were being dispatched in all compass directions from a conglomeration of terminals in that city. Shortly after the 1876 completion of its line between Chicago and the Twin Cities of St. Paul and Minneapolis, Minnesota, the Chicago, Milwaukee & St. Paul—The Milwaukee Road—established through service with an overnight train that in 1888 received electrically lighted rolling stock and in 1898 was finally named *Pioneer Limited*. Not to be outdone, the competing Burlington offered its *St. Paul-Minneapolis Limited Express* between Chicago and the Twin Cities, claiming it to be, according to an 1899 timetable, "The Finest Train in the World." On the Illinois Central in the late 1800s, the *New Orleans Special* was the hottest passenger train on the IC between Chicago and its namesake city on the Gulf. Locally known as the "Cannonball," this run would forever be immortalized in the annals of railroad history when engineer John Luther "Casey" Jones on the fateful early morning of April 30, 1900, rammed a disabled freight. Though he had successfully slowed the Cannonball enough to prevent passenger deaths, Casey himself had died.

In the West, shortly after the 1869 completion of the Chicago & North Western-Union Pacific-Central Pacific "Overland" transcontinental route, a train known simply as the *Express* and later the *Pacific Express* began galloping through the isolation and grandeur of the new American West, delivering travelers to new homes and towns that were springing up between Omaha and Sacramento. Its eastbound counterpart was the *Atlantic Express*, even though it fell short of that ocean by nearly 1,400 miles. In 1888, UP unveiled "The Finest Train in the World," the *Golden Gate Special*, catering to upper-echelon travelers with plush cars and exemplary service. The *Golden Gate* had been preceded by a more democratic run known as the *Overland Flyer*, inaugurated on November 13, 1887, between Omaha/Council Bluffs and Oakland (San Francisco). Known variously over the years as the *Overland Flyer*, *Overland Limited*, or simply the *Overland*, this train ascended to premier status on the Overland Route.

On the future world-famous Atchison, Topeka & Santa Fe, passenger service had been instituted in 1869, but its first true named train didn't appear until late 1892. The *California Limited* established a Chicago–Kansas City–Los Angeles passenger-train service of high reputation that would not be overshadowed until the coming of the *Chief* fleet in the mid-1920s.

On a less glamorous side of passenger service, though arguably no less important, the suburban or commuter train was also coming of age, proving instrumental to easing the suffocation of large urban centers like New York and Chicago. In 1869, Illinois Central's five scheduled suburban trains in each direction between downtown Chicago and Hyde Park, about six miles, sufficiently met the needs of commuters. Most people of that era lived right downtown and had little need for a suburban-type train. But as city centers grew and became more crowded, suburbs sprung up to harbor folks who worked downtown but didn't want to live there. By the end of the 1880s, when Chicago's population passed the one million mark, IC was operating 114 suburban trains on work days, carrying some four million commuters annually. This passenger count would more than double by the turn of the century and in 2001 the IC was the busiest commuter-rail line in Chicago. During the same period on the East Coast, the Long Island Rail Road, chartered in 1834 to serve as a link (via a ferry connection across Long Island Sound) between New York and Boston, was fast becoming the nation's most famous commuter railroad, serving the "bedroom" communities of New York strung out the length of Long Island.

As the sun set on the nineteenth century, the American passenger train was heading into its "golden age."

## TRAIN TIME ON THE CM&STP

In a turn-of-the-century scene of railroading, an eastbound Chicago, Milwaukee & St. Paul train—possibly the *Pioneer Limited*—rolls to a halt at the Gifford Road station on the railroad's Twin Cities–Milwaukee line near Oconomowoc, Wisconsin. Folks stand nearby, awaiting the arrival of loved ones as a buggy at left stands ready to take detraining passengers to their ultimate destinations. Station personnel are on the platform prepared to load and unload parcels and baggage. This was a scene that was once commonplace throughout America, all day, every day. CHUCK PORTER COLLECTION

# The Passenger Train Reigns Supreme in America: 1901–1933

The coming of the railroad was perhaps the most important event of nineteenth century America. More than any other factor, the railway was instrumental in the growth and shaping of the continent. Without rail transport, lands beyond the Atlantic Seaboard could never have been so quickly settled, much less unified into the strong republics they are today. In 1800, few people, if anyone at all, in the likes of Philadelphia, New York, and Boston even knew what railways were. In 1900, few could imagine life without them.

After governmental controls had been established late in the 1800s to curb the excesses and corruption of the then-burgeoning railroad companies, more revenues were diverted into the railroads themselves rather the pockets of the era's rail barons. The result? A 30-year period—from about 1880 to 1910—of exceptional growth, rehabilitation, and standardization. During that span, America's total rail mileage boomed from 93,000 miles to 240,000 miles before it leveled off. And a vast portion of that mileage hosted passenger service in one form or another.

Until the onset of World War I in the mid-1910s, most "intercity" transport—that is, between principal cities, versus commuter travel within a metropolitan area—was by rail, freight or passenger. The importance of the passenger train itself early in the twentieth century

### COLUMBIAN TRAIN DRUMHEAD

Named trains of the Golden Age often carried a lighted "drumhead" on their rear car as a sort of visual punctuation. The *Columbian* was the premier coach train on Baltimore & Ohio's Jersey City–Chicago route. BALTIMORE & OHIO

### HEAVYWEIGHT NICKEL PLATE PASSENGER TRAIN

Although photographed in 1956 during what is referred to in this book as the "streamliner era," this Boy Scout special speeding along over the New York, Chicago & St. Louis ("Nickel Plate Road") main line west of Valparaiso, Indiana, is a fine example of a passenger train from railroading's Golden Age. Hudson-type locomotive No. 170 was built by Brooks Locomotives Works in 1927 (although it was modernized in 1946), and it pulls a train of heavyweight cars from the "Roaring Twenties" painted in austere Pullman Green. Although the Golden Age ended with the start of the Depression, numerous cars and locomotives from the period survived decades beyond. SANDY GOODRICK

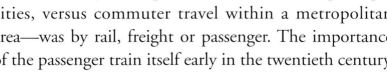

is underscored by the simple fact that close to 100 percent of U.S. intercity travel was by rail. Never in the history of transportation has one mode—not even the automobile—held such domination in such an expansive country. Even with the popularity of air travel today, the airline's market share of U.S. intercity travel is only about 15 percent.

Nothing is forever, of course. By 2000, the passenger train's astonishing prominence had shrunk to about 2 percent (including commuter), with over 80 percent of America traveling by private auto. America at the turn of the twentieth century was truly entering the "golden age" of the passenger train—a grand conveyance of electric-lit cars with plush seating and luxurious sleeping accommodations, sumptuous dining service, stately lounge and club accommodations, and a heady dose of speed. New York to Chicago? In 1800 it might have taken 24 days (although there was no Chicago at that time, only the "Chickago" River); in 1900 it was less than 24 hours.

And so the passenger train brought new promise to the new century, while the new century brought promise to the passenger train. The new century also ushered in . . . the new *Century*—New York Central System's *20th Century Limited*. To this day, transportation historians generally agree that this New York–Chicago run was among the greatest passenger trains—if not *the* greatest—ever to roll across the good green earth. For purposes of our story, the *Century* serves as a barometer for the American passenger train in the twentieth century.

Making its debut on June 15, 1902, the *20th Century* ("Limited" was not officially added to its title until five days later) separated New York and Chicago merely by an afternoon of hobnobbing among fellow esteemed travelers, and a good night's rest—after some fine dining, a good cigar, and a sip of cognac, of course. The new speedster rolled off the route's 960 miles of host New York Central & Hudson River and affiliate Lake Shore & Michigan Southern in

**HIGHBALL FOR CHICAGO, 1911**

A shiny clean high-wheeled New York Central 4-6-2 has just replaced an electric locomotive that moments earlier brought the *20th Century Limited* out of Grand Central to High Bridge, New York, on a late August afternoon in 1911. The handsome five-car train will arrive at Chicago's La Salle Street station the following morning. CAL'S CLASSICS

**NETWORKING, RAILROAD STYLE**

In this early twentieth century colorized scene at Hastings, Nebraska, three trains congregate at the Chicago, Burlington & Quincy depot to exchange passengers. At a time when passenger trains plied nearly all rail routes, it was not uncommon for trains to "hub" (to borrow a current airline term) at larger cities so that passengers could interconnect from one line to another, be it on the same railroad or that of another carrier. MIKE SCHAFER COLLECTION

20 hours flat, departing its endpoints in early afternoon for a next-morning arrival. As a scheduled service, the train was new but not its rolling stock, comprised mostly of reconditioned cars originally built by Pullman and Wagner for the *Lake Shore Limited*, the predecessor New York–Chicago flagship on Commodore Vanderbilt's fledgling New York Central System. Painted in austere Pullman green (Vanderbilt had banished bright colors and ornate trim from his railroads' locomotives and rolling stock to divert attention from the fact his empire was raking in mountains of money), the cars were restenciled with *Century* markings. Two sets of equipment were necessary to protect the schedules. Each set—electrically lighted—included a combination buffet-smoker-library car that also featured a barber shop; two 12-section, 1 drawing-room, 1 stateroom cars; a 30-seat dining car; and a 6-compartment open-platform observation-lounge car. There were no coaches; in terms of passenger accommodations, the *Century* was an all-first-class, all-sleeping-car train.

Interior design included seat fabrics, wall coverings, and carpeting in colors that harmonized with hardwood trim

(Santiago mahogany in the diner), but gone were the intricate carvings, ornate metalwork, and general Victorian gaudiness that had earmarked budding luxury trains of the late 1800s. The new *Century* correctly forecast that simplicity would be a hallmark of passenger-train design for the entire new century.

Above all, the *Century* meant service. The train catered to high society (a then-pricey Extra Fare of $8 per passenger applied to *Century* patrons as of its 1902 inaugural), and it was thus necessary for train staff, which included NYC and Pullman employees, to cater to passengers in the manner to which they were accustomed; whether it was how whiskey sours were presented in the lounge car or how the Long Island scallops were prepared in the diner. Clearly, the societal rockwork of the new-century America, for better or worse, now had strata.

The service aspect extended to the overall train's operation as well. The *Century* had priority over all other trains on the railroad, as on-time performance was an obsession with Central management. Standby locomotives were always positioned at the ready at strategic locations in the event of

By the onset of the twentieth century, most of North America's "classic" railroads had been built and were operating fairly extensive passenger services. Since many are referenced throughout this book, the best-known are noted below along with their formation dates. Most would last the majority of the century.

Atchison, Topeka & Santa Fe (1863)
Atlantic Coast Line (1900)
Baltimore & Ohio (1827)
Boston & Maine (1835)
Canadian Pacific (1881)
Chesapeake & Ohio (1867)
Chicago & North Western (1859)
Chicago, Burlington & Quincy (1855)
Chicago, Milwaukee & St. Paul ("The Milwaukee Road," 1874)
Chicago, Rock Island & Pacific (1866)
Erie (1859)
Great Northern (1889)
Illinois Central (1851)
Kansas City Southern (1900)
Lehigh Valley (1855)
Louisville & Nashville (1850)
Missouri Pacific (1879)
New York Central (1914, although it had unofficially been called "New York Central" for many years previous)
New York, Chicago & St. Louis ("Nickel Plate Road", 1881)
Norfolk & Western (1881)
Northern Pacific (1864)
Pennsylvania Railroad (1846)
Seaboard Air Line (1900)
Southern Pacific (1884)
Southern Railway (1887)
Union Pacific (1862)
Wabash (1877)
Western Pacific (1903)

## BURLINGTON'S NO. 1

Premier train of the Chicago, Burlington & Quincy at the turn of the century was No. 1, the *Chicago–Denver Express*. In 1901, the railroad issued a striking promotional brochure for the train, the cover of which featured an engineer at the throttle. JOE WELSH COLLECTION

failure in the assigned *Century* motive power. Refunds were given to passengers for each hour the *Century* was late, which was a rare circumstance during the early part of the twentieth century. (Curiously, though, "on time" in NYC terms then was anything less than 55 minutes late.)

In a twenty-first century world, it's hard to believe that a regularly scheduled passenger train could make money—almost nowhere in the world today does any scheduled passenger train network operated for the public, turn a profit. But things were different almost a century earlier.

The *20th Century Limited* made money from the start, and by the end of 1905 its revenues had reached the $1 million mark with an estimated profit of some $300,000. Earnings would peak at close to $10 million in 1928. Some of the revenues were not from passengers, but from . . . paper. The train's Railway Post Office (RPO) car carried not only letters (for next-day delivery at the terminal cities—faster than conventional mail service today between New York and Chicago) but also banking papers and securities from Wall Street concerns in Manhattan and La Salle Street banks in Chicago.

The *Century* quickly earned a prestige unequalled by other exalted luxury trains, and its clientele reflected that. Throughout most of its history, the train had a passenger manifest that read like a Who's Who of modern society. Passenger manifests are common today on trains and planes, but for different reasons. Back then, the *Century*'s list alerted the staff that particular passengers—business tycoons and movie stars, for example—should be given extra special attention.

Like other premier trains, the *Century* periodically was equipped with new rolling stock, the first time being little more than a year following its inauguration. All-steel "standard" or "heavyweight" sleepers arrived in 1910. Likewise, the train's schedule saw revampings from time to time, such as in 1905 when its running time was cut by two hours. In addition, the *Century*'s popularity often required that it run in "sections" (extra, separate trains run several minutes

apart) to accommodate all the riders, and sometimes these extra sections were added with only a couple hours' notice. Two to three extra sections were the norm for many years, with a record seven sections on occasion. Consequently, the railroad had to maintain quite a pool of extra cars that were of acceptable standards for *Century* service.

Beginning in 1910, NYC and Pullman began re-equipping the *Century* with all-steel rolling stock. The *Century* periodically received new heavyweight equipment up through 1930, when the Depression began to take hold and railroads started to hold back on capital expenditures.

NYC's east-west routes were rife with name trains other than the *Century*, including the *Commodore Vanderbilt* (the *Century*'s esteemed running mate on virtually the same schedule), *Chicagoan, Mohawk, Wolverine, Iroquois, New York Special,* and the venerable *Lake Shore Limited,* which, in terms of schedule, still operates today under Amtrak. All of these were primarily Chicago–New York runs via either Cleveland or Detroit. There were also Boston–Chicago and New York–St. Louis runs.

The *20th Century Limited* was not without peer. Rival Pennsylvania Railroad itself featured a four-track "Broad-Way" main line linking New York and Chicago, but via Philadelphia and Pittsburgh, and when the *Century* first sailed in 1902, the Pennsy likewise unveiled a new, deluxe New York–Chicago train the very same day. The *Pennsylvania Special* (initially referred to by some as the *Twenty-Hour Special*) was a virtual twin to the *Century*: a first-class-only,

all-sleeping-car train of exceptionally high standards. In 1912, the train was renamed *Broad-Way Limited*.

The *Broad-Way* and other selected luxury-type trains were discontinued during World War I, but Pennsy's finest was restored (with "Broadway" appearing as one word) following the war, with all-steel rolling stock. It was joined by a Chicago–Washington running mate, the *Washington-Broadway Limited,* later renamed *Liberty Limited.*

As with rival New York Central, the PRR fielded a wide array of east-west trains. Between Chicago and New York, travelers could choose between the *Manhattan Limited, Pennsylvania Limited, Metropolitan, Golden Arrow, Commercial Express,* and other trains. Between New York and St. Louis or Cincinnati, PRR offered trains like the *American, St. Louisan, Gotham Limited,* and *Cincinnati Limited.* Add to that trains of the Baltimore & Ohio, the Chesapeake & Ohio and the Erie Railroad, Midwest–East Coast travelers had dozens of trains to choose from, in each direction every day, with departures throughout the day. This is hard to contemplate in today's world, where there are but five Amtrak trains a day between Chicago and the East Coast.

## MOVING THE MASSES

Passenger-train historians have long focused on these two rival trains, and thousands upon thousands of words of prose, some in entire book form, have been written about the elite pair. The danger is that readers may be led to
*Continued on page 26*

## LIFE ABOARD THE CARS ON BURLINGTON NO. 1

The booklet issued by CB&Q for train No. 1 (its eastbound counterpart was train No. 6, but the guide applied to both) presented a series of elegant art renderings of car interiors. Although idealized like so many publicity photos that would propagate later, the scenes do illustrate what rail travel was like at the start of the new century. From left to right, beginning on the facing page: chair car showing the latest in cushioned, walkover seating; dining in opulence (note gas lights); interior of open-section Pullman sleeper in day seating mode; and the men's wash room. JOE WELSH COLLECTION

# from Podunk to Pinnacle:

### SMALL-TOWN CLASSIC

LEFT: Built by the Fort Worth & Denver, the wood-frame depot at Tomball, Texas, is a perfect example of an early twentieth century small-town depot. TOM KLINE

### MEDIUM CITY, WITH FLAVOR

ABOVE: The Southern Pacific depot at San Antonio, Texas, features the Spanish mission style so popular in the Southwest. TOM KLINE

### SOLID AND BUSINESSLIKE

BELOW: Stately brick depots such as this on the Chicago & North Western at Belvidere, Illinois, circa 1912, implied permanence. MIKE SCHAFER COLLECTION

Chances are, most railroad depots that survived into the new millennium were built during railroading's Golden Age, which in this book we've arbitrarily defined as 1901–1930. The terms "station" and "depot" are often used interchangeably by the public, but technically, as far as railroads themselves are concerned, a "station" is a specific, named location along a railroad's route. Whether or not there is a station building housing the railroad's local office—that is, a "depot"—at the station location is more or less irrelevant. In fact, most railroad stations today are merely signposts, and many locations where passenger trains still stop for passengers offer no depot facilities.

Traditional railroad depots served both freight customers and passengers, and during the Golden Age, depots were often the social epicenter of a community, regardless of its size. Passengers heading out of town purchased their transportation at their home depot(s), whose agents represented the railroad company. For out-of-town passengers arriving at a station, the depot served as a sort of gateway to the village, town, or city.

The extent of services offered at a depot had much to do with the size of the community and/or the number of trains serving the depot. At its

# Golden Era Railroad Depots

**WASHINGTON UNION STATION: BEAUX ARTS AT ITS BEST**

Opened in 1907, Washington Union Station remains a vibrant railroad depot and a wonderful example of the Beaux Arts style of architecture found on many early twentieth century city terminals. BRIAN SOLOMON

**GRAND CENTRAL TERMINAL, NEW YORK CITY**

Perhaps the most famous railroad depot of them all, New York Central's Grand Central Terminal, has been a monument to rail travel since it opened in 1913. NEW YORK CENTRAL, C. W. NEWTON COLLECTION

basic level, a staffed depot had a ticket counter, waiting room(s), and rest rooms. (Early depots often had separate waiting rooms for men and women, while Southern depots segregated the races.) The ultimate depot—those found in very large cities—offered everything from restaurants and barber shops to shower facilities and movie theaters (to entertain passengers waiting between trains). Such depots were often referred to as terminals because so many trains originated or terminated there.

During the early twentieth century, as railroads spent huge sums of money rebuilding their infrastructure, scores of dilapidated frame stations dating from the nineteenth century were wiped out and replaced with more substantial depots of wood, stone, or brick construction. In selected large cities, huge, ponderous Victorian piles of railroading's Rail Baron

era of the late 1880s were razed to make way for modern transportation temples—many of them built in the Beaux Arts style that had been popularized during the World's Columbian Exposition in Chicago in 1893. Through the doors of these thousands of depots spread across the lands, countless travelers have boarded and detrained from the famous and not-so-famous trains of past and present.

With rare exception, these early twentieth century depots were built with private capital, and many are still in service today, albeit almost all under new stewardship. Having been vacated by the passenger train, many have new uses (for example, restaurants, chambers of commerce, or museums), but some still serve in their intended function: as an interface between passenger and passenger train.

## MIXED BLESSINGS, STEEL AND WOOD PASSENGER CARS

Regal in wine red, heavyweight all-steel sleeping car *Rutherglen* trails a steam-powered mixed train about to depart St. Andrews, New Brunswick, on August 23, 1958. Ahead of the sleeper is an all-steel day coach; the RPO-baggage car ahead, however, is a wooden classic. Once out of the station, the train will pause at the St. Andrews yard to pick up a string of freight cars, which will be placed ahead of the express cars. Steel passenger cars like this pair could be found in regular service on U.S., Canadian, and Mexican trains from the 1910s well into the 1960s. JOHN DZIOBKO

*Continued from page 23*

believe these trains, as well as their posh, near contemporaries on other railroads—Santa Fe's *de-Luxe*, Seaboard's *Seaboard Florida Limited* and rival Atlantic Coast Line's *Florida Special*, and the UP-SP *Overland Limited*, for example—had become the norm in early twentieth century rail travel. They were, in fact, brilliant exceptions rather than the rule, demonstrating the excellence of service railroads were capable of for those patrons who could afford it.

In reality, a vast majority of intercity trains during the first half of the twentieth century were work-a-day runs, democratically equipped with day coaches, basic dining services, and, if their schedules took them into the night hours, sleeping accommodations, most of which by this time were offered by the Pullman Company (chapter 3). Mail and "express"—that is, relatively portable, time-sensitive shipments—had become a staple of passenger trains everywhere and were usually handled in baggage-type cars or special express boxcars equipped with high-speed passenger-type trucks and steam-line connections for train heating.

As is the case today, nearly all regularly scheduled passenger runs were assigned numbers, usually even-numbered for east- or northbound trains and odd for west- and southbound. Some of these runs were identified only by numbers, like airline flights and Amtrak's "corridor" runs in the Northeast U.S., while an increasing number were christened with titles—often incorporating the term "express" or "limited"—for marketing purposes or to emphasize the train's service territory.

When the twentieth century got under way, most of North America's rail routes had been built, and virtually all "classic" American railroads had been or were being established (sidebar); most operated a respectable network of passenger trains covering most of their lines. These companies, together with a host of smaller lines, often regional in nature, blanketed the U.S. at the turn of the century with well over 200,000 miles of track reaching into a vast majority of American villages, towns, and cities. U.S. railroads were poised to become the greatest, most comprehensive passenger and freight transportation network the world had ever known. For the passenger train, it was a drastically different world than we know now. For all practical purposes, as of 1900, the passenger train competed with virtually no other mode of transport over medium and long distances, save for—in rather isolated instances—lake boats on the Great Lakes and sternwheelers on such waterways as the Mississippi and Ohio rivers. The passenger trains of just about any given railroad only competed with those of another.

America was almost totally reliant on the railroads, so nearly every line or branch, no matter how obscure and even if it was the only railroad in town, usually offered some form of passenger service, if only a single daily two-car train in each direction. Non-competing railroads—usually "end-to-end" carriers—were able to readily cooperate with each other, scheduling trains into terminals to connect with departing trains of a "friendly" (non rival) connection. Thanks to standardization of track gauges following the Civil War, and the standardization of rolling-stock components later in the 1800s, adjoining carriers soon learned that pooling their efforts to jointly operate a through passenger train would improve service by eliminating the hassle of train changes where one railroad met another. At the turn of the century, there was no single railroad linking Chicago and Florida, but the new *Florida Flyer* carried travelers through from Chicago to Jacksonville with "no change of cars." The Chicago, Indianapolis & Louisville Railway ("Monon Route") handled the train out of Chicago in late evening and the following morning handed it off to future B&O

*Continued on page 31*

## NO BRIDGE? NO PROBLEM

Until the Mississippi River could be bridged in Louisiana, Southern Pacific passenger trains had to be ferried across the waterway to reach New Orleans. This colorized view, circa 1910, shows a train, divided into three sections, riding the SP barge *Mastodon* into Avondale, Louisiana, near New Orleans. Once the train is off-loaded, it will be reassembled to continue its trip west toward California. MIKE SCHAFER COLLECTION

## HELL GATE BRIDGE, NEW YORK CITY

Spanning the East River in Queens, Hell Gate Bridge is a prime example of long-lasting, major infrastructure improvements made by American railroads early in the twentieth century. Prior to Hell Gate's opening in 1917, some through trains bound from Philadelphia to New England were ferried—like the SP train at right—across the Hudson River from Jersey City and up the East River to the Bronx. Today, Hell Gate Bridge is a critical link in Amtrak's Northeast Corridor route. The venerable bridge was 80 years old as Amtrak's *Nutmeg State* flew high above a baseball game on Wards Island in 1997. JOE GREENSTEIN

Baggage, mail, and express have been riding aboard passenger trains nearly as long as people have. Early on, railroads began handling baggage, mail, and express ("express" being defined as parcels requiring expedited delivery) in cars built specifically for that purpose. Such cars traditionally were positioned between the locomotive(s) and passenger-carrying cars, so they have long been referred to as "head-end" cars—although they can often be found at the rear end of the train.

Rare is the intercity traveler who travels without even a modicum of baggage, and for those taking baggage in excess of what they could carry aboard, the railroads accepted "checked" baggage to be handled in baggage cars. This was usually done free of charge—as long as the baggage was handled on the same train as the passenger (otherwise it would be considered an express shipment)—as a means of enticing passengers off competing forms of transportation.

Baggage handling was a non-revenue venue for railroads, but a necessary nuisance; however, mail and express was quite lucrative. Like rail passengers, mail and express requires timely, expedited passage, and early in the 1830s, railroads began handling mail in bulk. In 1838, the U.S. Congress designated all rail lines to be official postal routes. The most well-known type of mail car was the Railway Post Office—very much a rolling post office, staffed with postal workers sorting mail while the train sped from city to city. George B. Armstrong, assistant postmaster in Chicago, developed the RPO in 1857, reportedly with the help of a couple of mice. In those days, mail was shipped by train in bags and then sorted and redistributed at selected post offices en route. Under this arrangement, bags of mail tended to languish at intermediate sorting points, making them ideal havens for refuge-seeking rodents. In one case, two romantically inclined Chicago mice had made their home in a bag of mail destined for Ontonagon, Michigan, chewing up letters for nesting material. When the bag arrived there, the pair had started a family.

**RAIL MAIL**

Bags of sorted mail are unloaded from the RPO car—this one a veteran of the heavyweight era—on Chesapeake & Ohio's *Night Express* having just arrived at Grand Central Station, Chicago, from Grand Rapids, Michigan in 1967.

**MAIL ON THE FLY**

A bag of mail hangs ready for retrieval by the RPO car of Frisco train No. 4, the *Will Rogers*, at Spencer, Oklahoma, in 1948. A special device on the the side of the RPO will hook the mail bag and sweep it into the car without the train ever slowing down. PRESTON GEORGE, COURTESY BERNICE ARGO

**EXPRESS AWAITS THE TRAIN**

Horse-drawn express company wagons and employees line pose at Chicago & North Western station at Dixon, Illinois, circa 1912. MIKE MCBRIDE COLLECTION

The Ontonagon postmaster alerted Armstrong, who soon became obsessed with solving the dilemma of slow mail processing. Inspired by the success of enroute mail sorting already commonplace on English railways, a makeshift "traveling post office" was put into service between Chicago and Clinton, Iowa, on the Chicago & North Western. The idea caught on, and by the mid-1860s the first purpose-built Railway Post Office (RPO) cars appeared. Mail-storage cars, basically traditional baggage cars, worked shoulder to shoulder with RPOs to carry mail that did not need to be sorted en route as well as bags that did or had been sorted.

Mail became an important revenue producer in a passenger train's operation, and railroads often operated trains that were primarily mail and express with limited (or no) accommodations for passengers. By 1915 there were some 20,000 postal clerks (provided by the railroads, not the U.S. Post Office, however) working on some 5,000 mail cars operating on over 216,000 route-miles. Although RPO service lasted in the U.S. until the late 1970s, RPO operations began to decline during the 1920s as mail-sorting methods improved at stationary post offices while some mail movement began to be shifted to trucks. The steepened decline in passenger trains after the stockmarket crash of 1929 forced the Post Office to consider alternative transportation, and as the U.S. rail passenger market really began to unravel in the late 1950s and 1960s, the Post Office shifted ever more mail movement to trucks and rapidly expanding airlines. When the U.S. Post Office unveiled its ZIP sorting procedures in the 1960s, it was all over for the RPO, and RPO contracts ended on most railroads in 1967–68. Nearly all mail that still moved in bulk over long distances went to trucks or dedicated freight trains. Mail would not return to passenger trains on a significant scale until later in the Amtrak era (chapter 7).

Paste Delivery Sheet on Back of this Tag

*A valuable shipping tip...*

RAILWAY EXPRESS AGENCY

HAVE SHIPMENTS CARRY INSIDE ADDRESS WHERE POSSIBLE. THUS, IF THE OUTSIDE ADDRESS SHOULD BE TORN OFF OR OBLITERATED, WE WOULD STILL BE ABLE TO DELIVER YOUR SHIPMENT TO CONSIGNEE.

SEND YOUR SHIPMENTS BY THE RELIABLE 2-WAY SHIPPING SERVICE.

No extra charge for pick-up and delivery within regular vehicle limits in all cities and principal towns.

*Complete Nationwide Rail-Air Service*

Passenger trains also hauled huge volumes of packages and other items that required expedited transport. Initially, this business involved a number of independent express companies, but during World War I most were consolidated into the American Railway Express Agency—renamed Railway Express Agency in 1927. REA parcels moved between cities on scheduled passenger trains in REA's own baggage-type cars or express boxcars (equipped with high-speed trucks, tightlock couplers, and steam lines so as to be compatible with passenger cars) or in similar cars provided by the railroad. At stations, parcels were offloaded and distributed locally by REA trucks, and vice versa.

The REA was to early and mid-twentieth century America what couriers like United Parcel Service and FedEx are today. However, REA was in effect a monopoly sanctioned by the Interstate Commerce Commission under the provision that REA—unlike UPS, FedEx, and their kin—had to accept shipment of *anything*, be it live chicks, fresh fruits, or explosives. REA thus became one of the most comprehensive, reliable, expedited shipping endeavors in American history. Green REA trucks meeting passenger trains during station stops or making deliveries about town were once a common sight in America.

The deterioration of America's rail passenger network in the 1950s and 1960s would prove fatal to REA, compounded by the rise in UPS, FedEx, and other couriers using their own trucks or planes and even employing freight railroads. In the 1990s, Amtrak reinvented the once-successful concept, developing a mail and express business that is tied in directly to Amtrak's scheduled trains. As in the "old days," the express moves in baggage-type cars and express boxcars attached, fore and aft, to passenger-carrying consists; as well, some Amtrak express is carried in truck trailers that can ride either on rails behind Amtrak trains or on highways behind traditional truck tractors.

## BALTIMORE & OHIO AT HARPERS FERRY

A vast majority of America's long-distance trains during the Golden Age of railroading ran between the East Coast and major Midwestern cities like Chicago, St. Louis, Cincinnati, and Detroit. By far, the Pennsylvania Railroad and the New York Central System fielded most of them, with Baltimore & Ohio a distant third, followed by Erie, Chesapeake & Ohio, and Norfolk & Western. Hampered by its circuitous route between New York (Jersey City) and Chicago that swung south through Washington, D.C., the B&O nonetheless harbored a faithful clientele who enjoyed B&O's exemplary service and wonderful scenery. In this scene from the 1920s, three B&O trains meet at Harpers Ferry, West Virginia, as viewed westward from the cliffs of Virginia. Prominent in this scene is the historic Potomac River and Chesapeake & Ohio Canal (hard against the Maryland bank of the Potomac at right). BILL HOWES COLLECTION

## PENNSYLVANIA RAILROAD LEADS THE WAY

Credit the mighty Pennsylvania Railroad with leading the industry into the steel-car era with its P-70 coaches, two of which, behind a combine and baggage car, trail a PRR K-4-class 4-6-2 hoofing out of Pittsburgh with a local train in the 1920s. Another P-70 coach can be seen to the right of the train. MIKE SCHAFER COLLECTION

*Continued from page 26*

component Cincinnati, Hamilton & Dayton at Indianapolis, Indiana. At Cincinnati, Ohio, CH&D relayed it to the Queen & Crescent Route (a future addition to the Southern Railway) to take on to Chattanooga, Tennessee. From there, the Southern hosted the *Flyer* on through Atlanta to Tifton, Georgia, where the Plant System (a future component of the Atlantic Coast Line Railroad) took over for the remainder of the trip to Jacksonville, with the train arriving there on the second morning.

The competition between railroads, of course, provided the impetus to continue improving trains and services, particularly between city pairs served by more than one railroad and where there was a great demand for service, such as New York–Chicago, Chicago–St. Louis, New York/Jersey City–Washington, and Chicago–Denver.

The early years of the twentieth century also witnessed the rise of great railway terminals. With more trains and travelers came the demand for larger and more-modern depots at major cities. One of the best-known new sprawling terminals was New York's Pennsylvania Station, opened in 1910 to give the great Pennsylvania Railroad direct access to Manhattan. Not to be outdone, of course, Vanderbilt interests over at the New York Central erected the

third rendition of Grand Central Terminal at 42nd Street, replacing a ponderous, inefficient old GCT in 1913. Also hosting trains of tenant New Haven Railroad, this all-new Grand Central rose to prominence as one of the most-famous terminals in all the world—a monument to a time when passenger trains ruled American transportation. Similar grandiose stations rose in other cities, often replacing older, outdated structures. Among these new monuments were the mammoth North Western Terminal in Chicago (1911), the Michigan Central Station at Detroit (1913), and Philadelphia's stately Thirtieth Street Station (1930).

In several large cities where numerous railroads converged, the union terminal had finally come of age. The concept of a joint or "union" depot dated from 1853 when the original Indianapolis Union Station opened, consolidating the operations of several railroads under one roof. Continuing rivalries between carriers and the lack of standardization of railroad equipment had hindered the spread of union-type facilities until the twentieth century when railroads began to fully realize the potential cost savings of a consolidated facility—and the possibility that passengers would be more inclined to choose a railroad that offered greater conveniences at connecting points. The first 30

## STREET-SMART IN SYRACUSE

Interurbans were not the only trains to invade city streets. A classic heavyweight New York Central train, powered by one of the road's handsome Hudson-type locomotives, cautiously eases through the streets of Syracuse, New York, prior to NYC's 1936 relocation of its busy New York–Chicago main line to a bypass route north of the city. Though the Depression was well under way, the permanent reroute, which exists to this day, was a necessary capital expense to improve service on the Water Level Route, which hosted dozens of trains each way between the East Coast and Midwest every day. CAL'S CLASSICS

# The Interurban Era

The refinement of the electric traction motor in the late nineteenth century led to the nearly explosive development of electric street railways within metropolitan areas. On the heels of streetcar systems came their close cousins, the interurbans, which provided welcomed local service between towns and cities in an era when mud roads were the rule and parallel steam railroads resisted providing comprehensive local service. Interurban trains, in fact, often used the tracks of streetcar companies to enter the cities and dovetail services with the local cars.

Initially, interurban companies were usually owned, and operated by utility companies, and most were built early in the twentieth century. A few grew to significant size, the largest—in terms of track-miles—being the sprawling Pacific Electric Railway which reached out in all directions from Los Angeles to communities as far away as San Bernardino. The largest interurban in terms of width and breadth was the Illinois Traction System (later, Illinois Terminal), which linked numerous central Illinois towns and cities with St. Louis, Missouri.

With rare exception, interurban trains were electric powered, and their passenger trains were usually comprised of one or more self-propelled cars or a combination of powered cars hauling "trailers" (non-powered car). As with regular "steam" railroads, the cars were of varying types, mostly coaches, but some also offering parlor, dining, and lounge services or equipped to handle mail, and express. The Illinois Traction System and the Indiana Railroad even offered sleeping-car service. The powered cars could also haul "trailers"—non-powered coaches, diners, and such.

The rise of the automobile in the 1920s quickly cut into interurban traffic, and the Depression of the 1930s wrought wholesale abandonment of interurban companies, most of which by this time had been divested from utility companies and therefore no longer had good financial backing.

A few lines survived into the post-World War II era, mainly because they served high-traffic areas. Notable in this regard was the Chicago North Shore & Milwaukee connecting its namesake cities with high-speed, hourly trains, including a set of streamliners known as the Electroliners. Abandoned in 1963, the North Shore had two sister companies, the Chicago Aurora & Elgin and the Chicago South Shore & South Bend. The "Roarin' Elgin" ended in 1961, but the South Shore Line remains as America's only surviving true interurban—and it's doing quite well, thank you.

years of the twentieth century saw new union facilities unveiled at numerous cities, among them Washington, D.C. (1907); Denver, Colorado (1912); Kansas City, Missouri (1914); Jacksonville, Florida (1919); St. Paul, Minnesota 1923); Chicago (1925); Toronto, Ontario (1927); and Cleveland, Ohio (1930). Five of these samples still serve as rail passenger facilities as of 2001.

One of the most important developments in rail passenger transport was the all-steel passenger car. The better part of a century has passed since the widespread acceptance of the steel car, and one might conclude that its development was logical, quick, and widely embraced. But the reality was that experimentation with metal cars began as early as 1846 and basically got nowhere until the twentieth century. The obvious drawback of wood cars was hardly lost upon the traveling public early on, as nearly every major passenger-train wreck of the nineteenth century resulted in some sort of conflagration whose fiery spectacle was vividly portrayed in early newspaper engravings.

Public outcry prompted inventors to build experimental metal cars of various design, and therein was just one of the problems: what the inventors—often non-railroad people—proposed and what the railroads wanted to build or operate were usually two different things. Then, as now, railroads were frugal to a fault, and metal construction in the 1800s was an expensive proposition while wood was cheap and plentiful. Metalworking was still in its infancy. Iron cars were exceedingly heavy, requiring more-powerful locomotives and therefore heavier, stronger rails—and the strength of iron rails was quite finite. Nor were iron cars comfortable for passengers. Without the natural insulating qualities of wood, metal cars became rolling ovens in summer and freezers in winter. Still, metal cars were more durable and safer in an accident, both in terms of strength and fire resistance. A number of railroads did buy and operate metal cars in the nineteenth century, but the industry as a whole was not quick to accept them.

A turning point was the refinement of steel-making during the last half of the nineteenth century. Steel is a refined iron that possesses greater strength, lighter weight, and more malleability than traditional iron, but until late in the nineteenth century, the process of making steel from iron was complex and expensive.

Steel was a boon to railroads, of course, but their acceptance of it didn't happen all at once. Although railroads quickly adopted steel in place of brittle iron rails, the complexities of car and locomotive construction prevented an equally rapid changeover for steel construction. Rather, the use of steel in car construction rose incrementally, first in obvious components like couplers, wheels, and brake rigging, then in center sills (the all-important "backbone" of a car) and flooring, and finally in the carbody itself.

For a short period, a "composite" car—that is, a car built of steel but sheathed with wood to make it appear to be all wood—was used. The idea was to pacify passengers who remained convinced that all-steel passenger cars attracted lightning and would electrocute their occupants. Ironically, railroads had been quick to accept all-steel freight cars in the late 1800s because steel freight cars could carry greater loads, which meant that fewer cars were necessary to haul a given amount of freight. Not so with passenger cars. A wood coach carried about the same number of passengers as an all-steel car. Safety would drive railroads to finally accept the all-steel passenger car.

The danger of wood or even composite passenger cars, especially in tunneled rights-of-way, was underscored by a tragic wood-car fire in the Paris subway around 1901. The tragedy prompted New York's then-abuilding Interborough Rapid Transit to order all-steel subway cars—a move partially sponsored by then-Pennsylvania Railroad president A. J. Cassatt. The PRR was at that time about to begin tunneling under the Hudson and East rivers as part of the construction of Pennsylvania Station in Manhattan. Cassatt was adamant about employing all-steel passenger rolling stock on trains using the new terminal.

The PRR's Altoona (Pennsylvania) Shops built an experimental all-steel car for the IRT in 1903. It was such as success that the PRR went on to develop an all-steel passenger car suitable for use on conventional trains. The result was one of the most famous families of steel passenger cars ever to serve the public: the P-70 coach. The first of these 80-foot rolling workhorses rolled out of Altoona in 1907 as part of a huge order—some 1,500 cars—of new all-steel rolling stock that also included diners, parlor cars, and sleepers to be built by Altoona Shops, American Car & Foundry, and the Pressed Steel Car Company. When the station opened in 1910, well over 300 of the cars had been built. Orders went in for still more cars, and by about 1913 the PRR had taken delivery of nearly 3,000 all-steel cars. By the end of the 1920s, the mighty Pennsy fielded over 5,500 steel passenger cars (more than twice as many cars as Amtrak has today for all U.S. service), and all wood cars had been pulled from regularly scheduled service.

LUXURIOUS AIR-CONDITIONED PORTLAND ROSE CLUB CAR
A BLENDED HARMONY OF COLOR AND DECORATION

### STANDARD-ERA LOUNGE CAR

Although the exterior of a heavyweight car might have been painted a mundane green, interiors were hardly as monochromatic. Union Pacific touted the club car on its Denver–Portland *Portland Rose* to be a "blended harmony of color and decoration." MIKE SCHAFER COLLECTION

## THE DRAW OF WARMER CLIMES

A 1930s-era folder promoting the *Dixie Flyer* and *Dixie Limited* between Chicago and Florida featured a detailed route map. Both trains had a St. Louis section, and both terminated at Jacksonville where connections could be made with Atlantic Coast Line and Florida East Coast trains.
MIKE SCHAFER COLLECTION

## BLOTTER ADVERTISING

Central of Georgia, one of the "relay" railroads in north-south rail traffic, gave away ink blotters showing Florida-bound train times at Atlanta.
MIKE SCHAFER COLLECTION

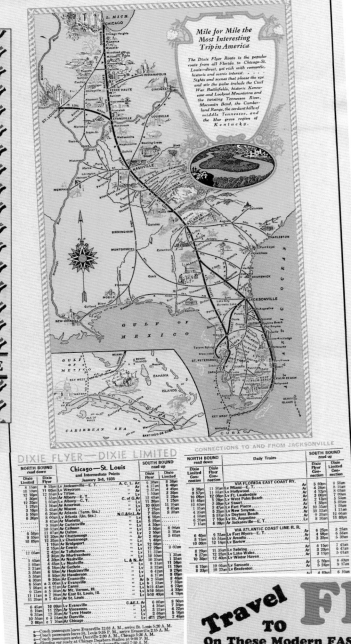

Already a powerhouse in American railroading when the new century started, the Pennsy thus became one of the leading forces in the move toward all-steel passenger cars. By 1910, American railroads overall had finally come to accept steel passenger-car construction, although some composite equipment was still being constructed, notably for the Santa Fe, which felt that they offered better insulation from the heat of Southwestern deserts.

In 1910, some 45,000 wood passenger cars still rolled on American rails while only 2,000 or so cars were all-steel or at least steel-framed. Thanks in part to the Pennsylvania's influence, the number of steel-frame and all-steel cars acquired by American railroads jumped to about 16,000 in 1915. By this time, orders for wood cars had all but ceased, although a number of railroads still resisted ordering new steel cars, content to get the most from their existing fleet of wood cars—or they simply could not yet afford new cars.

The American passenger train had now entered the "standard era" of its Golden Age. Although thousands of new steel passenger cars of all formats—coaches, sleepers, diners, lounges, and parlors—were being churned out by carbuilders and some railroad car shops, construction had settled on overall traditional designs that had been established in the previous century: a boxy carbody; clerestory roof; vertical, rectangular windows; and four- or six-wheel trucks. In later years, the clerestory or "monitor" roof gave way to the simple arch roof on some railroads.

The standard era also ushered in more-standardized train climate control and lighting. By the early years of the twentieth century, dangerous stove-powered heating in cars had largely given way to steam heat supplied by a central source—the train's locomotive, most of which then, of course, were steam. The steam was piped throughout the train via "steam lines" linked to each car's radiator system. In instances where electric locomotives powered trains for extended distances, the locomotives were equipped with small boilers for generating steam.

# Rocky Mountain Views
## of the Rio Grande. The Scenic Line of the World

As of the turn of the century, gas lighting had become the most popular means of interior car illumination. Compressed gas was stored in tanks beneath the carbodies and piped to adjustable lighting fixtures, providing each car with its own lighting system. Railroads had already dabbled with electric lighting, but for a car to have its own independent electric lighting system required huge, cumbersome, wet-cell batteries that required constant attention and recharging. Some railroads—notably The Milwaukee Road—employed special "head-end power" cars (usually converted baggage cars) that housed a dynamo which generated electricity fed to the entire train. Students of passenger railroading know well that this approach was destined to be the way of the future, but back in the late 1800s head-end-power technology was still crude and expensive,

### SCENIC LINE OF THE WORLD

In 1917, the Denver & Rio Grande Western issued a stunning souvenir album (actual size, 12 x 10 inches) featuring 23 color lithograph views of scenes along the railroad's spectacular Royal Gorge Route between Denver and Glenwood Springs. The book could only be purchased aboard Rio Grande trains. MIKE SCHAFER COLLECTION

### "ALONG THE RIO GRANDE"

A time-worn snapshot taken out the window by a passenger riding what was probably D&RGW's *Scenic Limited*—with double-headed locomotives—circa 1925 was lost to time until unearthed at a flea market in 2001. Penciled on the back of the photo is "Going thru Royal Gorge." MIKE SCHAFER COLLECTION

*Along Rio Grand*

**QUEEN OF THE COASTLINE**

It remains to this day one of the all-time great rail trips in North America—a ride along the former Southern Pacific Coast Line route between Los Angeles and San Francisco/Oakland. SP's *Daylight*s plied the Pacific Ocean coast from 1922 to 1971; Amtrak does likewise today with its *Coast Starlight*, running on approximately the same schedule as the *Daylight* of yore. JOE WELSH COLLECTION

so many railroads simply skipped electric lighting experimentation and moved directly from oil lighting to gas lighting, the latter being incredibly cheap to operate.

The popularity of gas lighting was of short duration. After about 1910, breakthroughs in electric train lighting shifted the balance. Now gaining widespread acceptance was an arrangement whereby axle-driven generators supplied current to lights when the train was in motion, and a bank of now-reliable dry-cell batteries took over when the train was stopped or moving at slow speed. As for the concept of head-end power—that would largely slide into dormancy until the streamliner era.

Another hallmark of the standard era was the radical shift in the direction of cosmetic car design. With the death of George Pullman in 1897 came the death of Victorian "splendor" and all its gaudy excesses and almost funereal overtones. Highly varnished car exteriors with elaborate pin-striping and lettering yielded to more-economical "dip" paint jobs in which the whole car was painted one color (usually dark green). Car interiors went from featuring intricately decorated or sculptured woodwork, fussy curtains, leaded glass, and floral-patterned upholstery to a combination of simple but elegant woodwork and large expanses of plainly painted walls and partitions, or walls of finished, but unembellished, natural wood. And so it would remain until the streamlined era.

The new rolling stock of the standard era, whether owned by the many railroads then in the passenger business or the Pullman Company, bore a remarkable similarity throughout the country, with most rolling stock wearing Brewster green. In 1901, this dark (and some would say monotonous) color had been adopted by Pullman as its official car color (the color thus also became known as Pullman green); Pullman sleepers by now had become a regular part of many trains from coast to coast, border to border. Most of the ballyhooed differences from train to train focused on interior appointments, service, and schedules. A few railroads did deviate from Pullman green. Chicago & Alton's *Alton Limited* of 1924 had all-steel cars painted in red and maroon—some of which lasted into the Amtrak era. No surprise, then, that the *Limited* became known as the "Red Train." Similarly, some of the Baltimore & Ohio standard-era rolling stock was painted blue, and just about every passenger car on the Pennsylvania Railroad wore the company's signature color, Tuscan red.

## GOLDEN AGE SAMPLER

With the flood of new composite or all-steel cars as the new century unfurled came a legion of new name-train services, or the upgrading of existing name trains. Spurred by the 1902 inaugurals mentioned earlier of two of America's most famous trains, the *20th Century Limited* and the *Broad-Way Limited*, more name trains than ever—too numerous to mention all here—were launched during the first 30 years of the new century.

### North and South

With the "discovery" of Florida in the late nineteenth century—largely through the efforts of Henry M. Flagler, who developed the East Coast, and Henry Plant, who developed the interior—came the tourists. Florida's unprecedented growth during the early years of the twentieth century resulted in a barrage of new trains out of the Northeast and Midwest, especially during frigid winter months. The New York–Florida market was especially thick with standard trains, almost all of them spawned by the Atlantic Coast Line and rival Seaboard Air Line. These railroads only reached as far north as Richmond, Virginia, so to tap deeply into the market of shivering Yankees, the Richmond, Fredericksburg & Potomac agreed to relay ACL and SAL trains between Richmond and Washington, D.C., where the Pennsylvania Railroad took them on to New York City, and vice versa.

In the popular north-south market, venerable Louisville & Nashville unveiled the *Pan-American* on December 5, 1921, between Cincinnati and New Orleans via Louisville, Kentucky, Nashville, Tennessee, and Birmingham and Montgomery, Alabama. Named for L&N's participation in trade between North and South America, the "Pan", as it was known for short, featured a baggage-club car, coaches, chair cars, dining car, Pullman sleepers, and parlor-observation car, all wheeled along by lanky Pacifics that had been built at L&N's South Louisville Shops. In 1925 the Pan was shorn of its coaches and re-equipped with new sleepers, making it an all-Pullman train.

L&N also served as a critical link in Chicago-based north-south service. The famed *Dixie Flyer* and its alter ego, the *Dixie Limited*, were primarily Chicago–Jacksonville runs (with St. Louis–Evansville connecting trains) operated jointly with Chicago & Eastern Illinois (Chicago–Evansville), Central of Georgia (Atlanta–Albany, Georgia), and Atlantic Coast Line (Atlanta–Jacksonville and other Florida destinations). Florida East Coast handled Miami-bound cars out of Jacksonville.

### Through the Rockies

The Panama-Pacific Exposition at San Francisco in 1915 inspired three cooperating carriers—Missouri Pacific, Denver & Rio Grande, and Western Pacific—to introduce one of the earliest great standard-era transcontinental trains that crossed the Rocky Mountains. Borrowing the name from an earlier Denver–Ogden, Utah, train of the Rio Grande, MP-D&RG-WP's new, all-steel *Scenic Limited* linked St. Louis and Oakland, California, by way of Kansas City, Denver, Pueblo, the Royal Gorge, Salt Lake City, Utah, and WP's line across the Utah-Nevada desert and through the then-obscurely known Feather River Canyon in Northern California. The *Scenic Limited* was purposely scheduled to traverse the most scenic parts of its journey during daylight hours.

## Up and down the West Coast

Elsewhere on the West Coast, more new standard trains were being launched. Southern Pacific's *Daylight Limited* was launched on April 28, 1922, linking San Francisco and Los Angeles—470 miles—with a 13-hour daytime run with no scheduled stops. What was then SP's fastest train featured a simple consist of coaches plus dining car, but the train's popularity resulted in the addition of lounge-observation cars in 1923. In 1924, unique "All Day Lunch" cars—coaches with a lunch counter at one end—were added. Parlor cars came in 1930, as did a short-lived train livery that was a distinct departure from somber Pullman green. For one season, the *Daylight* was painted in a lustery light gray Pyroxilin lacquer, the idea being to reflect the intoxicating heat of California sunshine. Air-conditioning was still a virtual unknown in transportation.

The *Lark* was SP's overnighter on the same route. The all-sleeping-car train commenced service on May 8, 1910, and became quite popular with the high-brow society of the San Francisco Peninsula. The best of Pullman's sleepers were assigned to the *Lark* in the 1920s, and additional new cars and services were added to the train even as the stock-market crash of 1929 began to take its toll. The new lounges that came in 1930 featured card-playing areas, soda fountain (Prohibition still being in force), barber shop, showers, and—the omnipresent status symbol of any worthy standard-era train—valet service. Car interiors were done in a very attractive Mission style. In 1931, an Oakland section was added to the *Lark*, being switched into (southward) or split from (northward) the main section at San Jose.

## Fit for the gods: Milwaukee Road's **Olympian**

On the northern tier of the wide band of Midwest-to-West Coast routes, three carriers vied for passengers: Great Northern with its *Oriental Limited*; Northern Pacific and its *North Coast Limited*; and latecomer (its line to the Pacific Coast not having been completed until 1909) Chicago, Milwaukee & St. Paul—The Milwaukee Road, which would shortly change its name to Chicago, Milwaukee, St. Paul & Pacific to reflect its new role as a transcon.

H-1510   HOTEL EL TOVAR, GRAND CANYON NATIONAL PARK, ARIZONA

(GN and NP did not reach Chicago, thus their transcontinental trains were relayed between Minneapolis/St. Paul and Chicago by Chicago, Burlington & Quincy and, briefly for NP only, Chicago & North Western.) Appropriate to any important line of that era was a flagship passenger train, and for the Milwaukee's newest route, it was the *Olympian*, in reference to Greece's Mount Olympus, mythical abode of the Greek Gods. A secondary companion train, the *Columbian*, operated on a schedule that complemented the *Olympian* by serving the route at more or less opposite times. Running time from the shore of Lake Michigan to Puget Sound was about 72 hours.

The first incarnations of the *Olympian* and the *Columbian* departed the terminal cities of Chicago and Tacoma on May 28, 1911. These were the Northwest's first all-steel trains, and the equipment was built by Barney & Smith and the Pullman Company, although Milwaukee Road—not Pullman—operated the sleepers. Early *Olympian* consists included coaches, "tourist" sleepers (limited-amenity section sleepers for the budget-minded), regular sleepers, and a diner. The train's feature car was the observation-lounge, boasting a women's tea room; a smoking room for the cigar-chomping, handle-bar-mustached male crowd; a buffet for lighter fare meals; library; barber shop; and bathing facilities. In a pleasant departure from traditional exterior paint (read, Pullman green), the *Olympian* was painted orange and maroon—colors that would remain closely associated with the railroad until the 1950s.

The *Olympian*, *Columbian*, and other services that would come and go along the Pacific Extension were

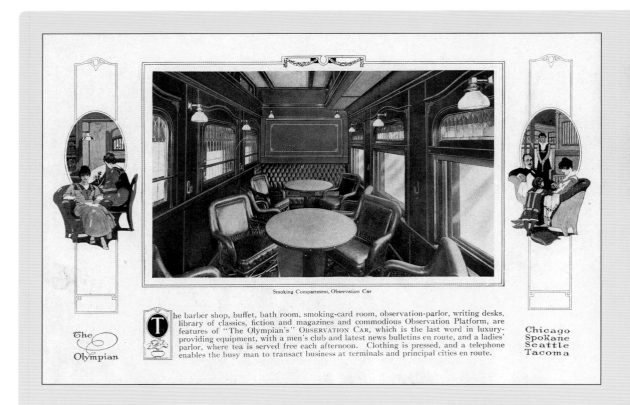

Smoking Compartment, Observation Car

**T**he barber shop, buffet, bath room, smoking-card room, observation-parlor, writing desks, library of classics, fiction and magazines and commodious Observation Platform, are features of "The Olympian's" OBSERVATION CAR, which is the last word in luxury-providing equipment, with a men's club and latest news bulletins en route, and a ladies' parlor, where tea is served free each afternoon. Clothing is pressed, and a telephone enables the busy man to transact business at terminals and principal cities en route.

The Olympian

Chicago
Spokane
Seattle
Tacoma

## OLYMPIAN OBSERVATION CAR

A booklet issued by the Chicago, Milwaukee & St. Paul Railway for its new Chicago–Tacoma, Washington, *Olympian* in 1911 featured finely executed artwork and photos of the train's features, such as the smoking compartment of the observation car shown (ABOVE), and scenes along the route. An exterior view of the train in 1928 (RIGHT) shows passengers and crew on the platform of observation car *City of Everett*. MILWAUKEE ROAD, COURTESY MILWAUKEE ROAD HISTORICAL SOCIETY

## BI-POLAR ON THE OLYMPIAN

The cover of a 1930 *Olympian* brochure featured one of The Milwaukee Road's heroic Bi-Polar locomotives that effortlessly moved the *Olympian* and sister train *Columbian* over electrified portions of the railroad's Pacific Extension. JOE WELSH COLLECTION

among a select group of American trains powered by electric locomotives for a significant portion of their runs. Between 1915 and 1917, the Milwaukee electrified some 440 miles of main line through the Rocky Mountains in Montana and Idaho and another 216 miles over the Cascade Range in Washington. Electric operation in these segments allowed the railroad to speed up schedules and operate special open-air observation cars.

On August 1, 1927, the *Olympian* was re-equipped with new heavyweight rolling stock and Pullman took over operation of the sleepers and lounge cars. Schedules were speeded up again significantly, and, during the final years

*Olympians of the past and*

# THE OLYMPIAN

*of the present*

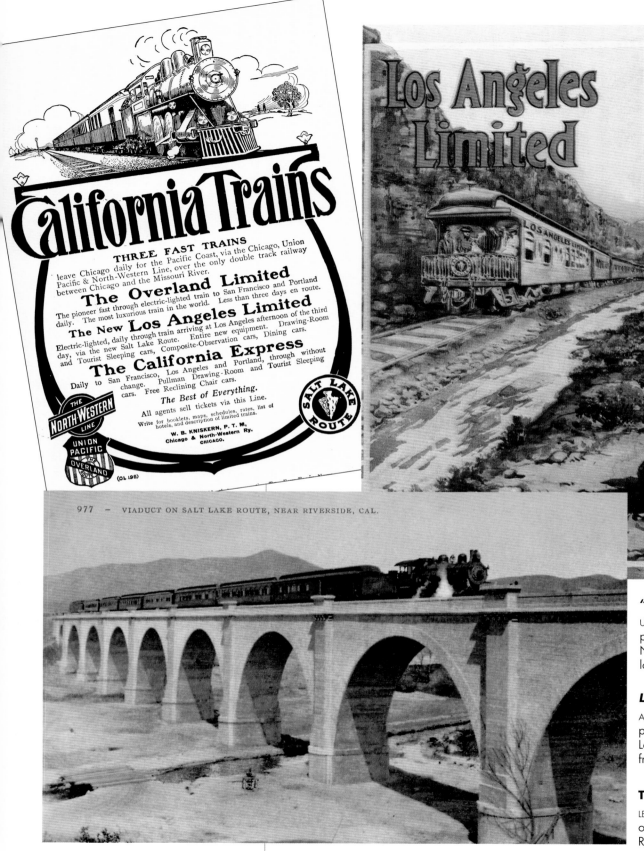

### "CALIFORNIA TRAINS", 1905

UPPER LEFT: A magazine ad from 1905 shows the premier trains on the "Chicago, Union Pacific & North-Western Line" (sic). Curiously missing is the logo for Southern Pacific. MIKE MCBRIDE COLLECTION

### *LOS ANGELES LIMITED*

ABOVE: A scowling Native American witnesses the passing of the *Los Angeles Limited* on the Salt Lake Route as depicted on the cover of a brochure from the early 1900s. JOE WELSH COLLECTION

### THE SALT LAKE ROUTE

LEFT: The *Los Angeles Limited* crosses a new viaduct on the San Pedro, Los Angeles & Salt Lake near Riverside, California. MIKE SCHAFER COLLECTION

leading to the Great Depression, through sleeping cars to Yellowstone Park were handled by the *Olympian* to Three Forks, Montana, where they were relayed by a branchline train down a 32-mile spur that ended at the Gallatin Gateway Inn—Milwaukee Road's hotel at the doorstep of the famous national park.

## Via Overland Route

Since its Gold Rush days, California continued to be a prime destination for transcontinental travelers, and a great many of them rode trains plying the famed Overland Route between Chicago and the San Francisco Bay Area: Chicago & North Western and Milwaukee Road (Chicago–Omaha on either line); Union Pacific (Omaha–Ogden, Utah), and Southern Pacific (Ogden–Oakland). At the start of the new century, the *Overland Limited* was the premier train on the route, and it also had a Portland section which was split from the main section at Odgen.

In its all-Pullman form during the early years of the century, the *Overland* was to Chicago–West Coast service what the *20th Century Limited* was to Chicago–East Coast service. This Chicago–California flyer was joined in 1905 by the new *Los Angeles Limited* between Chicago and Los Angeles via the Overland Route as far west as Ogden, then the new San Pedro, Los Angeles & Salt Lake to Los Angeles via Las Vegas, Nevada. Both trains established a reputation for high-class travel that would last until they were overshadowed by new streamliners in the 1930s.

## Santa Fe's unparalled transcons

No coverage of Midwest–California rail travel would be complete without spotlighting the legendary Atchison, Topeka & Santa Fe which until 1970 was the only railroad that reached all the way from Chicago—hub of the American passenger train network—to the West Coast. Santa Fe's flagship train between Chicago and Los Angeles was initially the *California Limited*, launched on November 27, 1892. With the arrival of railroading's standard era came a complete re-equipping of the train circa 1910. The new rolling stock included a twin-unit diner (kitchen car coupled to a dining-room car), club-lounge with a soda fountain and barber shop, and posh sleeping cars. The popularity of this train is underscored by the fact that it routinely operated in sections to accommodate demand; the record reportedly was 23 sections dispatched from Chicago on one day!

Clearly, Santa Fe realized from this that extra-luxury service could fill a niche and in 1911 introduced the *de-Luxe* as a complement to its *California Limited*. At the time, the *de-Luxe* represented the ultimate in first-class transportation.

There was but a single set of equipment, thus only one departure from each terminal each week for the 63-hour run, and only during the winter season. Passage was limited to just 60 passengers, allowing for a high ratio of service personnel to pampered passenger. At least one car featured sofas. Passengers read books from the library car while lounging in wicker chairs, or they could refresh themselves from desert dust with a bath or shower. The railroad charged an extra fare of $25—a lordly sum in those days. World War I brought an end to this and other luxury trains in 1917 during the government's wartime control of most U.S. railroads through the newly formed United States Railroad Administration.

The *Chief* name is synonymous with the Santa Fe, and it usually conjures up images of a gleaming stainless-steel streamliner. But the original *Chief* was very much a classic all-steel heavyweight train. The first run rolled out of Chicago's Dearborn Street Station on November 14, 1926; it was a daily all-Pullman operation with a $10 extra fare and a consist—Pullmans, diner, club-lounge—not unlike those of its peer carriers, although one of the cars sported a cigar store. In an unusual twist, service in the diner was provided by famous Fred Harvey Corporation rather than the railroad. Fred Harvey had been serving meals to Santa Fe patrons since 1893 and would continue to do so until the end of 1968.

## SANTA FE'S *CALIFORNIA LIMITED*

In a postcard scene sponsored by Fred Harvey Corporation circa 1920, Santa Fe's heavyweight egalitarian flagship of the road's Chicago–Kansas City–Los Angeles market, the *California Limited*, crosses Johnson's Canyon in Arizona. Composite (combination wood and steel) cars still ruled on the *California Limited* and other Santa Fe trains until air-conditioning became commonplace, because the railroad felt wood carbodies provided greater insulation from desert heat. MIKE SCHAFER COLLECTION

## AN INVITATION TO THE AMERICAN SOUTHWEST

Early on, Santa Fe employed Native American theming for its trains—a concept that would last until 1971. The excellent artwork used on the cover of this 1912 brochure for the *California Limited* reflected Santa Fe's penchant for panache. JOE WELSH COLLECTION

Santa Fe

*The* **Grand Canyon Limited**

*The* **California Limited**

The *Chief* made the 2,228-mile run in 63 hours, but by the end of 1930 this timing had been reduced to 56 hours, and the train re-equipped with new all-steel cars. "The *Chief* is Still *Chief,*" Santa Fe promotions touted, along with the fact that it was the fastest train between Chicago and California. The *Chief* and *California Limited* were the star players on the route, but not the only passenger runs. The *Navajo*, the *Missionary*, the *Grand Canyon Limited*, and the *Fast Mail Express* among others borne of the standard era catered to a public enamored with California.

The *Grand Canyon Limited* circa 1930 provides a great example of how complex train operations could get in the standard era. In reality, the *Grand Canyon Limited* represented a service that comprised a network of trains and through cars rather than just a train. It was a service that, in part (and as the name implied), focused on getting travelers to and from Grand Canyon National Park. Westbound, for example, the main section of the *Grand Canyon Limited*, train 23, ran between Chicago and Los Angeles. At Kansas City, through cars were pulled from No. 23 to be forwarded to Wichita, Kansas. At La Junta, Colorado, a train connecting from No. 23 took through cars up to Denver. At Williams, Arizona, through cars from 23 were set out to be taken by a connecting train up the 64-mile branch that ended at the endtrance to Santa Fe's El Tovar Hotel at the rim of the Grand Canyon. At Ash Fork, Arizona, No. 23 set out still more through cars that were forwarded to Phoenix on a connecting train. At Barstow, California, No. 23 was split into two trains, with one leg continuing to Los Angeles (via Cucamonga and Azusa, of Jack Benny fame) and the other up to the San Francisco Bay Area via Bakersfield and Fresno. Expeditious train handling and efficient switching were paramount to keeping everything reasonably on schedule; one delay in the operation could have a domino effect that could be felt all the way to California.

### *Bucking the Depression: C&O's* George Washington

One of the last new trains launched before the start of the streamliner era, which for purposes of this book was 1934, was Chesapeake & Ohio's *George Washington*, born on April 24, 1932—the 200th birthday of the first U.S. president. This stellar overnight train between the East Coast and Midwest was another example of a "network" service rather than a single train. Westbound, the main or "New York–Washington Section" of the train operated between New York City and Cincinnati, with the "Virginia Section" from Phoebus (greater Norfolk) joining the main section at Charlottesville, Virginia. The Pennsylvania Railroad handled through cars for the *George* out of New York's Pennsylvania Station to Washington on one of its regular trains. Toward the other end of the *George's* run, a Louisville section was cut from the main train at Ashland, Kentucky. Once the main leg of the *George* had arrived at Cincinnati, station switchers busily transferred the Chicago and St. Louis through cars to their connecting New York Central trains. Eastbound, this whole ritual happened in reverse.

The new *George* was a silver lining for the dark clouds of Depression when other railroads had begun to discontinue trains. The *George* joined a family of previously established Tidewater–Midwest C&O name trains that included the *Sportsman* and the *Fast Flying Virginian*, their geographical span similar to that of the *George*. The *George* quickly ascended as C&O's signature train, which it would remain until C&O handed its operation over to Amtrak in 1971.

Despite the Depression well under way, the American passenger train would soon see another silver lining—streamliners. The Depression had ended the Golden Age of the passenger train, but streamliners and diesels would launch a whole new era.

*The George Washington*

THE MOST WONDERFUL TRAIN
IN THE WORLD... *CREATED BY THE*

CHESAPEAKE AND OHIO

## THE SLEEPING CARS

Every car on THE GEORGE WASHINGTON bears a name related to some point, person or place in George Washington's part in the making of the United States. They are named Yorktown, Valley Forge, First Citizen, Potomac, Mount Vernon, Williamsburg, Von Steuben, Fairfax, Rochambeau, Lafayette, Cornwallis, Ferry Farm, Pohick Church, Monmouth, Monticello, Mary Washington, Wakefield, and so on.

The interior of every car is decorated with the reproduction of some famous painting, or the likeness of an historical personage or event suggested by the name of the car itself. If, for instance, you were to occupy a room in the Valley Forge, you would find the rooms named Anthony Wayne, Nathaniel Greene and Light Horse Harry Lee, the three com-

manders who were Washington's stay and support during that terrible winter when success of the cause trembled in the balance. You would find the interiors of those rooms suggesting the memories of those gallant men. Should you occupy a berth or a section in any of the Pullman cars, you would find the surroundings suggesting something of the person, place or event for which the car has been named.

## LIBRARY OBSERVATION LOUNGE CARS

The Library Observation Lounge Cars have been named Commander-in-Chief and American Revolution. You will see there Leutze's immortal picture, Washington Crossing the Delaware, and the historically famous Signing of the Declaration of Independence.

### THE COLONIAL LOOK

Colonial-motif dining cars became a hallmark on both the Chesapeake & Ohio and neighbor Baltimore & Ohio. Leaded-glass windows make this B&O colonial dining car from the 1920s seem like a high-class restaurant. B&O, BILL HOWES COLLECTION

### ANTI-DEPRESSANT

C&O's promotional brochure for the new *George Washington*—launched in the depths of the Depression—featured handsomely rendered inviting interior views of the train's feature cars. Shown are a portion of one of the train's Pullman section sleepers and the living-roomlike surroundings of the library-observation-lounge car. Note the bust of President Washington above the door. JOE WELSH COLLECTION

**QUIET**

IS REQUESTED FOR THE BENEFIT
OF THOSE WHO HAVE RETIRED

THE PULLMAN COMPANY

Imagine, if you would, a coast-to-coast hotel chain that slept 100,000 guests every night—and, in the process moved them from one city to another, or from their hometown to a national park, or from the Atlantic to the Pacific. Such was the Pullman Company at the peak of rail travel in America during the 1920s.

To many who can recall the era of Pullman travel, which ended on the eve of December 31, 1968, when the century-old company closed its (vestibule) doors, the name "Pullman" was synonymous with a sleeping car. And, though that's as it should be, there has always been some confusion in the matter. A Pullman was not so much a type of sleeping car as it was a sleeping car *operated* by the Pullman Company. In a sense, the Pullman Company was a railroad. True, Pullman did not own its own tracks (except for those within its huge shop complex on Chicago's South Side and at its plant in Worcester, Massachusetts), much less locomotives and stations. But it did own a vast fleet of sleepers and sundry other first-class-type cars, and it employed its own conductors and car attendants, the latter popularly known by the now unpolitically correct term "porters." Pullman relied on North American railroads to actually move the cars, usually attached to a carrier's regularly scheduled trains.

At its pinnacle, Pullman's operation was indeed an amazing transport system, interlinked so that Pullman

**QUIET IS REQUESTED**

The dark blue placards hanging on aisle walls in sleeping cars were an icon of Pullman travel. MIKE SCHAFER COLLECTION

**PULLMANS ON GM&O'S MIDNIGHT SPECIAL**

An airline strike during the summer of 1966 swelled the number of Pullmans on Gulf, Mobile & Ohio's *Midnight Special*, loading at Chicago Union Station on August 3 of that year, from the usual one to three. Not having enough GM&O-painted Pullmans to draw upon, the Pullman Company on this day has pressed a blue-and-white Missouri Pacific sleeper into service for the overnight run to St. Louis.

travelers could travel between any two points in the country where Pullman-equipped trains were scheduled to stop, and do so with but a modicum of layover time at train-change points, if there were any. The company referred to its service in terms of "car lines"—specific routes and schedules traveled by assigned cars. Most of Pullman's car lines were simple point-to-point operations—say, Chicago-to-St. Louis—that required only one railroad and one train to move the car(s) between the two designated endpoints. (In the case of Chicago–St. Louis and numerous other city pairs, however, there was more than one major carrier between the two cities, and each might have offered Pullman sleeping-car service on its night trains). Other car lines could be considerably more complex, involving more than one carrier and several trains. For example, in 1915, car line No. 3103 linked New Orleans and Denver. The Pullman assigned to this run began its journey at New Orleans in the evening as part of Texas & New Orleans train No. 11, which took it overnight to Houston. There, the car was transferred to Houston & Texas Central trains 15 and 83 to be carried, during the day, to Fort Worth. Fort Worth & Denver City train 7 ferried the car to Texline, Texas, where affiliate Colorado & Southern continued train 7 on to Denver for an early morning arrival. Despite the four different railroads and five different trains, through travelers using car line No. 3103 never had to vacate their Pullman sleeper until Denver. Passengers headed beyond Denver had a choice of connecting Pullman car lines there that would take them west, north, or east.

The average modern American traveler has little notion that this incredible network even existed, much less that it survived—albeit greatly decimated—almost into the 1970s. Today's air-travel network performs much the same function, only considerably faster—but at the expense of beds, relaxation, great food, and other creature comforts. Before the airline industry came of age, sleeping-car travel was simply a way of life in America. In that era, nearly all business-related overnight travel was by rail, so it was important that the business traveler had accommodations

that provided a restful night's sleep and a place to change clothes and freshen up for his or her 10 A.M. meeting. The Pullman car was truly a hotel on wheels.

Not all sleeping cars were Pullman-operated. A few railroads, particularly after World War II, elected not to subscribe to Pullman services and instead directly operated their own sleeping cars.

## HISTORY

George Mortimer Pullman did not invent the sleeping car, as is sometimes assumed. When he was born in 1831, in Brockton, New York, the idea for a railcar outfitted for sleeping had already been around for at least a decade. And when the Cumberland Valley Railroad began operating what is often considered to be the first sleeper—the *Chambersburg*—George was but 6 or 7 years old.

Born into a family of farmers and mechanics, the future sleeping-car magnate spent his young adulthood as a cabinet-maker. He later entered a contractor operation that moved houses and other buildings—an enterprise which in the late 1850s took him to Chicago where much of the downtown city infrastructure was in the process of being raised above the level of Lake Michigan.

Through some twists of fate, George teamed with a longtime associate, Benjamin Field, in a franchise arrangement in which they operated sleeping cars they had arranged to have built by America's first sleeping-car firm, T. T. Woodruff & Company, founded in 1857. Based in Chicago, Field and Pullman approached the Chicago, Alton & St. Louis Railroad about remodeling two coaches into sleepers. The newly revamped cars debuted in 1859, and eventually the Alton Route acquired additional cars from Field and Pullman, who now had founded their own company. Although it appears Field was satisfied with the fledgling endeavor, Pullman seemed less than enthusiastic and wanted to move on to bigger and better things—and not necessarily the sleeping-car business. He took a hiatus and headed west, but in 1863 he rejoined Field and they bought a luxurious new "palace" sleeping car for service on the CA&StL.

During the relatively short duration of Pullman's leave of absence from the partnership, the railroading scene had shifted dramatically. Civil War notwithstanding, the railroad boom was well under way—including the start of a "Pacific Railroad" to the West Coast. Pullman was a visionary, and he saw a future in long-distance rail travel as well as the need for better sleeping cars. Probably feeling hamstrung by the terms of the franchise with Woodruff, Pullman decided that if there was going to be an ultimate sleeping car, he was going to have to design and have it built himself. In 1865, car "A" was born, the biggest and most expensive sleeping car—about $20,000 or about five times the cost of a coach—built to that date. The ostentatious, 16-wheel, 12-section car was eventually christened *Pioneer*.

The *Pioneer* is somewhat steeped in legend as having many firsts, such as folding upper berths, an invention that actually dated to the 1830s (though the specifics of berth design had been patented by Field and Pullman). Nor was the *Pioneer* necessarily the most luxurious sleeper ever built—earlier cars of other sleeping-car operators could arguably be considered just as luxurious. However, it does appear that the *Pioneer* may have been the largest sleeper built at the time of its outshopping. The car was supposedly a foot wider and over two feet higher than its predecessors (in part to accommodate the folding upper berths), which reputedly kept it off the lines of carriers whose lineside clearances could not accommodate its passage.

The *Pioneer*'s real claim to fame was that it was supposedly included in the consist of President Abraham Lincoln's funeral train in 1865 and that its use required Chicago-area railroads hosting the special to rebuild station platforms and bridges to accommodate the car's girth. The publicity thus generated helped Pullman further establish his reputation in the realm of sleeping-car providers—of which there were many by the late 1800s.

Only a few weeks after serving on the slain president's funeral train, the *Pioneer* made its first trip on the Chicago & Alton, and—together with special excursions extolling Pullman-Field's newest sleepers and services—garnered still more publicity. By the end of 1866, nearly every major railroad serving Chicago was a subscriber to Pullman-Field sleeping-car operations. But despite this encouraging surge in business, Benjamin Field decided it was time for him to step aside, and George Pullman was now on his own.

Undeterred, Pullman marched on, incorporating the Pullman Palace Car Company in 1867. His established reputation as an astute businessman garnered him much support from far-flung financial circles that included the likes of Andrew Carnegie and Marshall Field. Backed by these and other financial principals, including some from the war-ravaged South, Pullman aimed for the top: a national network of sleeping-car lines.

He also had the backing of a public whose desire for luxury travel escalated right along with the great railroad building boom that followed the Civil War. Pullman had an overpowering belief that public travel should be an event rather than a nightmare of squalor in coaches, and it was quite obvious that a large segment of the traveling public agreed. Save for short-term dips from a couple of panics and recessions in the late 1800s, overall growth in Pullman-car patronage would continue unabated until the 1920s.

A myriad of sleeping-car companies flourished throughout the land at the time of the birth of the Pullman Palace Car Company, companies with names ranging from the perfunctory (Southern Transportation Company) to the whimsical (Rip Van Winkle Line), and more companies were formed afterward as well, some as late as the early 1900s. In addition, several railroads established their own sleeping-car service, including the Great Northern; the Chicago, Milwaukee & St. Paul (Milwaukee Road); and the New York, New Haven & Hartford.

One by one, however, the sleeping-car companies either disbanded or fell to Pullman control or outright acquisition. Wagner and the Central Transportation Company were Pullman's two most powerful competitors, both of them wielding a stronghold on Eastern sleeper services. But they, too, fell to Pullman: CTC in 1870 and Wagner at the end of 1899.

After the CTC acquisition, Pullman's cars were, nationwide, the rule and not the exception on trains offering sleeping-car service, and by about 1890 Pullman had clearly emerged as the dominate force in first-class rail transportation. The complexity of the Pullman empire grew exponentially between 1870 and the 1890s. In 1870, and

### PULLMAN CREW ON THE B&O

A Pullman crew—possibly on hand for the 1923 inaugural of the *Capitol Limited*—stands at attention for their portrait within the train shed of Grand Central Station in Chicago. Pullman operations of this era often included food service, hence the chef and attendant at far left. The eight crew members, left to right, in this scene were in the charge of the Pullman conductor at far right.
BALTIMORE & OHIO, BILL HOWES COLLECTION

in order to exercise even more control over its products, Pullman opened a car works in Detroit; no longer would Pullman have to rely exclusively on outside contractors to build and maintain cars. This move brought Pullman into the commercial car-building field as well.

In the early 1870s, Pullman operated some 800 cars over some 30,000 route-miles and fielded about 2,000 employees. About half the cars were operated through an association that had been established between Pullman and 14 individual railroads, notable among them the Atlantic Coast Line; Chicago, Rock Island & Pacific; Delaware, Lackawanna & Western; Missouri Pacific; Northern Pacific; Santa Fe; and Southern Pacific. Eventually, Pullman bought out most of the contracts of the "Association" railroads.

Growth and demand for new cars outstripped the ability of the Detroit plant to crank out new rolling stock, and in 1881 Pullman opened a new plant on Chicago's South Side, an operation sometimes referred to as the Calumet Works (because of nearby Calumet Lake). But the new facility was more than a railcar factory—it was in fact a whole town, and it represented new manufacturing methods as well as a new way of life. Pullman, Illinois, was America's first planned industrial community. Set upon 3,600 acres 14 miles south of downtown Chicago, Pullman featured broad, tree-lined streets, beautiful parks, rows of solidly built company houses, churches, and a centerpiece brick hostelry, the Hotel Florence (named for

George Pullman's daughter). The sprawling factory complex was designed by still-noteworthy Chicago architect Solon Spencer Beman, who also designed Chicago's Grand Central Station. The Pullman Car Works represented the first application of mass production via assembly line.

Workers and management were assigned their housing (placed according to hierarchy within the company; i.e., a common laborer would not be housed next door to a manager)—and were expected to follow strictly enforced rules set forth by Pullman within the community. In this sense, Pullman was a "dry" town, as no taverns were permitted.

The irony of this brief attempt at industrial idealism emerged in 1894 when, following the onset of a depression in 1893, some 4,000 workers were laid off and the wages cut of those remaining—with no commensurate reduction of rent owed by workers for their housing. A brutal strike ensued—complete with bloodshed—and spread to rail lines on which Pullman cars operated. President Grover Cleveland finally had to call in federal troops to quell the rioting—the first time in U.S. history that federal force had to be used in a labor problem.

The strike proved devastating to George Pullman and likely contributed to his death in 1897, only months before his company achieved its ultimate victory in the climb to becoming a giant in American railroad history: acquisition of the Wagner Car Company. George M. Pullman was laid to rest in Chicago's Graceland Cemetery,

## A PULLMAN CLASSIC: THE "12-1"

Trailing a streamlined consist (except for the heavyweight lounge car midway in the train) is a 12-section 1-drawing-room heavyweight Pullman on Pennsylvania Railroad's eastbound *General* at Englewood, Illinois, on April 12, 1941. At this time, the eastbound General carried a Boston-bound 12-1 from Chicago to Pennsylvania Station, New York, where it was transferred to New Haven train No. 182. The 12-1 sleeper was once the most common type of Pullman car. JOE WELSH COLLECTION

## CLASSIC PULLMAN SECTION SLEEPER

Section sleepers provided the most basic accommodation of first-class travel. For a nominal accommodation charge above the first-class fare, passengers occupied "sections" with facing seats during daytime travel. At night, the facing seats folded to form a lower berth, while the upper berth folded down from the ceiling (right). Passengers purchasing upper-berth accommodations were obliged to sit in the rearward facing sections seats during day travel while lower-berth passengers occupied the forward-facing seat. The view below shows daytime section arrangement on Union Pacific's *City of Denver*. UNION PACIFIC, MIKE SCHAFER COLLECTION

## MAKING UP THE BERTHS IN A SECTION SLEEPER

In the evening, as Pullman passengers sipped cognac in the lounge car or lingered over a late-night snack in the Pullman buffet, porters made up the berths throughout the sleeping-car section of the train. This Pullman attendant has just transformed section seating into upper and lower berths and is in the process of hanging the heavy, dark curtains that will privatize the sleeping areas. Day or night, passengers were obliged to use restrooms at the ends of the car. The upper berth, which was windowless, was accessible by a ladder. For these reasons, the upper berth was the cheapest way to travel in a Pullman. MISSOURI PACIFIC, MIKE SCHAFER COLLECTION

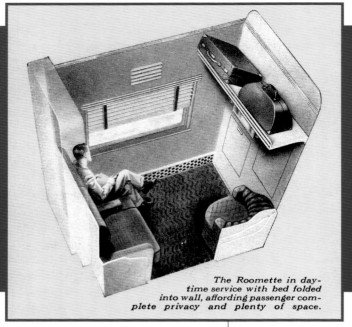

The Roomette in day-
time service with bed folded
into wall, affording passenger complete privacy and plenty of space.

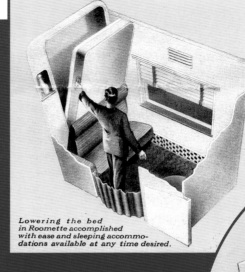

Lowering the bed
in Roomette accomplished
with ease and sleeping accommodations available at any time desired.

## THE ROOMETTE

The roomette was a relatively recent innovation (1937) that addressed a growing demand for more-private, individual sleeping accommodations. Since section sleepers often meant sharing facing seats with strangers—which, of course, had its advantages and disadvantages—and double bedrooms were too expensive for the lone traveler, the roomette filled a niche that after World War II would become the most popular sleeping-car accommodation. Travelers by day had a wide, plush seat and their own toilet facilities. At night, a bed folded out of the wall, and though it covered the toilet facilities, it gave the traveler a wall-to-wall, window-level bed. Roomettes doomed section accommodations in the U.S., with most of them gone by the end of the 1950s, although section space could still be had into the late 1960s in isolated instances. However, roomettes and sections both remained popular in Canada into the 1980s. PULLMAN COMPANY, AUTHOR'S COLLECTION

where ardent students of railway history still stop by his pillared memorial to pay their respects to a man whose name is more closely associated with American rail travel than any other. Even an Amtrak Superliner sleeping car, still rolling off the miles as this book goes to press, bears his name. Similarly, the town of Pullman was in the throes of renewed preservation efforts as the twenty-first century got under way.

The loss of Pullman himself did not deter his namesake company from continuing its role as a driving force in rail passenger transport. Robert Todd Lincoln—son of former U.S. President Abe Lincoln—assumed Pullman presidency and led the unimaginably rich company into the twentieth century, at which time the ostentatious "palace car" tag was dropped from the corporate title. It was now known simply as The Pullman Company.

Pullman's traffic expanded threefold during the first decade of the new century, and starting around 1910 began converting to all-steel construction. Virtually all the remaining competition was wiped out in the early 1900s, including nearly all the sleeping-car lines operated by the railroads themselves. (The last hold-out was the Milwaukee Road, which in 1927 finally sold out to Pullman.) For better or worse, the Pullman Company had evolved into a monopoly, a situation which would haunt the company until after World War II. Over the years, Pullman would be faced with protests of this situation, but usually offset them with the basically credible argument that, as a giant in the industry, customers stood to benefit from the economics of such a large endeavor, much in the same manner that companies today claim mergers and similar consolidations result in improved economics, which, presumably

were passed on to customers. For example, with its nationwide car pool, Pullman could move cars around to meet shifts in customer demand. Cars normally assigned to Western routes could be transferred to New York–Florida and Midwest-Florida routes in the dead of winter when Western travel dropped and sunbelt business boomed.

Further, competition between sleeping-car companies became less of an issue in the 1920s as a new type of competition—in part government sponsored—emerged: the automobile and motor coach, plying on a new national highway system. Nonetheless, the Roaring Twenties was Pullman's best decade in terms of the number of passengers hauled and profits. Every year during that period, up to 400 new cars were built and pressed into service to handle an average of 55,000 customers per night, being tended to by nearly 3,000 conductors and 12, 000 porters. By the end of the 1920s, Pullman had nearly 10,000 cars in service.

Despite any implications of monopoly, few could fault that Pullman had become synonymous with impeccable service. Car operation followed rigid standards that had been established by management under Pullman himself. The logistics of car operations, including the stocking of linens and blankets, spare parts, sanitary supplies, and such had been carefully planned and fully executed. And the service offered to patrons, kindly carried out in near militaristic form by Pullman porters, conductors, maids, barbers, and busboys has yet to be surpassed in any form of transportation, with the possible exception of trans-Atlantic oceanliners of yore. Detailed rulebooks outlined all the proper procedures for tending to customers, whether it was how to properly address boarding passengers or the serving of a beer (12 steps, including how to properly pre-chill the glass and turn the bottle so that the label faced the customer). As a result, Pullman employees were often sought to serve in the White House.

Perhaps the most notable change for Pullman in the 1920s was its 1924 split, turning manufacturing operations into a separate entity known as the Pullman-Standard Car & Manufacturing Corporation. This and The Pullman Company itself would eventually fall under the umbrella of holding company Pullman Inc., formed in 1927. These moves allowed Pullman Car & Manufacturing to better position itself in the lucrative freight-car building market and yet continue to produce passenger rolling stock for the Pullman Company. In 1929, PC&M merged with neighbor (in Hammond, Indiana) Standard Steel Car Company to form Pullman-Standard, and a new giant in railcar construction was born.

And then the bottom dropped out, not only from under the Pullman empire, but the country (and eventually, the

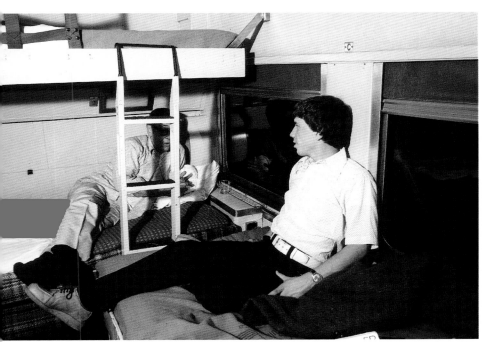

## THE DOUBLE BEDROOM

The double bedroom, with two beds, was ideal for two people traveling together. By day, the room featured either a long couch (as being tested by two potential parents on a New York Central Pullman) or two collapsible day chairs. At night, the couch folded into a bed that was crosswise to the rails while a second bed folded down from the ceiling to create a bunk-bed arrangement. Double bedrooms with two day chairs featured fold-down bunk beds that were parallel to the rails. In either case, the toilet annex remained fully accessible at all times. NEW YORK CENTRAL, COURTESY ROBERT YANOSEY, MORNING SUN BOOKS

## MASTER BEDROOM

Southern Railway passengers Dick Horstmann, John Graham, and author Schafer (out of view, taking the photo), en route from Washington, D.C., to Birmingham, Alabama, on the *Southern Crescent* in 1978, discuss the events of the day before retiring for the night in their master bedroom. A relative rarity in American rail travel, the master bedroom was a cousin to the drawing room, both accommodations featuring three beds, but master bedrooms included fully enclosed showers—a rarity on American trains until Amtrak's Superliner sleepers of the mid-1990s. Southern's buffet-lounge-sleepers, built for the original streamlined *Crescent* in 1950, featured two drawing rooms and one master bedroom. They were operated by Pullman until the end of 1968 when SR assumed their operation.

## DINING ABOARD A PULLMAN RESTAURANT CAR

During the 1930s, the Pullman Company rebuilt many of its heavyweight cars into parlor-"restaurant" or restaurant-sleepers to augment the railroad-operated full dining cars. Restaurant service provided by Pullman's commissary department was of a leisurely pace, available throughout the trip. Fare was simple items of the best quality available, prepared individually by the chef. In Pullmanland, presentation was everything. Pullman instructions to Commissary employees went into great detail concerning plate arrangement and garnish. On a September evening on Pennsylvania Railroad's Chicago–Cincinnati *Union,* a passenger is being served dinner by Pullman attendant Augustus Pringle. The dinner included a lettuce and tomato salad; fresh, crisp hash browned potatoes; and a house specialty, Charcoal grilled double lamb chops served with fresh peas seasoned with soft creamery-fresh butter, seasoned with salt and sugar. Pullman restaurant cars operated until the The Pullman Company itself quit on December 31, 1968. Nothing about it all was "fat free." ILLUSTRATION BY MITCH MARKOVITZ

world) as a whole with the Crash of '29 and the ensuing Great Depression. New car orders—freight and passenger—virtually vanished as railroads went bankrupt from coast to coast. Mushrooming unemployment slashed discretionary travel, and in 1932, for the first time ever, Pullman posted a loss in its sleeping-car operations. With patronage down by nearly 60 percent in 1933 (relative to 1929 ridership), Pullman had to take drastic measures, notably a draconian slash in employment and a cut in sleeping-car fares, to save itself. Had it not been for Pullman's long-held cash resources, accumulated through years of heady success, the company might have failed along with the multitude of those that did during this darkest of America's moments.

The silver lining in this cloud was actually painted Armour yellow and autumn-leaf brown. In 1933, Union Pacific contracted with Pullman-Standard to construct what would become America's first lightweight, streamlined passenger train, the M-10000 (later and perhaps better-known as the *City of Salina*). The train debuted in 1934 and, together with another, slightly younger streamliner—Burlington Route's *Zephyr* 9900—built by P-S's nemesis-to-be Edward G. Budd Manufacturing Company, ushered in the streamliner era.

With this new period of American history came a turnaround for both arms of the Pullman legacy. By the end of the 1930s, several railroads were scrambling to introduce new streamliners, and that meant new car-building business for Pullman-Standard and new customers to be handled by The Pullman Company in several hundred shiny new lightweight streamlined Pullman sleepers.

Alas, the bottom was about to fall out again, but this time the trap doors were directly under Pullman. In 1940, the U.S. Justice Department filed a complaint accusing the Pullman Company of being a monopoly in violation of the Sherman anti-trust act. Pullman's monopoly-like status of more than 40 years was hardly a revelation, but since the good of the traveling public had rarely been compromised by the highly respected carrier, legal forces apparently simply looked the other way toward more-important issues of the day.

This changed with the coming of age of the Budd Company, which, as it turned out, had prompted the suit. A relative newcomer to the railcar business, Budd was fast earning a reputation built on stainless steel and the company's patent for stainless-steel fabrication known as "shotwelding"—a patent that prevented Pullman-Standard from effectively producing quality stainless-steel cars of its own. (P-S did produce stainless-steel cars, but they were prone to corrosion.) A growing cache of railroads were eagerly approaching Budd for streamlined, lightweight, stainless-steel passenger cars, not only for their good looks, but also because of their durability and anticipated extended life expectancy (albeit at considerably higher prices).

The Chicago, Burlington & Quincy had been one of these roads. Thrilled with the success of its *Zephyr* 9900 of 1934, Burlington went full steam ahead on ordering new streamliners, all of them of fluted stainless steel and all of them from Budd. Among the cars were sleepers for the new (1936) *Denver Zephyr*. Pullman initially refused to operate these or any sleepers that had not been built by its sister company, Pullman-Standard. Eventually, both parties compromised, though largely in Pullman's favor: Burlington would purchase no more than ten sleepers from Budd (more than that, and Burlington would have to form its own sleeping-car operation to run all the sleepers on all its trains). The same situation developed between Santa Fe and Pullman shortly thereafter, and the outcome was the same.

Budd cried foul, and the federal government filed suit against Pullman for violation of Sherman-Clayton anti-trust laws. Budd also attempted to convince the courts that Pullman was using unscrupulous practices to seriously impede Budd's ability to garner new car orders. In 1944, the courts ruled in the government's favor, ordering Pullman Inc. to sell either its sleeping-car operation (Pullman Company) or its manufacturing firm (Pullman-Standard). In addition, Pullman was told it had to accommodate carriers wanting Pullman to provide sleeping-car service, regardless of who built the cars. Nonetheless, the courts also absolved Pullman of any predatory practices

Pullman Inc. chose to sell the Pullman Company, correctly forecasting a better future for freight-car construction than for rail passenger service. And the buyer? None other than 57 railroads, including Canadian lines, already offering Pullman service. The sale was made complete in 1947, and the terms of the agreement maintained that the railroads themselves buy the cars and lease them to Pullman for staffing and operation. Under new leadership, the Pullman Company forged ahead, fueled by postwar optimism and the fact that, despite an almost 40 percent drop in revenues since the close of the war, the company was in considerably better shape than during the Depression.

As many readers know all too well, this did not happen. Patronage continued to slip. Although Pullman ridership surged to 31 million passengers at the close of the war, as of the end of 1950 the number had dropped to prewar levels. New lightweight cars were indeed added to the fleet, but because most were built by the "big three" manufac-turers of passenger cars—Pullman-Standard, Budd, and American Car & Foundry—some of the economies of standardization were lost. That and new lighting systems, added plumbing (all-room cars demanded more privies than "section" sleepers required) and gadgetry meant that the newer cars were more expensive to maintain.

The decline in sleeping-car travel accelerated along with that of other classes of rail travel as the 1950s unfurled, forcing railroads to eliminate the worst-performing car lines, often those with convoluted routings linking secondary cities or in markets served by more than one route (i.e., Chicago–St. Louis). By the late 1950s, things really began to unravel as a few owner railroads began opting out of Pullman to operate sleepers on their own. The biggest loss during that period was the New York Central in 1958, which carried a large percentage of the nation's rail passenger traffic. This increased the financial burden of the remaining owner railroads.

By the end of the 1950s, intercity rail travel in general had been decimated by the new jet airliners and by automobiles and buses riding new "tracks"—the high-speed, limited-access highways built through government monies. First-class revenues mirrored the industry-wide peril, but Pullman travel was particularly affected, as the burgeoning airline industry had essentially eliminated the need for overnight business travel. Day coach trains would hold their own for a while longer, but overnight sleeper trains vanished into the darkness.

In 1965, losses neared the $22 million mark. Only one more nail would seal Pullman's coffin, and it came from the Pennsylvania Railroad when that legendary carrier pulled out of Pullman in 1967. At that point, the Pullman Company simply stopped staffing cars and collecting revenues after December 31, 1968. Pullman continued to maintain the cars for the railroads for a short time, but it was up to the railroads to staff them and eventually take over maintenance (they already owned them anyway). The 27 railroads that still offered Pullman service thus faced a choice: eliminate sleeping cars or run them on their own.

Ironically, more than 30 years after Pullman's demise, the carrier's legacy survives. Amtrak offers sleeping-car services on nearly all its overnight runs, and there remains a significant demand for sleeper space on long-distance trains. Interestingly, many Amtrak's sleeper customers still call them "Pullman" cars.

# Moving the People: What Makes a Passenger Locomotive?

Thousands of examples of early passenger-car motive power can be seen throughout the continent to this day. They are still used in a few major cities by constables on patrol; they are "standard equipment" for any respectable farm or ranch, and they are still used for many forms of entertainment, including racing. They are horses.

Horses (and mules, too) were a natural for moving the cars of the newfangled tramways and railways that began to sprout in early nineteenth century America. After all, they had served reliably for centuries pulling wagons of goods—and people. But no matter how large or strong the horse, it had its limitations on just how heavy a load it could pull and how fast it could pull it. As business grew on these infant railways, something faster and more powerful was needed to do the job. And that premise has pretty much driven locomotive development ever since.

In England early in the 1820s, experimentation was already under way with steam locomotives. On the Stockton & Darlington in September 1825, the first successful steam locomotive, the *Locomotion*, snorted off with its the first passenger train in the world powered by something that didn't need to be fed grass or hay. In October 1829, at a seven-day competition at Rainhill, England, several steam locomotives were tested for power and performance, the winner being Robert Stephenson & Company's *Rocket*. The *Rocket* streaked

### GG1 ELECTRIC

ABOVE. The most revered of all electric passenger locomotives is the GG1, created by the Pennsylvania Railroad with Baldwin Locomotive Works and General Electric. Wearing the Tuscan red heritage livery of PRR, GG1 No. 4877 hustles along with a New Jersey Transit commuter train in 1983.

### THOSE ESTHETIC E-UNITS

LEFT, TOP: in a colorized black & white photo taken in June 1941, early slant-nosed E-units of (left to right) Atlantic Coast Line, Florida East Coast, Seaboard Air Line, Southern Railway, and Baltimore & Ohio stand cheek by jowl at Washington, D.C. ELECTRO-MOTIVE

### MACHINERY AS ART FORM

LEFT, BOTTOM: The driving wheels of Milwaukee Road F7-class Hudson No. 100 at rest belie their speed potential. This and sister 4-6-4s could steam along with a *Hiawatha* at 100 MPH. MILWAUKEE ROAD, COURTESY MILWAUKEE ROAD HISTORICAL ASSOCIATION

## AMERICA'S FIRST "REAL" TRADITIONAL STEAM LOCOMOTIVE

Arriving from England in 1831, *John Bull* was the first "real" steam locomotive in America, with a horizontal fire-tube boiler and, added later, an ersatz pilot-wheel set and a "cowcatcher." *Bull* owner Camden & Amboy Railroad began building sister locomotives soon after the *John Bull* had proven itself, and by 1833 enough *Bull* clones had been built to allow the the New Jersey-based railroad to provide scheduled passenger service. This replica operating on the Strasburg Railroad in eastern Pennsylvania was built in 1940 by the Pennsylvania Railroad for public exhibitions. JIM BOYD

## THE LOCOMOTIVE THAT BUILT (AND MOVED) AMERICA: THE 4-4-0

Most passenger trains of the mid and late nineteenth century were in the charge of steam locomotives with the 4-4-0 wheel arrangement, known as "American Standard." Thousands of 4-4-0s were built from the late 1830s to the end of the century. These two restored 4-4-0s—City of Prineville No. 3 and Virginia & Truckee No. 22, the Inyo, are steamed up for Expo '86 at Vancouver, British Columbia. V&T 22 pulls Civil War era passenger equipment. JIM BOYD

along at 28 MPH—the fastest that man had ever moved over land at that time.

Only a couple months before these Rainhill Trials, the Delaware & Hudson Canal Company's *Stourbridge Lion* had become the first steam locomotive to operate in America, though only as an experiment. On December 25, 1830, on the South Carolina Canal & Railroad Company, the *Best Friend of Charleston* became the first locomotive to pull a scheduled passenger train in America (as well as the first locomotive to blow up and kill a crew man). The *Best Friend* and its predecessors and peers were all one-of-a-kind machines, but in 1831 America would see its first true "production" locomotive, in the form of the now-famous *John Bull*. Built in England, the *John Bull* was the first engine whose overall format would be followed by American steam locomotives for the next century plus: a horizontal boiler sitting ahead of a crew cab; driving wheels directly linked to cylinders which exhausted through a smokebox (to force a draft that would produce a hotter fire); and a crude "pilot" wheelset that helped guide the main part of the locomotive over the undulating, curving track.

Once stateside, the *John Bull* went to work on the Camden & Amboy, a New Jersey-based component of the future Pennsylvania Railroad, and 15 sister locomotives—built stateside to the *Bull*'s design—would join *John Bull* to handle the road's freight and passenger trains.

A vast majority of locomotives up to this time relied on four main driving wheels and little else in the way of wheels, but in 1837 a full-fledged swiveling pilot truck was introduced to engine design and soon widely adopted. The "4-4-0" (four pilot wheels, four driving wheels, no trailing wheels, with the zero pronounced as "oh") had been born. The 4-4-0 design, with its narrow boiler carried between the drive wheels and the smokebox weight carried by the pilot wheels, gained widespread acceptance on the multitude of new railroads mushrooming out of (or into) the wilderness to settle new lands. This wheel arrangement acquired the appropriate name "American Standard," and the 4-4-0 would reign supreme for much of the remainder of the century, hauling both freight and passenger trains. Often characterized by large diamond-shaped smokestacks (to reduce spark emissions), pointed "cowcatchers" (to push wayward livestock off the track), and oversize headlamps, the wood-burning 4-4-0 went down in history as the locomotive that settled America.

During railroading's infancy in America, the separation between freight and passengers often was indistinct, with both carried aboard a single train clanking through the countryside. However, as early as the 1840s, as locomotive evolution gained momentum, builders began to tailor a locomotive's design to specific duties. A locomotive designed expressly for freight service would have smaller drivers, putting more power and adhesion to the rails, at the expense of speed. Passenger locomotives featured large-diameter driving wheels to maximize speed. With 70-inch diameter drivers, a 4-4-0 could wheel a passenger train along at the unheard of speed of 60 MPH on well-laid track, though there was precious little of that to go around.

By the 1880s, builders were putting an additional set of drivers on new locomotives, and in the world of passenger engines the 4-6-0 or "Ten-Wheeler" was born, providing slightly more power and adhesion than the 4-4-0. Nonetheless, the 4-4-0 continued to rule the rails, and the pinnacle of its reign came on May 10, 1893, when New York Central & Hudson River 4-4-0 No. 999—cruising from New York to Buffalo with the *Empire State Express* and then bound for the Columbian Exposition World's Fair in Chicago—hit 112.5 MPH in Upstate New York. This was the first time a train had reached and exceeded the "century" mark of 100 MPH.

By this time, railroads were in need of more power as much as speed. Passenger cars were becoming larger and heavier, with iron and steel becoming more integral to car construction. More people than ever were riding trains, which consequently were becoming longer. In 1896, Baldwin Locomotive Works introduced the 4-4-2 wheel arrangement, named the "Atlantic" type because of its initial use on the Atlantic City Railroad in New Jersey. Trailing wheels allowed for a larger firebox (the trailing wheels

helped support the weight of the firebox) and therefore a more-powerful locomotive. The Atlantic format caught on quickly and was purchased and/or built by a number of railroads. Pennsylvania Railroad was among those, and its Juniata Shops in Altoona, Pennsylvania, along with Baldwin, built a number of Atlantics for the railroad's far-flung passenger network, including famous engine No. 7002. On June 12, 1905, this locomotive attained the astonishing—though arguably official—speed of 127.1 MPH while galloping across Ohio with the Pennsy's premier *Pennsylvania Special* en route from New York to Chicago.

An even more important type of passenger locomotive debuted in the late 1890s, although its popularity didn't catch on until early in the twentieth century. Like the 4-6-0, the 4-6-2 or "Pacific" type offered another set of drivers to deliver more power to the rails while maintaining high, sustained speeds. As with the 4-4-2, trailing wheels allowed for a larger firebox. The 4-6-2 was the near-perfect solution for the modern, all-steel, high-speed passenger train of the early 1900s, and the Pacific became the universal passenger power during the steam era of twentieth century America. In fact, 4-6-2s would be found heading U.S. passenger trains right nearly to the end of the 1950s.

Locomotive-building technology had advanced into the twentieth century with ever larger and more powerful locomotives in all service categories: passenger, freight, and "dual purpose" (passenger and high-speed freight). The early twentieth century saw three major steam locomotive builders come of age: venerable Baldwin Locomotive Works, dating from 1831; the American Locomotive Company (later known as Alco); and Lima Locomotive Works. Meanwhile, the shops of several railroads also continued to build locomotives.

## TEN-WHEELER BUILT FOR SPEED

Large driving wheels mean this pristine 4-6-0 of the Atlanta & West Point could hustle along with an average-size passenger train. This particular engine was built by Rogers Locomotive Works in December 1899. Still looking new, it is shown 40 years later, in 1939, with a passenger train pausing under the train shed of Montgomery Union Station. A&WP 273 may be long gone today, but the ornate train shed at this depot has been restored—although passenger trains no longer call at Alabama's state capital. JAY WILLIAMS/ BIG FOUR GRAPHICS COLLECTION

## PACIFIC ON THE *PACIFIC EXPRESS*

Pacific No. 2939 of the Erie Railroad heads up head-end-heavy train No. 7, the Hoboken-to-Chicago *Pacific Express*, pausing at Jamestown, New York, on June 16, 1940. The 4-6-2 was the most popular type of mainline passenger power during the steam era of the twentieth century. ROBERT F. COLLINS, COURTESY ED CRIST

## PACIFIC ALL DRESSED UP

To match its new *John Wilkes* streamliner of 1939, the Lehigh Valley applied streamlined shrouding to 4-6-2 No. 2101. The styling was done by noted industrial designer Otto Kuhler. A number of railroads applied shrouding to their steam locomotives during the early years of the streamliner era. Underneath, most were just another work-a-day steam locomotive. MARTIN S. ZAK, ANDOVER JUNCTION PUBLICATIONS COLLECTION

Any standardization of locomotive design prior to World War I occurred only at a very general level. Steam locomotives were still built to design specifics supplied by the customer, as every railroad had its own unique operating conditions and motive-power philosophies. However, this changed dramatically with the onset of World War I, when the federal government took over the operations of most railroads through its United States Railroad Administration. USRA's influence went beyond day-to-day operations; it also set out to standardize the components of American railroading. With this goal, the USRA developed standardized designs for new locomotives and freight cars that would be built during the war effort.

After the war, the USRA relinquished control of the nation's railroads, but its standardized designs generally were highly regarded and continued to be followed by many railroads until the end of the steam era. Of course, individual railroads still customized their USRA-design locomotives to a degree, but their overall appearances bore a family resemblance: a USRA Pacific heading Baltimore & Ohio's *National Limited* could pass as a kissin' cousin to one of Grand Trunk Western's USRA 4-6-2s pounding through Michigan with the Chicago-bound *Maple Leaf*.

There was life beyond the 4-6-2 in the realm of passenger locomotives. In 1911, Alco added yet another set of drivers to the 4-6-2 to produce the 4-8-2 "Mountain" type, a powerful dual-purpose locomotive ideal for heavy passenger runs in rugged territory and for high-speed freight service. Then, in 1925, Lima Locomotive Works of Lima, Ohio, introduced the four-wheel trailing truck, which allowed for an even larger boiler and firebox and led to the creation of the 2-8-4 "Berkshire" (named for that Massachusetts mountain range), primarily a freight locomotive. As the 1930s unfolded, the prototype 2-8-4 design was modified into a super-efficient machine through a larger boiler with a combustion chamber to produce higher steam pressure. The American steam locomotive had now entered the "super power" era.

The Berkshire was principally a freight locomotive, but the introduction of its four-wheel trailing truck had some great implications in the area of passenger locomotives. First was the 1926 introduction of the 4-8-4 on the Northern Pacific Railroad. These new heavy-duty, 73-inch-drivered "Northerns," as they would become known on most railroads, allowed the NP to eliminate the need to "double-head" (assign two locomotives to) passenger trains in mountain territory, thus greatly saving on crew and operating costs. This concept worked for the Santa Fe Railway as well, particularly with its popular new heavyweight *Chief* passenger train, introduced in 1926 on a high-speed schedule between Chicago and Los Angeles. Brawny 4-8-4s soon could be seen hustling passenger trains on roads like Union Pacific; New York Central; Chicago, Burlington & Quincy; the Milwaukee Road; and Southern Pacific.

Shortly after the introduction of the 4-8-4 came one of the most renowned steam passenger locomotives of all time: the 4-6-4, representing the next evolutionary step from the 4-6-2. Again, the four-wheel trailing truck allowed for a larger firebox—so the resulting engine would have about one third greater capacity than a standard 4-6-2, according the the calculations of New York Central's then-motive-power chief Paul Keifer. Calculations became reality on February 14, 1927 when Alco delivered the prototype 4-6-4 "Hudson"—so named for the state of New York's most famous river, shouldered by NYC main lines.

For railroads that needed speed and power but not necessarily the mountain-climbing capabilities of a 4-8-4, the

## GREAT BIG NORTHERN ON THE GREAT NORTHERN

Looming at the head end of Great Northern train No. 7 is 4-8-4 No. 2510, taking a brief respite from its morning-to-evening journey with the day local between Spokane and Seattle. The "Northern" type first appeared on GN rival Northern Pacific. Both railroads needed big locomotives like these to expedite heavy passenger trains through the Rockies and Cascades.
SANDY GOODRICK

## PENNSYLVANIA T1 DUPLEX

In some respects, Pennsylvania Railroad's T1 duplex 4-4-4-4 was the ultimate steam locomotive. Tremendously powerful, this sculptured locomotive could charge across the flatlands of Indiana and Ohio with the likes of the *General* or *Liberty Limited* at sustained speeds of 100 MPH and barely work up a sweat. Unfortunately, shop forces dedicated to keeping the T-1s in running order did work up a sweat, and the maintenance costs (and the coming of diesels) doomed these remarkable machines. BALDWIN LOCOMOTIVE WORKS, RAILFAN & RAILROAD COLLECTION

Hudson was perfect, and Central and other railroads took delivery of 275 Hudsons during the next several years. The 4-6-4 was a well-proportioned design, and equipped with 80-inch drivers, Hudsons could wheel a heavy passenger train along level track at nearly 100 MPH.

During the last 30 years or so of the steam era in America, which ended in the late 1950s, Pacifics, Hudsons, and Northerns ruled on passenger trains not affected by a new upstart that made headlines in 1934: the diesel-electric locomotive. There were some departures from this norm, and one in particular begs mentioning.

A diesel skeptic until well after World War II, the herculean Pennsylvania Railroad—whose passenger trains served nearly half the U.S. population—developed a rakish, semi-streamlined, "duplex"-type steam locomotive (two sets of drivers and cylinders) known as the T1, with a 4-4-4-4 wheel arrangement. Fifty of these behemoths were delivered at the end of World War II. These state-of-the-art racers developed some 6,000 hp and could easily replace double-headed PRR Class K4 Pacifics on a passenger train—and then hurtle that train along at more than 100 MPH! (American passenger trains back then overall were much faster than they are now.) Though generally superior in performance to its steam contemporaries, the T1s were subject to high maintenance costs. That coupled with the burgeoning success of postwar diesel-electric technology, doomed these awesome locomotives early on. In fact, no steam locomotive of the post-World War II era could beat

the prowess of the new diesel-electrics pouring forth from builders, especially in the realm of passenger service, where diesels made their first inroads in the 1930s.

## DIESEL-ELECTRIC LOCOMOTIVES

The use of internal-combustion power to move passengers dates to the first decade of the twentieth century when General Electric built a passenger-carrying railcar propelled by traction motors—linked to the car's wheels—that were fed electricity from a gas-powered generator. The result was the "gas-electric" motorcar, and the concept quickly caught on. These self-propelled vehicles, nicknamed "doodlebugs," were ideal for short branchline runs where patronage was light. They were much more economical to operate than even a one-car steam-powered passenger train.

GE exited the motorcar-building business in 1917, but in 1924 the slack was taken up by a new little Cleveland-based firm, the Electro-Motive Company. Using GE traction motors and generators, gas engines from Winton Engine Company, and railcar bodies fabricated by St. Louis Car Company, EMC assembled more than 400 motorcars before the Great Depression.

As a variation of this technology, in 1913 GE mounted two gas-powered generators in a non-passenger-carrying box-cab carbody to power traction-motor-equipped "trucks" (wheel assemblies), thus creating the world's first internal-combustion locomotive. Working with the Chicago, Rock Island & Pacific, EMC embarked on a similar

## ELECTRO-MOTIVE BOX-CAB LOCOMOTIVES 511-512

The boxy, ho-hum look of this EMC demonstrator locomotive set belies its importance in the evolutionary journey of the passenger locomotive. Shown testing at Boston in 1935, the duo is proving that diesel-electric locomotives can equal or surpass the steam locomotive in performance and efficiency while handling conventional passenger trains. BOB'S PHOTO

project in the late 1920s, producing reliable gas-electric locomotives that were used to switch or pull short freight or passenger trains. The drawback? There was (and is) a limit as to how much power a gasoline engine can generate.

GE had realized this as early as 1925 when it teamed up with Ingersoll-Rand to produce a line of fairly successful diesel-electric box-cab switching locomotives. However, diesel engines of this period were large and unwieldy in relation to their power output and difficult to fit inside a rail carbody. This all changed in 1934 when Electro-Motive and Winton—both having been purchased by General Motors in 1930—provided a new, more-compact Model 201-A diesel engine and traction motors to the Edward G. Budd Manufacturing Company in Philadelphia to power a new lightweight streamliner being built there: Burlington's *Zephyr* 9900. A rousing success, this little slip of silver became the world's first diesel-electric-powered, over-the-road, high-speed mainline train.

### SANTA FE E1A AND E1B

Electro-Motive's first E-units—the EA/EB and the E1A and E1B shown at the EMC plant in suburban Chicago in 1937, arguably illustrated the pinnacle of streamlined passenger diesels. Clad in the famous red, silver, yellow, and black "warbonnet" livery developed by Leland Knickerbocker of General Motors' Styling Section, Santa Fe's 11 E1s initially were assigned to the *Super Chief, El Capitan, Kansas Cityan, Chicagoan,* and *San Diegan.*
JIM BOYD COLLECTION

For the steam locomotive in America, *Zephyr* 9900 was a deadly silver bullet, proving that diesel technology could be applied to rail transport and be much more economical than steam power. Not immediately evident, though, was to what extent diesels could replace steam. Could diesel power be harnessed to pull "real" trains of conventional cars? The little 600-hp *Zephyr* was no match for a 3,600-hp 4-8-4 steam locomotive, which is what it took to move a 12-car standard passenger train over the road at sustained high speeds. But the format introduced by *Zephyr* 9900, with its 201-A Winton power plant, was a design still in infancy, and infants grow up.

Regardless, *Zephyr* 9900 and its peer, Union Pacific's distillate-electric streamliner, the M-10000, sparked a revolution in overall train design, and soon the Burlington, UP, and other railroads were ordering new, lightweight streamliners, all of them with diesel-electric technology. In most cases, the power cars of these new trains were designed specific to a given trainset and thus were not considered true locomotives—that is, independent motive-power units that could be assigned to any conventional train that had been assembled by coach-yard crews with the appropriate number of cars needed to accommodate the traffic demand for that day's trip.

Again, Electro-Motive set out to make a change. The company's design engineer, Dick Dilworth, spearheaded a crucial move in the diesel motive-power format that, in a sense, took a step backward: build an independent

### DIESEL POWER AS A SELLING POINT

Railroads used dieselization as a selling point for rail travel, as illustrated by this promotional ink blotter from 1941. The B&O pointed out which of its premier trains featured a clean, quiet, and smooth new motive and spoke of diesel-electric power being "so smooth, so quiet, it's like gliding—the perfect train ride." BILL HOWES COLLECTION

## ALCO DL-SERIES

Rock Island 621 was one of four DL-series units purchase by the CRI&P in 1941; it is shown leading the morning *Peoria Rocket* out of Chicago in 1967. As a dual-service locomotive, the DLs—styled by industrial designer Otto Kuhler— remained in production through World War II when other locomotive builders were restricted from building passenger diesels. Rock Island 621's three sisters were all retired by the early 1960s, but since the 621 had been re-engined by Electro-Motive in 1952, it lasted until 1968.

## ALCO'S CELEBRATED PA

Alco's 2,000-hp, single-engine PA/PB brought timeless design to passenger diesels, although its new 251-model engine proved to be a maintenance headache. The last PAs to operate in scheduled passenger service in the U.S. were those of Delaware & Hudson (cover), purchased secondhand from Santa Fe in 1967. The New York, Chicago & St. Louis (Nickel Plate Road) purchased eleven PAs in 1947–48 for its soon-to-be-streamlined *Nickel Plate Limited* and other runs; NKP crews dubbed the blue-and-light gray units "Bluebirds." The 190 is shown at the Alco plant in Schenectady, New York, upon its outshopping. ALCO, KEVIN HOLLAND COLLECTION

locomotive. Elaborating on the format employed by the GE/Alco/Ingersoll-Rand box-cab switchers of the late 1920s, Dilworth mounted four 900-hp 12-cylinder 201-A engines in two simple, semi-permanently coupled box-cab carbodies (with control cabs), each riding on two four-wheel power trucks to create a 3,600-hp locomotive set. Diesel-electric technology had then become a formidable adversary of the steam locomotive.

This new twin-unit box-cab locomotive, numbered 511-512, was successfully tested on Baltimore & Ohio passenger trains operating between Chicago and Washington, D.C. B&O was sold on the idea and, later in 1935, purchased its own box-cab, No. 50, for service on the Washington–Jersey City *Royal Blue*. Shortly after, the Santa Fe took delivery of two more box-cabs from EMC to power the new *Super Chief*, a hot, 39¾-hour Chicago–Los Angeles run equipped with heavyweight cars.

Things really took off for EMC following the debut of its box-cab diesel-electrics, and business began to boom, prompting Electro-Motive to open a huge new facility at LaGrange in suburban Chicago in the mid-1930s. At about the same time, in 1935, EMC began to produce "catalog" diesel-electric switchers that could be purchased "off the shelf" by any railroad, much like a person could buy an automobile. In terms of passenger diesels, many of EMC's orders in the late 1930s were for additional power cars for new streamliners. But at the same time, EMC also began offering catalog model passenger diesels, the first of which was the EA/EB model of 1937—the first of its famous and long-running (until 1964) E-series passenger diesel.

For this model, EMC developed a standardized, but very stylistic, streamlined carbody that was a distinct departure from the box-cab format: the crew cab was set high in the locomotive above and behind a bulbous, slant-

ed nose—an arrangement that provided considerable protection from whatever might wander in front of the train. The cab-equipped locomotives were known as "A" units, while the cabless—which had to operate in tandem with a cab unit—were considered "booster" or "B" units, hence the EA and EB designations.

Except for the stylistic carbodies, the early E models were quite like the box-cabs of 1935: the EA and EB both featured two 900-hp Winton 201-A prime movers, one for each traction-motor-equipped truck, for an 1,800-hp rat-

ing; the "E" in the model designation stood for "eighteen-hundred horsepower." Unlike the box-cabs, each E-unit truck assembly featured six wheels (three axles) rather than four to spread the weight over the rails; the center wheelset on each truck was unpowered.

By standardizing a locomotive model that could be purchased by any railroad, basically customizing only the paint scheme, EMC was able to offer quality locomotives at lower prices.

Baltimore & Ohio was first to purchase E-units, acquiring a dozen EAs and EBs in 1937–38. As EMC introduced variations and/or upgrades to the E series, the model number likewise was altered: e.g., E1, E2, and so on up to the 2,400-hp E9 model introduced in 1954 and remaining in the Electro-Motive catalog through 1963. Despite changes in horsepower, Electro-Motive kept the "E" designation. (One Electro-Motive technician suggested that, after the horsepower change, "E" came to mean "Express" locomotive instead of "eighteen hundred horsepower," but this has never been substantiated.)

The E-unit became the most successful diesel-electric passenger locomotive ever to speed along American rails, with well over 1,300 built in just over a quarter of a century—though only three were built for Canadian service. In addition, Electro-Motive offered customized passenger versions of the company's popular streamlined F-series freight locomotive as well as its utilitarian GP7/GP9 models, with high-speed gearing and steam-generators (both regular features on E-units), the latter for train heating.

For decades, GM's Electro-Motive Division (EMC was merged in 1941 to become a division of GM) reigned supreme in the realm of diesel-electric locomotives, both passenger and freight. But it did not have a monopoly, of course. Usually breathing the dust of Electro-Motive, the American Locomotive Company (officially renamed Alco in 1956) offered a well-remembered line of passenger

diesels. The company's first catalog model was its DL-series introduced in 1940. Featuring two 1000-hp prime movers in a distinctive streamlined carbody riding on two three-axle trucks, the DL format mirrored that of the E-unit.

Immediately following the war, Alco introduced one of the most celebrated passenger diesels of all time, the PA/PB series. Its carbody of modernistic, timeless design, riding on two three-axle trucks, housed a single, newly designed—and rather troublesome—2000-hp power plant which ultimately would prove this locomotive's undoing. Only 297 units were built, between 1946 and 1953. Nonetheless, PAs lasted in North American passenger service almost to the end of the twentieth century, though the survivors had been re-engined with non-Alco power plants.

As with EMD, Alco and its Canadian subsidiary, Montreal Locomotive Works, sold their catalog freight locomotives in passenger versions.

America's oldest locomotive builder, Baldwin (Baldwin-Lima-Hamilton after a 1950 merger), began offering an interesting lineup of passenger diesels at the close of World War II. Most radical (and largely unreliable) was its 20-wheeled, 6,000-hp "Centipede," produced from 1945 to 1948. In accordance with the successful format established before the war by EMD's E-unit and Alco's DL, Baldwin also produced its own version of a six-axle, double-engine, 2000-hp passenger unit, the DR-6 series. This series, produced only from 1945 to 1948, was unusual in that it was available with a cab at one or both ends (making it bidirectional); it was also available in two distinctly different carbody styles: the "babyface" version (its ample windshields and pug nose looked like a baby's face) and the "sharknose" version, with a rakish snout.

Latecomer in the locomotive field, Fairbanks-Morse had been building opposed-piston-style power plants for marine application since 1932, with a few power plants supplied for Southern Railway passenger railcars in 1939.

## THE UBIQUITOUS E-UNIT

Electro-Motive E-series passenger diesels dominated U.S. passenger train operations for more than a quarter of a century. The most popular E-series model was the E7, with over 500 units sold between the end of World War II and 1950. An A-B-A (cab-booster-cab) set of Southern Pacific E7s, all in different paint schemes (the lead unit is wearing the rarely photographed experimental "Halloween" scheme), are in charge of moving mail-and-express train No. 40 over SP's Sunset Route main line at Phoenix, Arizona, in Feburary 1959. JOHN J. BECHT

## FAIRBANKS-MORSE/CLC
## PASSENGER C-LINERS

ABOVE: Back-to-back Canadian National CPA16-5 locomotives from Fairbanks-Morse subsidiary Canadian Locomotive Works are at speed with CN passenger train near Moncton, New Brunswick, in 1958. Built in 1954–55, these units had a two-axle front truck and—to carry the extra weight of a steam generator—a three-axled rear truck.
JOHN DZIOBKO

## BALDWIN "BABYFACE"

ABOVE RIGHT: Baldwin's line of passenger diesels included this unusual variation of its DR-series, a DR6-2-10 built for the Chicago & North Western in 1948. Shown arriving in Rockford, Illinois, with the daily "Capone Local" from Chicago (the famous mobster was a regular passenger on this run), the unit sports a built-in baggage compartment (note baggage door) where the second engine normally would have been positioned. Thus, this unit contained only a single 1,000 hp engine instead of the usual two. T. V. MAGUIRE, MIKE SCHAFER COLLECTION

## BALDWIN "SHARKNOSE"
## PASSENGER DIESEL

RIGHT: A pair of PRR Baldwin DR6-4-20s in the "sharknose" carbody style rumbles across the Passaic River Bridge on the approach to Newark, New Jersey, Pennsylvania Station with a New York & Long Branch commuter train in September 1958. JOHN DZIOBKO

F-M did not begin offering a line of true locomotives until 1944, and its first passenger diesel, the "Eries" (F-M was based in Beloit, Wisconsin, but these locomotives were assembled at GE's plant in Erie, Pennsylvania), appeared in 1945. Like the EMD E-unit, the Alco DLs, and the Baldwin DRs, the imposing Eries were 2,000-hp streamlined carbody units riding on two three-axle trucks, but with a single engine. Beginning in 1950, F-M produced the CP series ("Consolidated Line, Passenger") locomotive, which came in varying horsepower and truck arrangements.

One of F-M's most legendary locomotives, the 2,400-hp Train Master, debuted in 1953, and although it was primarily touted as a powerful freight locomotive, its ability to rapidly accelerate with a heavy train made it a worthy (if boxy looking) passenger locomotive. Several railroads had Train Masters for passenger service.

The aforementioned diesel-electric locomotives allowed American railroads to fully dieselize their steam-powered passenger services by the end of the 1950s. But the rush to build a better passenger diesel had virtually stopped early in the 1950s when it became alarmingly clear that the American passenger train was headed for trouble. Suddenly there was no more large-scale demand for new passenger locomotives of any type, and Alco, Baldwin, and FM conceded what little remained of the market to Electro-Motive. The decline era of the American passenger train would be played out largely with durable E- and passengerized F and GP units, a modest stable of Alco PAs, and an oddball survivor here and there.

### Latecomers in the streamliner era

As the passenger train sped toward virtual oblivion in the 1960s, a few passenger-friendly railroads realized that some of their older locomotives—even their sturdy war-era Electro-Motive products—were simply at the end of their service lives and would need replacement. With this in

mind, Electro-Motive began offering passenger versions of their later-model SD- and GP-series freight locomotives in 1964. Though non-streamlined, the SDP35s, SDP40s, SDP45s, GP40Ps, and GP40TCs provided a low-cost option when new passenger power was a must. And, perhaps more to the point, they could be (and were) readily converted to freight service.

EMD and new-kid-on-the-locomotive-building-block General Electric introduced a new generation of passenger diesels later in the 1960s. For EMD, it was the fully-cowled 3,600-hp FP45, which hit the rails in 1967 on Santa Fe and Milwaukee Road. In 1966, GE first offered the U28CG, a passenger-ized version of one of its Universal-series freight locomotives, and then in 1967 introduced a full-carbody, streamlined passenger diesel, the U30CG. Only Santa Fe purchased these two models.

### EMD SDP35

Seaboard Air Line was one of three railroads that opted for Electro-Motive Division's passenger version of its SD35 freight locomotive: the SDP35, produced in 1964–65. The main difference on the SDP version was a longer carbody (but not frame) to house a steam generator for train heating, and high-speed gearing. SAL 1106 is on northbound Atlanta–Washington mail/express/passenger train No. 4 at Raleigh, North Carolina, in December 1964. WARREN CALLOWAY

## RENAISSANCE-ERA PASSENGER LOCOMOTIVES

The passenger train in America bottomed out as the 1960s closed, but the 1970s signaled the start of a new era. Nearly all intercity trains in North America would be operated by Amtrak (U.S.) and VIA (Canada), while dozens of new public-sponsored agencies—from Chicago's Regional Transportation Authority to New Jersey Transit—would assume commuter-train operations. These new operating entities were committed to improving passenger service, and that meant buying new equipment. In the span of a decade—the 1970s—there arose a big-time need for new passenger locomotives.

When Amtrak started operations on May 1, 1971, it had been left a hodge-podge collection of aging E-units, a motley crew of passenger Fs, a stable of elderly GG1 electrics, and little else. Brand-new power was based largely on the tried-and-proven steeds of the recent past. Amtrak's first new locomotives, ordered in 1972, were $68 million worth of Electro-Motive's new SDP40F, cousins of EMD's popular SD40–2 freight locomotive in terms of prime mover, electrical equipment, and frame, but with a semi-streamlined, cowled carbody virtually identical to the FP45 of the 1960s. Then, in 1974–76, GE delivered new 6,000-hp straight electric locomotives (E60Cs) and 3,000-hp diesel-electrics (P30CHs)—the later essentially a cowled version of GE's U30C freight locomotive with high-speed gearing and an HEP (head-end power) generator for train lighting, heating, and air-conditioning as Amtrak began the switch to all-electric train climate control and central-source lighting.

Coinciding with the U.S. Bicentennial in 1976 was the arrival of a locomotive destined to be—at least in terms of widespread use, popularity, and durability—the E-unit of the renaissance period: Electro-Motive's F40. Like the E-unit, it featured a full-width carbody, but beyond that, it had little in common with its classic predecessor. The F40 was a short, four-axle locomotive with a single 3,000-hp, constant-speed V16 power plant that generated power for the unit's four traction motors as well as for train lighting and climate control.

*continued on page 70*

### EMD FP45

Streamlining did return to new passenger diesels late in the 1960s in the form of Electro-Motive's new FP45, built for Santa Fe and Milwaukee Road in 1967–68. Even at this late date, these two still-passenger-conscious railroads wanted motive power that was at least semi-streamlined. Aided by two freight F45s in blue and yellow, Santa Fe FP45 No. 5940 arrives in Chicago with the *El Capitan-Super Chief* in 1970. JIM HEUER

### NEW YORK CENTRAL T-MOTOR

New York Central's fleet of T-class electrics were built between 1913 and 1926. Unit 273 is handling a rake of head-end cars at the NYC's coach yard at Mott Haven Junction near New York City in 1960. JOHN DZIOBKO

### NEW HAVEN EP4 PASSENGER ELECTRIC

LEFT: A heroic artistic rendering commissioned by General Electric dating from the 1930 depicts a New Haven EP4 passenger electric streaming along the railroad's electrified main line west of New Haven.

Electric passenger locomotives deserve special mention because, in the long run, pure electric propulsion has been more instrumental in rail passenger service than freight. As of 2001, little in the way of rail freight in America moves by straight electric locomotives anymore, yet the use of electricity is expanding in the passenger realm.

In 1835, just as steam locomotion was gaining recognition as the new miracle of motive power, the electric motor debuted in America. The first electric-powered locomotive appeared a dozen years later, with huge, crude, wet-cell batteries supplying current to the motor; in 1860, generators proved a better source of electrical power. The first electric locomotive to power a train of passengers may have been that built by Thomas Edison in 1880 and operated on a 1,400-foot loop of test track at Menlo Park, New Jersey.

The evolution of the electric locomotive took a significant advance in 1885 when Frank Sprague developed the "traction motor," which could be hung on a truck assembly and directly geared to a driving axle, with as many motors as there were axles. The powerful torque of a traction motor was ideal for powering drive wheels.

Electric power could be obtained to feed to the traction motor in three basic ways: (1) via an overhead trolley-wire distribution system in which the power was collected by a trolley pole or sliding "pantograph" atop the locomotive or railcar; (2) from a third-rail distribution system in which the power was collected from a shoe attached to the truck of the locomotive or railcar; or (3) from a gasoline or (later) diesel-powered generator carried aboard the locomotive. As the No. 3 format reveals, a so-called diesel locomotive is really an electric locomotive that carries it own electrical supply, since all diesel-electric locomotives have traction motors.

Sprague's traction motor made possible the electric streetcar ("trolley") and interurban train, a practical electric locomotive, and the self-propelled "m.u." car (chapter 5). General Electric built the first successful commercial electric locomotives in 1893–94—and none too soon. Smoke-abatement ordinances in some major cities, principally New York, would soon force railroads into electrification. In 1895, the Baltimore & Ohio took delivery of the first mainline electric locomotive—or "motor," as they are sometimes referred—to haul passenger and freight trains through its Howard Street Tunnel in Baltimore, Maryland.

Once such heavy-duty electrification endeavors proved themselves, railway electrification projects began to propagate, usually in urban areas where traffic was dense or in mountainous territory where there were arduous grades and/or long tunnels. Elsewhere, electrification tended to be too expensive in return for the benefits.

Among the earliest electric power built for passenger service were New York Central System's "center-cab" S-class motors: compact but powerful (3,000 hp and capable of speeds in excess of 80 MPH) locomotives built early in the twentieth century to haul conventional passenger trains in and out of both the old and new Grand Central Terminals in Manhattan. Larger, more powerful electrics for NYC—the T class box-cabs—began to arrive in 1913 to handle a growing number of all-steel passenger cars. Central also had 22 box-cabs built for the electrification of its new Cleveland (Ohio) Union Terminal in the late 1920s. These P-class motors migrated to New York terminal service after Cleveland Union Terminal was de-electrified early in the 1950s. They outlasted the NYC, powering Penn Central and, briefly, Amtrak passenger trains into the 1970s.

NYC rival Pennsylvania Railroad entered mainline passenger electrification in 1909 when the first of its stalwart Class DD1 electrics, built by PRR's Juniata Shops, came on line for the new Pennsylvania Station in Manhattan; they operated off third rail. In the mid-1920s, two dozen L-class box-cabs entered New York terminal service.

Pennsy's massive electrification expansion project—beginning the late 1920s—turned out to be the largest in North America, with nearly 800 route-miles under "catenary" (trolley contact wire supported by a messenger wire, an arrangement necessary for high-speed mainline electric operation). By the end of the 1930s, high-speed electric passenger locomotives were moving PRR passenger trains between New York, Philadelphia, Washington, and Harrisburg at near-100 MPH speeds.

To handle all the passenger traffic on the newly electrified main lines, the PRR relied upon a large fleet—some 90 units—of new P5-class box-cabs built by Baldwin, GE, and PRR's Juniata Shops. Alas, the P5s developed unforeseen problems, leading the PRR to develop what many rail historians consider the greatest electric locomotive ever built: the GG1. The prototype GG1 emerged from Baldwin (with help from GE) in 1934. Its success led to the eventual purchase of 138 more GG1s.

Although used in both freight and passenger service, the "G" was best known as a passenger locomotive. Under its double-ended, streamlined

**PENNSYLVANIA RAILROAD P5a ELECTRIC**

The Pennsylvania ordered P5a electrics to handle fast passenger trains on its newly electrified main lines early in the 1930s, but design flaws soon sidelined a number of them, prompting the PRR to use K4 steam locomotives as substitute power until new electrics—the GG1s—could be built. The P5a's were then relegated to freight duties, except for the occasional excursion, such as this at Lancaster, Pennsylvania, in 1961; a modified P5a with a streamlined carbody is at left. JOHN DZIOBKO

## TWO GENERATIONS OF PASSENGER ELECTRICS

Former Amtrak GE E60CP No. 972, with ownership having been transferred to commuter agency New Jersey Transit by the time of this 1983 scene, stands with veteran GG1 4877 at South Amboy, New Jersey. To celebrate the 4877's heritage, it had been painted in the famed pinstriped Tuscan red livery of the late, lamented Pennsylvania Railroad. It is shown on the eve of the final run of a GG1 in regularly scheduled passenger service. JIM BOYD

carbody (refined by industrial designer Raymond Loewy) was a power-house of electrons—5,000 hp worth that could rapidly accelerate the *Broadway Limited* or *Afternoon Congressional* to speeds in excess of 100 MPH (128 MPH was the reported tops).

Pennsy's partner in Northeast Corridor passenger operations, the New York, New Haven & Hartford, began electrifying its lines between New York City and New Haven, Connecticut, in 1905, completing that electrification in 1914. In 1917, the railroad extended through, electrified passenger service into Pennsylvania Station via the new Hell Gate Bridge to link up with the PRR and make through Boston–Washington service possible.

For more than sixty years, EP-series ("Electric Passenger") locomotives of varying classes sped New Haven trains like the famed *Merchants Limited* and *Colonial* into the heart of Manhattan. The early EPs were all of double-ended box-cab format. With streamlining all the rage beginning in the mid-1930s, the new EP4 model of 1938 appeared with a streamlined cab carbody (also double-ended). In 1955, NH took delivery of its last passenger "pure" electrics, ten handsome high-tech, 4,000-hp EP5s capable of 90 MPH. (Shortly after, NH ordered new FL9 diesel-electric/straight electric locomotives from Electro-Motive. The FL9 could operate as a regular diesel-electric locomotive or off of third rail as a "straight" electric.)

Outside the densely populated urban areas of the Northeast, electric-locomotive-powered passenger trains were relatively rare in American railroading. The most notable were those traversing Milwaukee Road's Pacific Extension, two segments of which were electrified to facilitate the crossing of the Rocky Mountain and Cascade ranges in Montana, Idaho,

and Washington. Initially, box-cab electrics built by GE-Alco in 1915–16 hoisted the likes of the *Columbian* and *Olympian* over mist-shrouded mountain passes. In 1918, five GE articulated 3,480-hp "Bi-Polar" passenger electrics added distinction to the Milwaukee's electric passenger operations. These were supplemented by ten behemoth Baldwin-Westinghouse 4,200-hp passenger box-cabs in 1919. A dozen streamlined GE "Little Joe" electrics arrived in 1950, two of which were equipped with steam generators for passenger service.

Great Northern also relied on electric motive power to move its trains over Western mountains, but its electrified territory was much shorter—about 73 miles versus Milwaukee Road's 660-plus route-miles. Freight and passenger trains were assisted through Cascade Tunnel by a quartet of box-cab sets delivered in 1909. When the second Cascade Tunnel and approach trackage were built in the late 1920s and the electrification was extended all the way over the backbone of the Cascade Range between Skykomish and Wenatchee, Washington, additional box-cabs were purchased to relay trains over the lengthened electrified district. Two giant, 5,000-hp W1-class streamlined electrics were delivered by GE in 1947 and painted to match the streamlined livery of the new *Empire Builder*. They made easy work of lifting passenger trains over the mountain. Dieselization ended the GN electrification in 1956.

Elsewhere, electric-locomotive-powered passenger trains could be found between Port Huron, Michigan, and Sarnia, Ontario, via the St. Clair Tunnel under the St. Clair River; between Detroit, Michigan, and Windsor, Ontario, under the Detroit River; through Boston & Maine's

## ELECTRO-MOTIVE/ASEA/BUDD AEM7

They are strictly utilitarian in looks, but the AEM7 has proven a worthy successor to the celebrated GG1 electric. In 1999, an NJ Transit AEM7 hums along at Newark, New Jersey, with a Manhattan-bound commuter train. JOE GREENSTEIN

## AMTRAK BI-DIRECTIONAL ELECTRICS

New HHP8 double-ended electrics laying over between runs at Philadelphia's Thirtieth Street Station in December 2000. JOE GREENSTEIN

Hoosac Tunnel in the Berkshire Mountains of Massachusetts; on the Butte, Anaconda & Pacific Railway in Montana; on the Virginian Railway in West Virginia and Virginia; and on the Canadian National through the north approach tunnel to Montreal Central Station.

Despite the superb power and efficiency, cleanliness, and quietness of electric locomotion, it never quite caught on the way it did in Europe, where electric railways blanket the continent, and many of the above-named installations have been abandoned. Pure electric propulsion in rail transportation requires large capital investment and greater maintenance costs on the infrastructure, particularly the power distribution system. The advantages are far-reaching and long-lasting: longevity (electric locomotives are less complex and last longer than diesels) and very low air and noise pollution. However, since no dollar amount can be attached to the benefits of lower pollution, there is less of an incentive to electrify, particularly in a political and corporate environment where short-term financial benefits overrule long-term financial and quality-of-life benefits.

Electric locomotion has fared best in America along the Northeast Corridor and its branches and almost totally in the realm of the passenger train. Since the passenger train did not die in America as expected, the need for electric locomotives has persisted. The first new passenger electrics in the renaissance era (post 1970) were E60-series models from GE for Amtrak. Strictly utilitarian in design, 26 of these pondering, double-ended, 6,000-hp locomotives arrived on the scene in 1974–75 for

service on the former-PRR and New Haven main lines. Tracking problems and slow acceleration diminished the E60s' usefulness, and Amtrak sought another type of electric to replace the decades-old GG1 fleet.

It came in the form of a diminutive but highly successful locomotive known as the AEM7, built by GM's Electro-Motive Division under license from ASEA, a Swedish builder that had established the locomotive's design years before it emigrated to America. A legion of these 7,000-hp brutes were built throughout the 1980s for Amtrak, SEPTA (Southeastern Pennsylvania Transportation Authority), MARC (Maryland Department of Transportation), and New Jersey Transit.

The story of electric passenger power in America has a happy ending. Amtrak completed the electrification of its former-New Haven Railroad main line between New Haven and Boston in 2000—a route that now hosts 150-MPH trains. For this new high-speed service, Amtrak purchased state-of-the-art motive power in the form of double-ended units for hauling conventional rolling stock, and single-end power cars for its new *Acela Express* trainsets, with one power car at each end of the train. The new motive power, built by Alstom, features super-sleek carbody styling, AC traction technology, and the agility required to bring American passenger trains into the twenty-first century. Alas, the aging electrical-distribution infrastructure between Washington and New Haven—some of it more than 90 years old in 2001—has hampered the new trains' ability to strut their stuff. But that's another story.

*continued from page 65*

The reign of the F40 and its variants (including models with restyled noses) would last into the new millennium, not only on Amtrak, but on VIA Rail Canada and numerous commuter carriers, with the traditional F40PH becoming a classic in its own right.

The evolution of the F40 carried into the F59, with its more-efficient engine and two different carbody styles, including one with a new "isolated" cab design to lower engine noise in the crew cab. Although the latter—the F59PHI model—features a streamlined nose/cab design, the panache of streamliner diesel styling of the late 1930s and 1940s clearly remains dormant.

Another radical departure from earlier renaissance-era passenger diesels, at least in terms of styling, is represented by GE's Genesis Series diesel (model Dash B40–8WH), introduced in 1993 and still in production as of 2001. In essence, this creature is a GE 8–40-series freight roadswitcher heavily customized (at the behest of its primary purchaser, Amtrak) for passenger service. The 4,000-hp locomotive, with its custom-designed four-wheel trucks and unitized carbody, features an imposing, robotic face with a steeply sloping, angular nose that at once resembles the looming countenance of a Boeing 747 and a European high-speed train. One variation of the Genesis provides for dual powering: it can be run as a standard diesel-electric locomotive or as a straight electric locomotive on electrified lines leading into Grand Central Terminal and Pennsylvania Station in Manhattan.

Even Alco, in a sense, provided diesels for renaissance-era passenger trains. Although this venerable builder left the locomotive-building business in 1969, its Canadian arm—Montreal Locomotive Works—survived and in the early 1980s built 34 low-slung, knife-prow diesels to pull new, Bombardier-built low-profile, lightweight trains known as LRCs (for "Light, Rapid, Comfortable"). Although LRC locomotives were styled to match LRC trains, their standardized couplings allowed them to pull conventional equipment, so they were true locomotives.

With the future of the passenger train in North America always in some sort of limbo, it's hard to predict the passenger locomotives of the future. Although most American diesel-electric passenger locomotives are capable of speeds of 100 MPH or more, most of today's rail passenger routes, outside the Northeast Corridor (Boston–Washington) and Toronto–Montreal–Quebec, aren't what they used to be, and 79 MPH tends to be the maximum speed, if that. If true high-speed corridor operation finally comes of age throughout the country, as has been long proposed, then the next generation of passenger power will likely be a locomotive—possibly double-ended for maximum efficiency—capable of rapid acceleration and the ability to cruise its train along at a sustained 125 MPH . . . or better.

## GENERAL MOTORS LTD. FP59PHI

Though streamlined, the Electro-Motive DE30AC—illustrated by Long Island Rail Road No. 410 on a bilevel commuter train at Long Island City, New York, in 2000—is strictly utilitarian in looks, except for the fluting, an added touch requested by the LIRR. Relatives of the boxy F59PH popular with some newer commuter carriers, the LIRR units were developed by EMD through consultation with the LIRR in view of the carrier's special needs in braking and acceleration. Purchase of these and other new locomotives and passenger cars for LIRR's far-flung commuter operation was funded by the Metropolitan Transportation Authority, which oversees a number of passenger transport operations in the New York City area. JOE GREENSTEIN

## GENERAL ELECTRIC GENESIS

As the twentieth century waned, so did the prominence of the popular EMD F40. In its place was a new breed of passenger diesel, from Electro-Motive nemesis GE. Classed as a Dash B40–8WH, these imposing, 4,000 - hp passenger locomotives are better known as "Genesis Series" units, two of which roll along San Pablo Bay at Pinole, California, in 1999. The Genesis units reigned supreme on most Amtrak long-distance trains at the start of the new millennium. New York's Metro North Railroad was using a version that could run either off third-rail power or as a conventional diesel-electric. PHIL GOSNEY

## ELECTRO-MOTIVE F40

Following its introduction in 1976, the F40 series became the E-unit of renaissance-era passenger operations—both intercity and commuter—in North America. VIA F40 6418 leads the Ottawa–Toronto *Capital* at Smith Falls, Ontario, in July 1993. JOHN LEOPARD

# The Evolution of the Railroad Passenger Car in North America

America's earliest documented passenger-carrying rail cars were little more than horse-drawn carriages to which four flanged wheels and rudimentary couplings were applied. In fact, because these cars were constructed by carriage builders of the era, they closely followed the carriage format: inward-facing bench seats accessed directly by doors on the side of the carbody. These were "coaches" in their simplest form, offering spartan accommodation and a punishingly hard ride in common with the stagecoaches from which they were derived.

In the decade after the Baltimore & Ohio Railroad carried the nation's first paying passengers aboard such vehicles on January 7, 1830, distances traveled by rail were typically short. Transit times were long, however, given the rudimentary track conditions and resulting slow speeds of the day. So long, in some cases—such as in 1837 on the Cumberland Valley Railroad's 60-some miles between Harrisburg and Chambersburg, Pennsylvania—that something beyond a coach seat was called for. Thus was born the sleeping car, in which "beds" (usually not much more than large, wooden shelves) and—usually—bedding allowed the travel-prone to, well, travel prone.

As public confidence in railroads as a new mode of transport grew through the 1840s and 1850s, so did passenger cars—in both size and appointment. The coach and the baggage car were—and over 150 years later,

## A NOSE FOR NEWS

ABOVE: Tracing its roots back to the early 1950s *Train X* concept, the turbine-powered, articulated *TurboTrain* made headlines during testing in the late 1960s and eventual revenue service for Canadian National and Amtrak. More telling, however, were the darker headlines drawing attention to the fires, service failures, and perennial unreliability that plagued these aircrafts-on-rails. One of CN's trainsets fueled at Toronto in May 1975. KEVIN J. HOLLAND

## GROWING PANES

LEFT: After World War II, evolution and revolution went hand-in-hand as America's railroads and carbuilders sought to outdo each other by wooing passengers with ever-more-creative "feature" cars. Chief among these was the dome car, envisaged in concept as far back as the late nineteenth century, but first executed in modern guise by the Chicago, Burlington & Quincy during the rebuilding of a "flat-top" prewar Budd coach in 1945. The dome bandwagon eventually included "short" and "long" configurations from Budd and Pullman-Standard. Builder ACF also entered the fray, and Southern Pacific even tried its hand at a group of homegrown "long" dome rebuilds, like No. 3604 in this 1971 view in the company of the CB&Q "pattern dome" that started it all, *Silver Dome*. Four-wheel trucks were an anomaly on typically heavy long-dome cars.

**A GOOD NIGHT'S SLEEP**

Lucas Sleeping Car No. 4 was a product of the Jackson & Sharp Company, and typified the ornate woodwork, open platforms, and four-wheel trucks of mid-to-late nineteenth century American passenger cars. George M. Pullman did not invent the sleeping car, but managed—through the takeover of competitors—to acquire a virtual monopoly on the cars' ownership and operation by the turn of the twentieth century. ANDOVER JUNCTION PUBLICATIONS COLLECTION

remain—the plebian duo, meeting the most basic needs of the traveling public. Then, as now, the basic day coach was augmented with a range of specialized car types ranging from parlors, diners, and lounges to the aforementioned sleepers.

## Form Follows Function

Ride quality improved when paired trucks, one at each end of the car, replaced the early four-wheel arrangement. Car length increased to 40, 50, 60 feet and beyond, establishing the basic passenger car profile seen for decades to follow. Early carbodies and underframes were crafted from wood and strengthened by truss rods. Car exteriors were often painted but invariably varnished to a high shine. The term "varnish," in fact, was to become a common industry nickname for passenger trains.

Open platforms and steps at each end of a typical car gave passengers access from adjacent cars as well as from station platforms. Heat was provided by an exposed coal- or wood-burning stove—a deadly hazard in the event of an accident. More than a few unlucky passengers survived minor derailments in the mid-nineteenth century only to perish in the ensuing fire from an overturned stove. Cooling and ventilation were initally made possible by open windows and nothing more, with any "fresh" air liberally mixed with locomotive smoke and cinders. But this new form of travel was so astonishly fast that travelers simply endured these discomforts—at least in the earliest years of rail travel.

George M. Pullman, whose name would become synonymous not only with railroad sleeping cars but with sumptuous travel in general, did not build his first sleeper until 1859. More innovator than inventor, Pullman refined the concept of overnight rail travel beyond the embryonic examples already in operation. His 40-foot-long sleeping car "No. 9" was one of two cars rebuilt from wooden Chicago & Alton Railroad coaches at Bloomington, Illinois. Ten upper and ten lower berths provided nocturnal accommodation, with fixed seats sufficing during the day. A toilet and a wood-stove were located at each end of the low-ceilinged car, and passengers choosing to read after dark had to make do by the flickering—and potentially disastrous—light of candles.

Five years later, Pullman's luxurious sleeping car *Pioneer* was completed. This car marked the transition to what would become the ubiquitous Pullman "section" of two facing settees that opened into a lower berth, with a smaller upper berth concealed in a fold-down ceiling compartment. Other far-reaching refinements aboard the 58-foot-long *Pioneer* were the clerestory roof, private room accommodations at each end of the car, and the removal of the noxious heating stoves to a position beneath the floor.

By America's centennial in 1876, the typical passenger car was 70 feet long and rode on a pair of well-sprung six-wheel trucks, although many coaches and "head-end" (baggage and mail) cars employed somewhat rougher-riding but less-expensive four-wheel designs. Oil lamps, air brakes, and hot-water heating systems all had been introduced to improve passenger comfort and safety.

A more visible safety improvement appeared in 1887. A "vestibule" enclosed the formerly open end-platform, making movement from one car to another a less-daunting proposition, even in good weather. The jostling no-man's-land between cars, above the couplers, was duly enclosed by mating bellows-like diaphragms, one on each end of every car. Originally only as wide as the space between the car-end step wells, the vestibule was soon widened to enclose the entire end-platform area. This necessitated the development of the folding trap door, which served as a platform floor above the step well while underway but folded upward to provide access to the steps during station stops.

Inside, twelve sections (along with a "drawing room" in which the beds folded away and the space became a private sitting room) had become the standard for sleeping cars.

## From Wood to Steel

Although passengers had benefitted from the strength of steel car frames since the late nineteenth century—they reduced the degree of destruction when wood-bodied cars were involved in derailments or collisions—the 1907 introduction of all-steel passenger cars was met with some trepidation. Passengers, it seems, were fearful of electrocution—whether from the overhead catenary on newly electrified lines or from thunderstorms—while traveling in the new steel cocoons that entered widespread service in 1910. It was a groundless fear, but a persistent one—so much so that carbuilders crafted the steel exterior sheathing on some of the earliest all-steel cars to resemble wood and thus calm nervous passengers. Electricity had already found its way into turn-of-the-century cars, however, as axle-belt-driven underfloor generators provided current for sputtering carbon-arc lights. Batteries, charged while the cars were in motion, were a standby during station stops.

By the end of World War I, passenger cars in North America had become standardized to a remarkable degree, largely through the efforts of The Pullman Company, whose cars criss-crossed the continent. The prewar flirtation with imitation wood sheathing had given way to the unpretentious solidity of sheet steel, rivets, and—for the most part—dark green paint that became known as "Pullman green" since it had become ubiquitous to that company. The products of different carbuilders and carbuilding railroads produced variations on the "standard" clerestory-roofed theme,

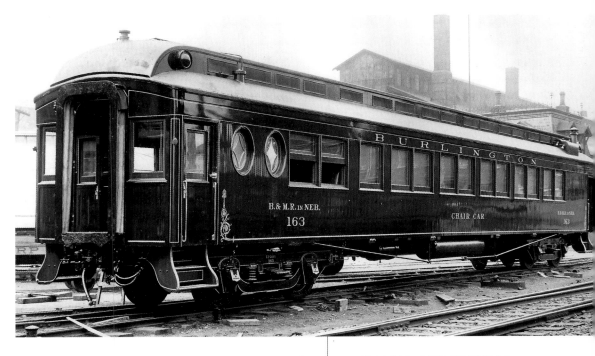

with the arch-roofed "Harriman" cars of the Union Pacific, Southern Pacific, and Illinois Central and the Santa Fe's distinctive carbody side-sill treatment among the more common examples.

In Pullman's world, close to 4,000 examples of the "12-1" (12-section, 1-drawing room) sleeping car were eventually built to a variety of subtly different heavyweight floor plans. Cars with this accommodation mix accounted for roughly 40 percent of the Pullman Company's heavyweight fleet at its zenith in the early 1930s.

Solitary overnight passengers desiring a suitably sized private room had to wait until 1927, when Pullman debuted its "single room" car. Inside the shell of this popular but rather inefficient floor plan were a mere 14 rooms, each designed to accommodate an individual passenger and providing private toilet and folding lavatory facilities along with a crosswise-mounted bed. No typical Pullman foldout, these beds featured stationary box springs and mattresses, a luxury previously found only aboard sumptuous private cars and the business cars of railroad managers. Reflecting their specialization and ultimate inefficiency, only 45 of this type were built. With the exception of a few in California, all were initially assigned to "carriage trade" overnight runs in the East and Midwest.

While the coach seat remained the most prevalent onboard "accommodation," generations of passengers—accustomed to sleeping behind nothing more than a heavy curtain, and waiting in line to use the washroom at the end of the aisle—immediately warmed to the idea of the self-contained private room. Pullman, in turn, sought ways to convert older cars to include room accommodations

### VESTIBULES AND VARNISH

With its leaded glass, delicate scrollwork, and heavily varnished sheathing, this CB&Q chair car was a classic example of the evolving wood carbuilders' art. ANDOVER JUNCTION PUBLICATIONS COLLECTION

## BRIDGING THE GAP

During the evolution from full open platforms on heavyweight observation cars to enclosed, high-windowed "solariums," vestigial railed platforms could be seen on railroads as diverse as the New Haven, Chesapeake & Ohio, and Canadian National. KEVIN J. HOLLAND COLLECTION

## WHAT A DIFFERENCE . . .

This 1927 Milwaukee Road *Olympian* coach was illuminated by a combination of kerosene and electric fixtures. Hinged panels in the clerestory augmented the ventilation provided by the opening windows. MILWAUKEE ROAD HISTORICAL ASSOCIATION COLLECTION

while still maximizing the passenger load (and revenue potential) of each new floor plan. A variety of plans resulted, many combining open sections with another new self-contained private space, the double bedroom.

Continuing its quest to fit as many single rooms as possible into a standard-length car and thus striking a balance between passenger appeal and revenue potential, Pullman introduced a pair of 16-room "duplex" cars in 1932. The *Nocturne* and *Eventide*, rebuilt from club cars, were the forerunners of a concept that would—with the exception of the streamlined "Slumbercoach" introduced in the 1950s—experience limited popularity and for only a brief period after World War II. "Duplexing" was a means of staggering rooms on two levels, one slightly overlapping its neighbor, but within the overall height of a conventional single-level passenger car. A token increase in revenue space resulted (in this case, two more rooms than in the first single-room cars of 1927), as did a telltale two-tier window pattern on the room-side of the car.

One of the most widely appreciated improvements to passenger trains of the early 1930s was neither structural nor cosmetic, but "atmospheric." Air-conditioning had made its Pullman debut aboard 12-1 sleeper *McNair* in September 1929, and found another early proponent in the Baltimore & Ohio. B&O diner *Martha Washington* was the first mechanically air-conditioned car, and the B&O's *Columbian* became America's first completely air-conditioned train on May 24, 1931.

Clerestory-roofed cars equipped with air-conditioning either as-built or retrofitted, typically sprouted tell-tale ductwork sections along the lower steps of their roofs. Air cooled by ice or mechanical means was circulated throughout the cars by fans and marked the end of a widespread need for operable passenger car windows. However, open-window cars could be found in regularly scheduled passenger service, usually commuter, in the U.S. well into the 1970s.

As the Depression's impact was felt aboard the nation's passenger trains, Pullman responded by incorporating compact dining, buffet, and lounge areas into some of its sleeping cars. In this way, the operation of two, three, or more less-than-fully occupied cars could be consolidated to prolong the viability of an otherwise marginal run. Instead of running a diner and a Pullman sleeper on a lightly patronized run, a single Pullman buffet-sleeper could do the job.

# A New Era Dawns

By the early 1930s, the concept of streamlining was sweeping across North America as an adjunct to the Art Deco movement, with everything from Coca-Cola™ dispensers and office machines to ships and trains emerging in sleek, aerodynamic sheathing (chapter 6). Although the wind resistance of products like soft drink machines and office duplicators was of course moot, the application of streamlining to transportation was aimed, at least in theory, to achieve economic as well as purely esthetic gain by way of reduced drag and fuel consumption. Names like Norman Bel Geddes, Henry Dreyfuss, Walter Dorwin Teague, Otto Kuhler, and Raymond Loewy became widely known through the 1930s as they personified the science of industrial design in the public's eye. Their collective work in the field of transportation—along with that of less-celebrated but equally talented colleagues—was sometimes more eccentric than practical. Nonetheless, they collectively pulled the design trend away from the more flamboyant tastes of the late nineteenth century and toward a clean-lined esthetic often bordering on austere. Theirs was a portable and widely sought skill, with Dreyfuss and Teague eventually making great contributions to railroad nemeses like Lockheed and Boeing—Dreyfuss as interior designer of Lockheed's graceful Constellation, and Teague's firm as cabin stylists of Boeing's 707.

The emergence of a new era for railroad passengers was clear when, in mid-1933, Pullman unveiled a gleaming sleeping car at the Century of Progress Exposition in Chicago. The *George M. Pullman* was unlike anything to have previously carried the company's name. It was, in retrospect, very much a hybrid of heavyweight design elements and the streamlined, lightweight forms to follow. An observation-lounge-sleeping car, the *George M. Pullman* offered its passengers an enclosed, round-ended observation room—the first of its kind—in place of the open platform or latter-day heavyweight solarium of its ancestors. Aluminum—in itself a symbol of modernity in the 1930s—was everywhere, from the unpainted, brushed exterior to interior accents. By virtue of its then-radical construction, the car was on the order of only half as heavy as its Pullman predecessors. Future trends were also implied in the car's as-built four-wheel truck design: rare was the streamlined lightweight car equipped with the old standby of six-wheel trucks, called for under the heaviest postwar dining and dome cars. The old passenger car hallmarks of paired rectangular windows, riveted belt rail, and exposed steps were all still present on the *George M. Pullman*, but with its low, arched roof, bullet-shaped solarium, and clean-lined Art Deco interior, the car was very much a glimpse of the future.

As futuristic as the *George M. Pullman* was, the earliest streamlined trainsets—as distinct from even earlier knife-nosed McKeen self-propelled cars—were decidedly snake-like in appearance and harkened back to Jules Verne's lunar-voyage imagery of six decades before. Articulation and full-width diaphragms between the new streamliners' cars created the impression of a single, lithe vehicle, particularly when these trains negotiated the complex trackwork at large terminals.

*The Streamliner* (a.k.a. *City of Salina*), the *Zephyr*, the *Hiawatha*, the *Comet*, the *Flying Yankee*, and their kin were all front-page news upon their debuts, offering America as exotic and futuristic a counterpoint to the reality of the Depression as did the "Buck Rogers" serials playing in theaters every Saturday afternoon.

Among the earliest large groups of streamlined conventional—that is to say, non-articulated—passenger cars in the U.S. were those styled by Teague, built by Pullman's Osgood-Bradley works in Massachusetts and delivered to the New Haven Railroad beginning in 1934. Promptly duplicated in model form as part of the New Haven-based A.C. Gilbert Company's "American Flyer" line of toy trains, these turtle-roofed Pullman-Standard cars—along with similar examples built for the Bangor & Aroostook, Lehigh Valley, Seaboard Air Line, and Cotton Belt railroads—became known unofficially as "American Flyer" cars.

## . . . A DECADE MAKES

Barely ten years later, this Lehigh Valley coach modeled the indirect fluorescent lighting and sealed windows in vogue after the mid-1930s. The streamlined era had arrived on America's railroads. JIM BOYD COLLECTION

## PUNCTUATION

The application of streamlining to the American passenger train was arguably nowhere as apparent as it was at the rear of the nation's leading trains. *American Milemaster* served in the Pullman pool after display at the 1939 World's Fair.

## PANACHE

Three years after the round-ended observation car made its debut in the guise of the *George M. Pullman*—a 1933 experimental car making widespread use of aluminum for structural and decorative purposes—Pullman crafted the *Green Diamond* for Illinois Central. This 1936 builder's view shows the Art Deco frenzy that was the *Green Diamond's* observation room. BOTH, PULLMAN-STANDARD; KEVIN J. HOLLAND COLLECTION

The Milwaukee Road's streamlined *Hiawatha* cars of 1934–35—introduced and home-built to compete against the likes of the Burlington's *Zephyr*—were a curious mix of styling elements, with details such as arched windows harkening to an earlier and decidedly unstreamlined era. The "second-generation" *Hiawatha* cars of 1936 abandoned the arched windows but were notable for their ribbed sides, a styling device that would also be used on some of the road's freight equipment and cabooses. The *Hiawathas'* markers were originally carried by cars whose end treatment was every bit as revolutionary as the *George M. Pullman's*. Squared-off rather than rounded in plan, the *Hiawathas'* unique "Beaver Tail" observation cars evoked the automobile and bus styling of the day with their slope-end profile and original smallish paired end windows. These evolved into a futuristic "Buck Rogers" design, complete with fins, created by Otto Kuhler for the 1939 edition of the *Hiawatha* (built in 1938). Guided by stylist Brooks Stevens, the Milwaukee Road would further reprise its reputation for eccentric but appealing observation car designs in the late 1940s.

North of the border, the Canadian Pacific Railway developed its own small fleet of lightweight coaches, parlors, and head-end cars in the 1930s, hauled by streamlined "Jubilee" steam locomotives in high-speed Ontario and Quebec services. These smooth-sided cars had a slight curvature of their lower sides (in cross-section), giving them a vaguely Continental look enhanced by their rich maroon paint. The CPR operated coaches, head-end cars, and even all-room sleepers built to a similar "custom" curve-sided design in the late 1940s.

Following its 1933 success stories—the *George M. Pullman* and teardrop-shaped, self-propelled *Railplane*—The Pullman Company made more headlines in 1934 with the introduction of the first lightweight, streamlined articulated sleeping cars—*Abraham Lincoln, Overland Trail*, and *Oregon Trail*—on the UP's M-10001 streamliner, the *City of Portland*.

Pullman's innovations notwithstanding, arguably the most dazzling—and far-reaching (in terms of effect on the industry)—streamlined passenger car designs to debut in the mid-1930s were the stainless-steel products of the Budd Company. Their striking fluted exteriors and the rakish shovel-nosed bodies of their power cars were a legacy of the Budd-Michelin experimental railcar of 1931 and its pneumatic-tire offspring built for the Reading, Pennsylvania, and Texas & Pacific by 1933. Budd's sleek, aerodynamic efforts, as first embodied in the Burlington's *Zephyr*, made turret-cabbed aluminum contemporaries like UP's *Streamliners* and Illinois Central's *Green Diamond* look like so many colorful but pug-nosed worms.

The B&O/Alton's AC&F-built *Royal Blue/Abraham Lincoln* of 1935, despite having a slope-nosed locomotive,

somehow still lacked the panache of a *Zephyr*. AC&F fared better, esthetically, with the Gulf, Mobile & Northern's *Rebels* of 1935. The first of the new wave of pocket streamliners to operate in the South, the two spot-welded, smooth-sided *Rebel* trainsets were non-articulated.

Esthetics aside, the enduring strength of Budd's design lay in the company's use of corrosion-resistant stainless steel throughout the box-girder carbody, assembled using the company's patented "Shotweld" process. With the Burlington's initial *Zephyr* and the Boston & Maine–Maine Central's *Flying Yankee* in the national spotlight, Budd made formal "Zephyresque" proposals to a number of railroads. Specifications were even produced for a double-ended version—for the perpetually innovative New Haven—but that railroad opted to make do with its pioneering, bidirectional Besler Steam Train and Goodyear-Zeppelin *Comet* instead.

As appealing as the new streamlined, articulated trainsets were to the public, their operating limitations soon became apparent to their owners. The ability to add cars to the trains' semi-permanently coupled consists to meet traffic demands ranged from difficult to impossible. The need for operational flexibility and interchangeability won out, and by the late 1930s the carbuilding industry's attention had turned to the continued development of non-articulated, lightweight cars.

This effort had already coalesced at Pullman-Standard in 1935 with a confidently named pair of articulated cars: 16-duplex room sleeper *Advance* and sleeper-lounge-observation *Progress*. Late in 1936, P-S built the *Forward*, embodying what would become the definitive architecture of the lightweight era. The *Forward's* fluted stainless-steel sheathing concealed a truss-supported, non-articulated body, and its unappealing collection of underbody-mounted mechanical equipment was concealed behind curved metal skirts that hinged up in sections for service access.

**FROM FORMAL . . .**

TOP: New chairs can't hide the prim Edwardian elegance of this Illinois Central lounge car. ALAN BRADLEY

**. . . TO FLOWING**

ABOVE: Milwaukee Road's "Tip Top Tap" lounges were a symphony of curves. MILWAUKEE ROAD HISTORICAL ASSOCIATION

non-articulated, streamlined, steam-powered train with a pug-ended observation car at each end.

Pullman did not rest on its considerable laurels. The 1937 introduction of the "roomette" brought the appeal of the individual sleeping car room to the lightweight era. A pair of 18-roomette demonstrators—named, in a fit of pragmatic creativity, *Roomette I* and *Roomette II*—gave railroads and the traveling public a taste of the modern accommodations awaiting them the following year with the inaugurations of the lightweight *20th Century Limited* and *Broadway Limited*. The roomette's success was immediate, and its combination with the modernized double bedroom (with enclosed toilet) in the 10 roomette-5 bedroom (10-5) and, later, 10-6 floor plans became the lightweight era's equivalent to the venerable 12-1.

For all the strides being made during the 1930s on lightweight passenger car design, though, the benefits were moot to those railroads lacking the resources to acquire new equipment, or the justification to allocate new cars to secondary or marginal routes. As a result, the 1930s saw old or obsolete heavyweight cars—and in some cases, entire trains—"modernized" by a number of railroads.

New York Central, hardly a pauper even during the Depression, rebuilt a group of heavyweight suburban cars under the direction of Henry Dreyfuss in 1936 to create the *Mercury*, a "streamliner" by just about every other definition. Other, less prosperous, roads following a similar "silk-purse-out-of-a-sow's-ear" approach before and after World War II included the Nashville, Chattanooga & St. Louis (*City of Memphis*) and Lehigh Valley (*John Wilkes* and *Asa Packer*), while the likes of Pennsylvania, Erie, Nickel Plate, Atlantic Coast Line, Soo Line, Texas & Pacific and Northern Pacific rebuilt cars for general service. For its part, The Pullman Company modernized hundreds of its own heavyweight cars inside and out after the war, producing in some cases the incongruity of clerestory-roofed cars with modern sealed picture windows.

## THE WAR ENDS ... AND THE BATTLE BEGINS

Unable to take delivery of new passenger-train equipment during World War II, railroads across North America wrung every possible mile, and then some, out of their existing car fleets while planning for widespread re-equipping at war's end.

The New York Central and the New York, New Haven & Hartford were among those passenger-oriented railroads anticipating strong peacetime markets, and both conducted extensive research on car types and amenities deemed desirable for postwar service. The New York Central circulated a hefty sleeping-car questionnaire booklet to passengers in 1944, soliciting travelers' opinions on everything from seat and toilet configurations to window sizes and exterior car finish.

Although *Forward's* exterior was sheathed in stainless-steel panels—a material that would prove to be P-S's Achilles heel after the war—the strong, corrosion-resistant metal had already become very much identified with the Budd Company, even at that early date.

Thwarted by Besler and Goodyear-Zeppelin from what would have been its bidirectional debut on the New Haven, Budd was able to win an order from the Reading Company to produce the *Crusader*, a noteworthy five-car,

A more obscure innovator in postwar passenger car design, but one with particularly far-reaching impact, was the combined research departments of the Chesapeake & Ohio, Nickel Plate Road, and Pere Marquette railroads. Among the innovations developed by this collaboration and first applied to lightweight cars built for the C&O and NKP were center bulkheads in coaches; air-operated sliding car-end doors; placement of more-expensive bedroom space in the better-riding center portion of sleeping cars; foot-pedal-operated sink faucets (said to be a result of then-C&O Chairman Robert R. Young's obsession with hygiene) and the use of cutaway beds in roomettes.

The latter was probably the C&O group's farthest-reaching passenger-car innovation, and was among the improvements adopted by Pullman-Standard in 1954 with the builder's "S-Type" roomette, a design also emulated by the Budd Company. It permitted the occupant of a roomette to lower or raise the bed without opening the door, and eliminated the need for the awkward and unreliable folding sinks found in various earlier roomette layouts. The porcelain sink was located atop a corner unit, convertible into a night table with the aid of a hinged Formica top. Three-way washstand mirrors were yet another S-Type improvement over prewar room designs.

Coach passengers' comfort was not ignored, though, as seating, lighting, and interior layout of these cars were also upgraded after the war. One of the most successful attempts to eliminate the "bowling alley" effect of a coach's interior was one of those C&O-initiated ideas. Placement of an offset bulkhead at the center of the car divided the seating area into two separate "rooms," with a dogleg in the passage through the bulkhead, blocking the view from one end of the car to the other. The bulkhead also typically housed a drinking fountain, literature racks, and decorative maps or murals. Cars of this type were originally built for the C&O and Nickel Plate, and eventually saw service with dozens of owners.

The introduction of the "Sleepy Hollow" coach seat followed more than two years of research sponsored by Heywood-Wakefield. In its public and trade advertising, the manufacturer made much of the fact that Harvard University anthropoligist Dr. Ernest A. Hooton had taken the measurements of thousands of passengers in order to calculate the dimensions of the "perfect" coach seat. The Sleepy Hollow design was widely adopted (and emulated) in postwar construction and—although Sleepy Hollow seats are no longer manufactured—to this day remains the standard by which all coach seats are measured.

## Show Time

Innovations in passenger car design of the 1940s were highlighted by the addition of "signature features" to the lightweight architecture established in the previous decade.

The performance of Budd all-stainless steel railway passenger cars again demonstrates the effectiveness of the Budd philosophy of combining imaginative, forward looking design, quality workmanship and the most suitable materials.

Railroads have found they can use these cars for many years and millions of miles beyond major overhaul schedules considered normal for cars not constructed of stainless steel.

The most critical inspections fail to discover any deterioration.

Parts which in cars built of other materials are notoriously vulnerable to rust, corrosion and excessive wear, remain unimpaired. And the superior strength of the stainless steel structure assures maximum safety for the railway passenger and increased availability for service.

Application of Budd ideas to the field of railway passenger transportation has proved as sound as it has in the field of the all-steel automobile body, the steel wheel and other automotive components. The Budd Company, Philadelphia, Detroit, Gary.

**PIONEERS IN BETTER TRANSPORTATION**

Chief among these was the dome car (sometimes mistakenly referred to as an "observation" car).

As appealing as observation cars were to passengers and—for their "punctuation" value at the end of a train—to passenger department marketing staff, they were a costly impediment to efficient operation, especially where cars were added or removed from a train during its run. In this scenario, an observation car had to be removed from the train and then restored to its trailing position after all other switching was complete—simply adding cars behind its glassed-in solarium would rob passengers of their view. Some roads removed observation cars altogether, while other added an ungainly tail-end diaphragm to permit car-to-car access when the cars ran in mid-train. Square-ended observation cars—either purpose-built or modified—helped maintain the "line" of a train while operating in mid-consist, but at the expense of the round-ended cars' visibility. Costly to build and operate, observation cars of any description inevitably proved to an an avoidable expense, and they gradually disappeared as the 1960s wore on, enjoying a brief revival under Amtrak until new equipment arrived.

In 1956, the Santa Fe introduced its Budd-built "Hi-Level" cars (on the heels of two 1954 experimental cars), a glass-roofed upper floor plan gave passengers a dome-like side and upward view from within the bilevel car, which was too tall to accommodate a "conventional" dome. These Santa Fe cars made headlines when they entered service on the all-coach *El Capitan*. Although the Chesapeake & Ohio (and possibly other American railroads) had examined the feasability of bilevel intercity passenger cars in the mid-1940s, and the Long Island Rail Road rostered ersatz bilevel commuter coaches, the "El Cap" was the first long-distance train to employ bilevel equipment in revenue service. Bilevel designs, particularly with coach floor plans, increase car capacity while reducing the weight per seat, a handy measure of car efficiency. With the entire upper level devoted to nothing but seating, other space-consuming (and revenue-killing) necessities such as vestibule areas, luggage storage, washrooms, and mechanical equipment could be located on the lower level.

Despite high hopes from carbuilders and industry pundits in the late 1950s, Santa Fe's would be one of only three such long-distance bilevel operations for almost another two decades. The Chicago & North Western also operated a modest intercity regional fleet of bilevel trains beginning in 1958, adapting a P-S bilevel commuter car shell for its bilevel reclining-seat coaches, lounge cars, and parlor cars. These cars, built new, were supplemented by older, single-level streamline diners and head-end cars rebuilt with false high rooflines to blend with the new intercity bilevel cars. In the third—and relatively unsung—instance, the Burlington received a series of Budd bilevels around 1960 that were equipped with toilets and more deeply cushioned
*continued on page 86*

# Pleasant Under Glass

**D**ome cars have come to symbolize the halcyon days of North America's postwar streamliners. They were indispensible on the great Western cruise trains, and even found their way east where clearances and managerial conservatism could be overcome. The dome, as the story goes, was invented in its modern form by a General Motors executive, C. R. Osborn, while viewing Colorado's mountain grandeur from the cab of one of his employer's diesel locomotives on the Denver & Rio Grande Western. The concept itself, however—permitting passengers to see ahead, behind, and above the train with ease—was not new. Designs had been proposed as early as the 1880s, and the Canadian Pacific Railway operated wooden sightseeing cars, equipped with twin cupolas, in the Rocky Mountains during the late nineteenth century.

First executed in the lightweight era by the Burlington on a rebuilt Budd coach at the railway's Aurora, Illinois, shops in 1945, the dome caught the fancy of the public and railway marketing departments alike in a big way with the nationwide tour begun by the P-S–GM *Train of Tomorrow* in 1947. This four-car E7A-powered train, each car of which—*Sky Dust, Sky View, Dream Cloud,* and *Moon Glow*—was equipped with a dome of flat-glass panels, was intended to showcase the features envisioned by P-S for its postwar offerings. Following their tour duties, the cars were sold to Union Pacific in 1950 for pool-train service between Portland and Seattle.

Pullman-Standard's high-profile *Train of Tomorrow* cars notwithstanding, Budd turned out the most dome-equipped cars, with P-S and ACF relegated to also-rans in the sales contest. "Short" domes appeared atop production cars ranging from coaches and diners to observation, lounge, and sleeping cars, and begat full-length versions with the 1952 debut of Milwaukee's P-S "Super Domes" and Santa Fe's 1954 Budd-built cars. The short-dome cars were marketed under a variety of names including "Astra Dome" (UP), "Planetarium Dome" (MP), "Scenic Dome" (CP), "Strata Dome" (B&O), and, most common of all (to the extent is has almost become generic), the "Vista-Dome", a name apparently coined by Budd rather than a specific railroad but popularized by CB&Q, GN, NP, Wabash, WP, and the Rio Grande.

The dome and observation car concepts coalesced in an unusual way with The Milwaukee Road's "Skytop" parlors and sleepers. Lacking domes in the conventional sense, these cars featured a unique glass-roofed streamlined solarium designed by Brooks Stevens. Other hybrid variations on the glass-roofed theme were the Seaboard Air Line's 1955 trio of sleeper-lounges— delivered as *Miami Beach*, *Palm Beach*, and *Hollywood Beach*—whose otherwise standard-profile lounge section incorporated extra-tall side windows and large glass roof panels.

Taller-than-normal side windows also found limited application in observation cars built by P-S, Budd, and ACF, creating what were dubbed "Lookout Lounges" for roads like New York Central, Great Northern, Southern, and Louisville & Nashville.

### ALL THAT GLITTERS

FACING PAGE: Budd became the uncontested champion in the postwar dome-car bonanza, and the company's *California Zephyr*—built for the CB&Q, D&RGW, and WP—was a wonderland of domes. Various *CZ* domes populate Amtrak's *Denver Zephyr* at Chicago in 1971.

### THE GREENHOUSE EFFECT

ABOVE LEFT: The glass-enclosed "Skytop" observation car, built exclusively for the Milwaukee Road in parlor (seen here) and sleeper configurations, was a novel twist on both the dome format and observation cars. MILWAUKEE ROAD, COURTESY MILWAUKEE ROAD HISTORICAL ASSOCIATION

### FLORIDA FLAT-TOPS

ABOVE: SAL ran a trio of glass-roofed Pullman-Standard-built sleeper-lounges between Florida and the Northeast. Dubbed "Sun Lounges," the cars featured a Tropical motif, complete with driftwood tables lamps. KEVIN J. HOLLAND COLLECTION

### WHAT DOME CARS WERE ALL ABOUT

LEFT: The view from one of the domes on Union Pacific's "Royal Gorge Steam Special" on June 22, 1997, illustrates what dome cars were all about. They were the ultimate way to view the passing countryside as well as the train. ALEX MAYES

## LOOKING IN

Heavyweight observation cars, for the most part, were subdued enclaves conducive to reading, conversation, and refreshments. These passengers aboard the Milwaukee Road's *Olympian* in January 1935 have turned their backs to the passing scenery.
MILWAUKEE ROAD, COURTESY MILWAUKEE ROAD HISTORICAL ASSOCIATION

## LOOKING OUT

Industrial designer Brooks Stevens' stunning Skytop observation cars were an engineering nightmare but a boon to passengers. Although, curiously, all seats still faced inward, occupants like those in this 1948 parlor car scene were hard-pressed not to have a view. Skytop lounges in the Milwaukee's *Creek*-series sleepers (later sold to Canadian National) included even more glass. MILWAUKEE ROAD, COURTESY MILWAUKEE ROAD HISTORICAL ASSOCIATION

## BUILT TO LAST

Even as passenger car architecture evolved through the mid-twentieth century, some older designs emerged as stalwarts. One of these was the Pennsylvania Railroad's P-70 coach, a heavyweight ark with few concessions to the streamline esthetic. This one brought up the rear of the eastbound *General* at Chicago in 1967.

## STAINLESS STEEL TO THE SUBURBS

A pair of New Haven electric multiple-unit cars—with an express car in tow—reach for the catenary in this 1955 view at Danbury, Connecticut, at the end of the then-electrified (now diesel only) Danbury branch. Cars such as these—offering greater operational flexibility than their locomotive-hauled counterparts—were common in electrified urban environments like New York, Chicago, and Montreal, although the snazzy stainless-steel sheathing embraced by the New Haven was atypical. JIM SHAUGHNESSY

## THE DETROIT INFLUENCE

The *Aerotrain* had a locomotive that evoked the futuristic lines of General Motors stylist Harley Earl's conceptual 1951 LeSabre automobile. And although spearheaded by GM as a panacea for the passenger train's ills—circa mid-1950s—it still met the same checkered fate as its contemporaries. After demonstrating across the U.S. and in Canada, the two *Aerotrains* (but three *Aerotrain* locomotives) ended up serving the Rock Island out of Chicago. One example survives as a museum piece in Green Bay, Wisconsin; another lives at the Museum of Transportation in St. Louis. KEVIN J. HOLLAND COLLECTION

*continued from page 82*

seats than their strictly suburban brethren. These cars were used for tour movements, to bolster regularly assigned consists on intercity trains during peak periods, and to handle group movements on regularly scheduled trains. The Burlington's *Morning* and *Afternoon Zephyrs*, among others, thus became bilevel trains on occasion.

The economics of bilevel cars were not lost on commuter operators—particularly in Chicago, where the Rock Island, Milwaukee Road, C&NW, and Illinois Central (the latter with electric m.u. cars) followed the Burlington's 1950 lead in bilevel suburban operations. Bilevel commuter operations—often employing a lozenge-shaped "trilevel" car (two main levels linked by two outer mezzanine levels) originally built in the late 1970s by Canada's Hawker-Siddely—can be found today in cities as disparate as Miami, Boston, New York, Los Angeles, Toronto, San Francisco, Seattle, Vancouver, and, of course, Chicago.

## DECLINE AND REVIVAL

The last cars of the exuberant postwar building spree had hardly carried their first passengers when the railroads—collectively and, for the most part, individually—began to recognize just how optimistic their postwar traffic forecasts had been. Whether for business or pleasure, Americans were traveling again—that much was true. Free of wartime restraints, though, they were availing themselves of the airways' speed and the highways' freedom. Domes and dependability were not enough for the railroads to maintain the intercity and long-distance dominance enjoyed prior to Pearl Harbor.

A select few railroads and routes continued to hold their trade in the face of the new competition, and new cars were being designed and built into the mid-1950s for service between the Midwest and Pacific Northwest, between the Northeast and Florida, and across Canada. By and large, though, the era of long-distance passenger car construction in North America would be dormant for almost two decades.

The 1950s are remembered for the flurry of activity—desperate innovation, really—yielding such ultra-lightweight passenger train concepts as the Talgo (a Spanish development promoted in the U.S. by ACF), General Motors' *Aerotrain*, Pennsy's Budd-built *Keystone*, and the C&O/Pullman-Standard *Train-X*. These low-profile trainsets, some of them articulated and reminiscent of the prewar *Zephyr*, *Comet*, and M-10000, amounted to a last-ditch effort by American carbuilders and railroads to ward off the bus and the private automobile. The similarity of the individual cars on these trains to buses, in size and ride quality, contributed to their undoing. Even in *Train-X's* 1960s incarnation as the United Aircraft *TurboTrain* (following the concept's mid-1950s locomotive-hauled debut as New Haven's *Dan'l Webster* and NYC's *Xplorer*) riders never really warmed to the equipment's cramped quarters and invariably rough ride. If railroad passengers were to endure aircraft-style seating and food service in these new-generation trains, most apparently opted for the aircraft's speed as well. The new generation, as envisioned by railroads and carbuilders in the 1950s, was stillborn.

Other, more conventional, passenger-car proposals were floated in the 1950s. Budd's "Siesta Coach" budget sleeper idea of 1953 entered service in 1956 on Burlington's re-equipped *Denver Zephyr* as the "Slumbercoach." By splitting the 24-inch-wide beds into two fold-down halves, Budd's designers were able to shoehorn 24 modular single rooms and 8 double rooms into a conventional 85-foot single-level carbody, providing cramped but economical sleeping-car travel for up to 40 passengers at a time. Even though Slumbercoach proponents saw the concept as an upgrade from coach rather than the potential degradation of profitable Pullman traffic—echoing a 1940 Pullman

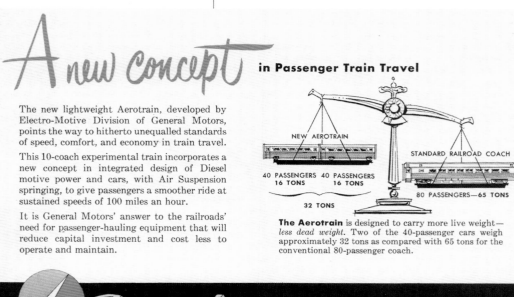

The new lightweight Aerotrain, developed by Electro-Motive Division of General Motors, points the way to hitherto unequalled standards of speed, comfort, and economy in train travel.

This 10-coach experimental train incorporates a new concept in integrated design of Diesel motive power and cars, with Air Suspension springing, to give passengers a smoother ride at sustained speeds of 100 miles an hour.

It is General Motors' answer to the railroads' need for passenger-hauling equipment that will reduce capital investment and cost less to operate and maintain.

**The Aerotrain** is designed to carry more live weight—*less dead weight*. Two of the 40-passenger cars weigh approximately 32 tons as compared with 65 tons for the conventional 80-passenger coach.

NEW AEROTRAIN

40 PASSENGERS   40 PASSENGERS
16 TONS         16 TONS

32 TONS

STANDARD RAILROAD COACH

80 PASSENGERS—65 TONS

**Aerotrain**—Center of gravity is 10 inches lower than in present standard railroad coaches — yet passengers ride no lower than in conventional trains and considerably higher than in other projected lightweight trains to provide a more enjoyable view of the scenery.

Having determined that a postwar market existed for a self-propelled car to replace aging gas-electric "doodlebugs" as well as to supplant uneconomical locomotive-hauled trains on secondary routes, the Budd Company introduced its Rail Diesel Car (RDC) in 1949.

Gas-electric cars typically rolled the various elements of multi-car trains into a single vehicle offering cost-effective coach, express, and even RPO service over lightly-traveled routes. Lifelines for many a rural community before the advent of reliable roads and widespread automobile ownership, the doodlebugs—sometimes pulling a trailer car or two—mirrored the architecture of contemporary heavyweight passenger cars with their riveted steel bodies and operable windows.

Although manufacturers such as ACF and Mack offered their own streamlined replacements for the "classic" gas-electric doodlebug before and after the war, the Budd RDC immediately became the market leader and was offered in five eventual variations. The RDC-1 was a full coach; the RDC-2 added a short baggage section, to which the RDC-3 added an additional RPO apartment; the short-bodied RDC-4 catered to mail, baggage, and express only; and the RDC-9 was a blind-ended custom job built for the B&M. A kitchen- and dinette-equipped RDC-2 variant was even produced for the B&O.

Budd's original RDC "package" was cosmetically and mechanically upgraded in 1956, with quieter and slightly more powerful engines and a restyled end treatment among the biggest improvements.

The RDC found applications ranging from high-density commuter operations in Boston (on the B&M) to rural branchline service (on roads like New York Central and Canadian National) and long-distance secondary mainline service (such as the B&O's *Daylight Speedliners* and Western Pacific's *Zephyrette*).

A variation on the RDC theme was created in 1957 when Budd produced the five-car *Roger Williams* for New Haven. Planned as a self-contained bidirectional trainset, the *Roger Williams* placed three cabless RDC coaches between a pair of pug-nosed single-cab end cars, all sheathed in atypical (for Budd) finely fluted side panels.

More typically, though, the stainless-steel "Budd Cars" were employed—consciously or circumstantially—as a transition between uneconomic locomotive-hauled trains and ultimate discontinuance of service on declining routes across North America.

### WARPAINT

UPPER LEFT: Budd's Rail Diesel Car (RDC) was particularly popular in Canada, serving, at various times, nine of the country's ten provinces. These Canadian Pacific cars met west of Montreal's Windsor Station in 1972. Speedy and silent RDC's were prone to grade-crossing mishaps, and a number of operators embraced gyrating warning lights and high-visibility end paint in attempts to make the cars more visible to motorists. Smaller end windows and a beefed-up pilot design were among Budd's "Phase II" responses to the same problem.

### PRAIRIE PREDECESSOR

TOP RIGHT: Illinois Central's fondness for streamlined self-propelled vehicles—like the ACF-built *Illini* of 1940 illustrated in this rare brochure—waned after a series of grade-crossing accidents. DON SARNO COLLECTION

### ALL-IN-ONE

ABOVE: Combining motive power, operator's cab, RPO apartment, baggage and express space and a coach section, this Grand Trunk Western car—possibly on the Detroit–Port Huron, Michigan, branch—typified the self-contained versatility and inherent economy of the gas-electric "doodlebug." GTW, KEVIN J. HOLLAND COLLECTION

## CHEAP SLEEP

Budd's 1953 proposal for a high-density economy sleeper, the "Siesta Coach", emerged as the Slumbercoach in 1956 and met with limited success. Burlington's *Silver Rest* had survived to see Amtrak service when it was photographed at Chicago in May 1972.

## AT YOUR SERVICE

Dining cars—like this Budd-built Canadian Pacific example—were the perennial loss-leaders of passenger train operation. Heavy to haul and expensive to staff, they were seen by management as a necessary evil.

coach-sleeper experiment pre-empted by the war—the design met with fairly limited acceptance. The New York Central embraced the idea by rebuilding existing cars—using some Budd components—into what it called "Sleepercoaches." UP took another approach by running surplus 21-roomette cars as economy sleepers. Interestingly, Slumbercoaches in Amtrak service seemed to have a popular following right up to their retirement in the late 1980s.

Budd attempted to counter the precipitous decline in late-1950s car orders with the "Pioneer III," a no-frills carbody design with closely spaced fluting, lozenge-shaped windows, and inboard-bearing trucks that saw some use—in electric m.u. form in suburban service—with the PRR and Reading. Budd's Pioneer III demonstrator coach was unveiled in July 1956 and had accumulated over 120,000 test miles on U.S. and Canadian railroads by the time the car's m.u. variant entered revenue service on the PRR in 1958.

It took an infusion of $90 million in federal government funds—in the form of the High Speed Ground Transportation R&D Act of 1965—to kick-start the "modern era" of passenger car design and construction. With some of this federal pie and $45-million of its own money, the Pennsylvania Railroad built on its relationship with the Budd Company to create what became the *Metroliners*, the high-speed electric multiple-unit trains built to serve the New York–Washington Northeast Corridor.

Budd's proven stainless-steel construction methods were applied to create slit-windowed carbodies with an almost tubular cross-section. The cars' sides curved outward to maximize interior width and strength, while the choice of window styling was a pragmatic one to minimize the "target" available to the rock-throwing denizens along the *Metroliners'* route.

When it came time for the recently created Amtrak—which had inherited the *Metroliners* from Penn Central—to procure its first new passenger cars, the *Metroliner*

carbody tooling was adapted by Budd for Amtrak (to save money and tooling time) for locomotive-hauled short- and medium-distance day service and "Amfleet" was born in 1975. Budd even adapted the so-called "Metroshell" to create the SPV-2000. With SPV standing for "Self-Propelled Vehicle," the car—only a handful of which were sold—was preferred by Budd as the next-generation replacement for the company's RDC.

Amtrak had also inherited the Santa Fe's Budd-built Hi-Level cars and opted to acquire its own new bilevel equipment for long-distance services where clearance limitations on the tall cars was not an issue. Dubbed "Super-liners," the first members of Amtrak's new stainless-steel bilevel fleet emerged from Pullman-Standard—after numerous delays and cost overruns—and entered service in 1978. They marked Pullman-Standard's troubled exit from the passenger car market, and the so-called Superliner II cars acquired by Amtrak in the mid-1990s were built by Bombardier (pronounced Bom-BAR-dee-ay).

Consolidation had been the order of the industry since the end of the "classic" era in the late 1950s and very early 1960s. Minority builders like St. Louis Car and AC&F dropped out of intercity passenger car production as the market evaporated. By the late 1970s P-S had no choice

The Metroliners
The Metroliners
The Metroliners

but to follow suit, and even Budd was forced to exit the market after bringing the Viewliner concept to fruition. Bombardier acquired patents and production rights for Budd and P-S designs and today is the only active North American builder of intercity passenger cars.

With the debut of Amtrak's original Superliner sleeping cars, the roomette disappeared from the carbuilders' repertoire, replaced by a two-person "economy room." While more versatile from a sales perspective, the economy room—hardly larger than the roomette it replaced—harkened to the "dark ages" of rail travel by forcing passengers to venture not just down the aisle but downstairs for toilet and washing facilities. One step forward, it seemed, was actually two steps back. Even though it also lacked toilet facilities, the "family room" was a noteworthy innovation in the Superliner sleeper design. Taking advantage of the lack of a through aisle on the cars' lower level, this four-person room occupied the full width of the car end, and was the first American sleeping car space to offer a private view from both sides of the train.

## CANADIAN CONTENDER

The LRC—for Light, Rapid, Comfortable—was developed in the early 1970s by the Canadian consortium of Alcan, MLW (later, Bombardier), and Dofasco. Despite demonstrating on Amtrak in the mid-1980s, the LRC's only customer was VIA Rail Canada, in whose service a consist is seen at Kingston, Ontario, in June 1998. ALEX MAYES

Another sleeping car space had long-since disappeared from U.S. trains by the 1970s—the open section. With the advent of "all-room" cars in the mid-1930s, U.S. passengers abandoned the sections' lack of privacy in droves. Very few lightweight sleeping cars incorporating sections were built for U.S. railroads. They were typically assigned to runs with a steady traffic of government-business travelers who were not authorized to travel at government expense in roomettes or more expensive sleeper space. Sections remained popular in Canada, however, and were well-represented in the mid-1950s lightweight cars orders placed by both Canadian National (from P-S) and Canadian Pacific (from Budd). Even the venerable heavyweight 12-1 plan remained in CN service until the early 1970s, and today's VIA passengers can still opt to trade a bit of privacy for the congeniality afforded by the classic open section.

While the Pennsy's Northeast Corridor efforts got the lion's share of passenger train-related media attention in the 1960s, Canadian National earned some significant headlines of its own on the passenger car front. For a 1967 re-equipping of Southwestern Ontario regional services, CN turned to the firm of Hawker-Siddely to produce 25 aluminum-bodied, head-end-power-equipped coaches, dinettes, and club (parlor) cars, marketed as *Tempo* service. Variations on this H-S body were also developed for commuter and export customers.

The use of head-end power (HEP) was a first in Canada, and had seen only limited application in the U.S. on such trainsets as the PRR *Keystone*. HEP produced a substantial reduction in individual car weight with the elimination of generators, batteries, steam lines and other related components—all replaced by current supplied by the locomotive or a dedicated power car. HEP came into its own with Amtrak's Amfleet and Superliner equipment, along with older steam-heat-era cars retained and converted by both Amtrak and Canada's VIA.

Canadian National (and, later, VIA) also gave the troublesome *Turbo Train* the closest thing it ever got to a fighting chance. Built by United Aircraft (and in conjunction with MLW—the Montreal Locomotive Works—in Canada), the gas-turbine-powered *Turbo* combined the "audio" of a jet aircraft with the "visual"—and the consist limitations—of the original serpentine streamliners of the 1930s. In concept, *Turbo* traced its origins to Alan Cripe of the Chesapeake & Ohio's postwar research department, and to the C&O/P-S *Train-X* demonstration car of 1952.

The LRC—for Light, Rapid, Comfortable—was an early Seventies attempt by a trio of Canadian railroad supply companies (Dofasco, Alcan, and MLW) to realize the elusive grail of a successful next-generation passenger train concept. The LRC prudently ignored the pitfalls of articulation in favor of locomotive-hauled cars, but staked its high-speed success on a troublesome inertial banking system.

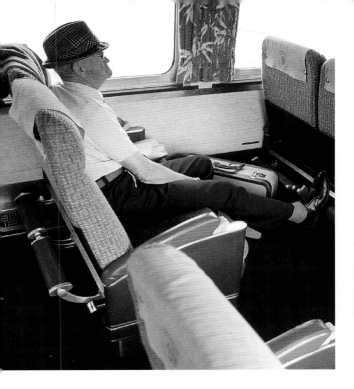

### THE BASICS

ABOVE LEFT: The cars may have changed over the decades, but the mechanics of coach travel were constant—a seat, a window, and a destination. This pensive traveler was aboard the Southern's Asheville–Salisbury, North Carolina, local in 1975.

### GENERATIONS

ABOVE: Just as the Santa Fe had embraced the efficiencies of long-distance bilevel equipment in the mid-1950s, Amtrak "looked up" in the 1970s when it created the Superliners with Pullman-Standard. A Superliner coach-baggage car, at left in this view, displayed its compatability with an elderly ex-Santa Fe Budd Hi-Level coach in this 1996 scene at Joliet, Illinois.

### THE NEW STANDARD

LEFT: Amfleet's tubular architecture, derived from the PRR *Metroliners*, is highlighted in this 1992 view of a *Metroliner Service* train near Newark, New Jersey.

## UP AND DOWN THE COAST

First developed in the late 1970s on behalf of Toronto's GO Transit, lozenge-shaped bilevel commuter cars such as these (on a Coaster suburban train at Del Mar, California, in October 1998) have become favorites of commuter agencies throughout North America. Cars such as these are, in effect, trilevels, with small seating areas above each truck adjacent to a staircase landing between the main upper and lower levels. A cab in the lead car controls the locomotive at the opposite end of the bidirectional train in "push" mode. ALEX MAYES

## WINDOWS ON THE FUTURE

The Viewliner, developed by Budd and Amtrak and finally executed by Morrison-Knudsen in the late 1980s, was designed to accommodate modular interiors within an Amfleet-like stainless-steel carbody. Both sleeping and dining car versions were built as replacements for Amtrak's well-traveled "Heritage Fleet", which were upgraded veterans of the post-World War II streamliner era. Two of the three prototype cars are shown being assembled at Amtrak's Beech Grove Shops near Indianapolis, Indiana, in 1988.

This was designed to tilt carbodies automatically and thereby enable curves to be negotiated at higher speeds than were comfortable with conventional cars. LRC cars echoed Amfleet's fish-bellied architecture—but with remarkably large windows—and were fabricated of aluminum alloys.

Back in the U.S., Amtrak spent much of the 1980s and 1990s on its own quest for the "next best." Continuing the trend begun in 1973 when it imported French RTG turbine-powered trainsets and subsequently evaluated French and Swedish electric locomotives, Amtrak borrowed and tested sleek trainsets from European and Scandinavian operators. Spanish-designed Talgo equipment—whose design concepts trace to the 1950s—was finally selected for Pacific Northwest corridor services, and high-speed locomotive-powered electric trainsets based in part on France's wildly popular TGV trains. The latter are being built in the U.S. and Canada by Bombardier through a licensing agreement with Alstom. A lot is riding on Amtrak's new tilt-body "bullet" trains, the *Acela Express*es, which, as this book goes into its first printing, were replacing the locomotive-and-Amfleet *Metroliners* on the Northeast Corridor (the original *Metroliners* having long since been demotored and converted to cab-control cars). The success of both the *Acela Express* and Talgo equipment may help determine the future path of an Amtrak currently in jeopardy, to say little of the passenger train in general in North America.

Evolution, whether biological or mechanical, is an imprecise adventure, fraught with perils and hard-earned experience. That the North American railroad passenger car continues to evolve at all as the twenty-first century dawns is pause for satisfaction among the mode's advocates, provided the lessons of the 1950s are heeded. As long as substance prevails over style, the story of passenger car development should continue to unfold.

**FUTURE SNACK**

The austere but airy interior of the cafe car in one of Amtrak's *Acela Express* trainsets in July 2001 typifies the styling tastes embraced by Amtrak designers in the late 1990s. The clean lines befit a train intended to zip between Boston, New York, and Washington, D.C., at up to 150 MPH.

# Passenger Train Design Reaches its Pinnacle as the Bottom Falls Out

A streamliner is a train designed with uniform, smooth, flowing contours that minimize wind resistance while providing a sleek, modern appearance. The emergence of streamliners in the mid-1930s ushered in a whole new era for the American passenger train, though that era would end in ruin.

For the purposes of this book, the streamliner era is arbitrarily defined as beginning in 1934 and ending with the start of Amtrak, the national railroad passenger carrier, in 1971. To say "streamliner" era is something of a misnomer, though, because it may imply that all passenger trains during this 37-year period were (or became) streamliners. Not quite so. True, streamliners and streamlining caught on in a flash, coast to coast, but the movement just as suddenly slacked off—twice, in fact; first at the onset of America's entry into World War II and, second, as the 1950s progressed, bringing on new American priorities—a focus on travel by car and air.

Ironically, for all the attention they garnered, streamlined trains were the minority of rail passenger equipment operating on intercity runs in the US, Canada, and Mexico during much of the streamliner era. Even at the very end of this period, some intercity trains and many commuter trains still sported heavyweight equipment. Streamlined equipment was expensive and the railroads tended only to streamline and upgrade their top trains.

**THE ULTIMATE STREAMLINER PAINT SCHEME**

ABOVE: Among the most celebrated streamliner-era paint schemes of all time was that created by Leland Knickerbocker of General Motors Styling Section for Santa Fe's new streamliners of 1937. Now popularly known as the "warbonnet" livery, Knickerbocker combined bright colors and flowing shapes to simulate an Indian headdress on the nose of the locomotive, in this case AT&SF E6A No. 13 at Kansas City in 1965. MIKE MCBRIDE

**EAST IS EAST AND WEST IS WEST . . .**

. . . and never the twain shall meet. But in this 1966 view at Chicago, East and West *are* meeting. Representing the former is the 1949 edition of Pennsylvania Railroad's *Broadway Limited*; and representing "Everywhere West" Burlington Route is the 1956 *Denver Zephyr*. ALAN BRADLEY

## MEAN MCKEEN

INSET: One streamliner precursor of note was the wedge-nosed McKeen car developed for the Union Pacific early in the twentieth century. The aerodynamic shape of these foreboding-looking self-propelled gas-electrics supposedly lowered wind resistance, although the cars probably never operated regularly at speeds high enough to make a difference. UNION PACIFIC

## "LITTLE ZIP" ON TOUR

America's first true lightweight, internal-combustion streamliner—UP's M-10000—was a hit with the public, if the crowds awaiting a glimpse of "Little Zip" (as UP crews called it) at Los Angeles in 1934 are any indication. The yellow-and-brown train was on its nationwide exhibition tour, traveling to points both on and off home rails. UNION PACIFIC MUSEUM COLLECTION

As the economics of the passenger (and freight) business soured during the 1950s, the railroads remained cautious about spending money to upgrade any further, and there was a tendency to hang onto the older equipment.

The start of Amtrak operations on May 1, 1971, makes for a convenient closure to the streamliner era that had been launched by America's common-carrier railroads, since the national carrier was a whole new operating entity unlike the private-sector railroad. But the streamliner era really didn't end in May 1971. Amtrak inherited a large fleet of stream-lined rolling stock from the railroads that joined Amtrak, and successive new rolling stock acquired by the carrier over the years, including its new *Acela Express* high-speed trains delivered in 1999–2001, has been very much in the realm of streamliners.

## Seeds of an Idea

Industrial designers have dabbled with streamlining, as applied to railcars, since the 1830s. In 1900, Baltimore & Ohio used fluted shrouding to remodel an entire train of wood cars into an ersatz streamliner. It reached speeds of up to 85 MPH, presaging another feature of the future streamliner—speed. Inexplicably, the shrouding was removed after only a couple of months. It was a false start for the streamliner era.

About six years after the isolated B&O experiment, William R. McKeen Jr., superintendent of motive power for Union Pacific, designed a self-propelled railcar based on the U.S. Navy's new high-speed torpedo boats that had so inspired E. H. Harriman, UP's chief executive officer. The result of UP's effort were a fleet of sinister-looking, knife-prowed motorcars pulling coach trailers. These McKeen cars, as they became known, were assigned to lightly patronized runs, often on branch lines. Other self-propelled railcars—some of them with rudimentary streamstyling—began to appear soon after on other railroads, but none, including the McKeen cars, ever quite captured the public's fancy.

## THE STREAMLINER BLOSSOMS

Beginning in the 1920s, there had been warning signs that all was not well for the American passenger train. A growing number of travelers began opting for auto or bus travel over an expanding new highway system sponsored by federal and local governments. In 1921, with the advent of the Federal Highway Act, Congress declared a goal of linking every county seat in the country with improved roads. Auto registration grew from 8 million in 1920 to 23 million in 1930; during the same ten-year period railroad passenger revenues dropped by 41 percent.

Then came the stockmarket crash of 1929 and the ensuing Great Depression. The railroads were hit hard. Between 1929 and 1934, U.S. railroad passenger revenue fell by 50 percent. At first, the industry grappled with this alarming loss by cutting some services outright and, on selected routes, cooperating with rival carriers to reduce duplicating services. Improvements such as air conditioning were added to attract passengers. But the service cuts and minor technical upgrades couldn't make up the difference. The "enemy" no longer was the other railroad; it was the automobile.

There was a solution to be had, and two pioneering railroads—Union Pacific and rival Chicago, Burlington & Quincy—simultaneously tackled the two-sided problem. Both felt the best approach would be to entice passengers back to the rails, at the same time reducing the cost of carrying them to their destinations. UP and Burlington laid their bet on a new type of conveyance that could do both: the lightweight streamliner.

Since World War I, rail motorcars already had successfully addressed the problem of lower operating costs (see "A Self-Propelling Prophecy," Chapter 5), especially on short-haul runs and branchline routes. Motorcars hardly had the pizazz needed to attract patronage, though. But what if you dressed one up in a radical new style of clothes? That's what had happened with the Rail Plane, a super-streamlined internal-combustion motorcar which incorporated aeronautical construction techniques like welded tubular framing and aluminum shrouding. Sponsored by Pullman Car & Manufacturing, the Rail Plane debuted in 1932 and turned heads when it reached speeds of 90 MPH in test runs. The train caught the attention of W. Averell Harriman, UP's chairman of the board and grandson of the Harriman who earlier had sanctioned the development of the McKeen car. W. A. Harriman wanted a flashy new hot-rod train for the UP similar to the Rail Plane, and in 1933, UP placed an order with PC&M for a four-car train that was destined to become North America's first internal-combustion-powered, high-speed, streamliner. (The Rail Plane's motorcar status kept it from being considered a true "train.")

The yellow-and-brown speedster—designated M-10000 ("M" for motor train)—was delivered in February

MODERN *Streamlined Beauty* OUTSIDE...

THE NEW AIR CONDITIONED *DeLuxe Passenger Coaches* OF THE NEW HAVEN R.R.

## NEW CARS FOR THE NEW HAVEN

Aside from introducing its own lightweight, articulated streamliner, the *Comet*, in 1935, the New York, New Haven & Hartford also unveiled a fleet of newly built streamline conventional cars the same year. Built by Pullman Car & Manufacturing's plant in Worcester, Massachusetts, the new rolling stock featured rounded contours and large windows, emphasized in this promotional folder from the period. JOE WELSH COLLECTION

## FIRST CITY OF DENVER

UP's M-10000 streamliner ushered in a whole series of "City" streamliners for the railroad. West of Omaha in 1936, one of the two new *City of Denver* trainsets poses for the company photographer. UNION PACIFIC MUSEUM COLLECTION; CITY OF DENVER BAGGAGE DECAL, MIKE MCBRIDE COLLECTION

THE *Streamliner*
CITY OF DENVER
WORLD'S FASTEST LONG DISTANCE TRAIN
CHICAGO & NORTH WESTERN UNION PACIFIC

1934 and immediately embarked upon a 12,625-mile exhibition tour through 22 states as well as Washington, D.C., where President Franklin D. Roosevelt made a personal inspection of it.

The 204-foot train was comprised of four semi-permanently coupled cars: a power-baggage-mail car, a coach, a sleeping car, and a buffet-coach. (Inexplicably, the sleeping-car rarely appeared with the train.) The M-10000 was articulated; that is, adjacent cars shared a common truck to reduce overall train weight and provide a smoother ride. (A conventional three-car train would have ridden upon six trucks not including the separate locomotive required to pull it; the M-10000 had four trucks total, including the motored front truck of the power car.)

The M-10000 won the race to become America's first lightweight, streamlined train, but only by a nose. CB&Q's own streamliner was under construction at the

same time as the M-10000, but Burlington's approach was decidedly different. The train was being built by the Edward G. Budd Manufacturing Co. of Philadelphia. Burlington's vision called for a carbody of stainless steel, a tough, new, lightweight "miracle metal", but one that was difficult to assemble through ordinary welding. Budd had solved this fabrication problem with its newly patented "shotwelding" process.

To power the train, Burlington took another bold step, choosing a diesel-electric power plant. Interestingly, motor-car builder Electro-Motive Corporation supplied the power plants for both new streamliners, but for the M-10000, UP opted for a readily available Winton spark-ignition engine fueled by distillate (a semi-crude petroleum fuel) to ensure that it would have its streamliner ready first. Diesel-electric power had proven successful, but only in stationary engines. Burlington's liberal management

convinced a reluctant EMC to modify one of its Winton stationary diesel-electric engines for use in the train, whose carbody was already under construction.

Christened as the *Zephyr*—after Zephyrus, the Greek god of the West Wind—the three-car streamliner emerged from Budd in April 1934. The 197-foot-long articulated train, given the number 9900 by proud parent Burlington, featured a power car that included a Railway Post Office and mail-storage compartment, a baggage-coach, and a coach-parlor observation car.

Both new trains were a public sensation, thanks in part to extended exhibition tours and speed runs, the most notable being that of the *Zephyr's* nonstop run between Denver and Chicago on May 26, 1934. The train departed Denver at 5:05 A.M. for a well-publicized dawn-to-dusk run, flashing past spectators lining the tracks of towns and cities all along the 1,015-mile route. At 8:09 P.M. the same day, the train arrived amidst a bedazzled, cheering audience at the at Chicago's Century of Progress.

The *Zephyr* became the first streamliner in revenue service when it began its first daily round trip over CB&Q's 250-mile Lincoln–Omaha–Kansas City route on November 11, 1934. All along, Burlington had intended its streamliner—in reality, a glorified motorcar train—to replace a steam-powered train on a money-losing secondary run that had been suffering declining patronage. Theoretically, the new *Zephyr* would reduce operating costs and attract enough new patronage so the run could possibly break even. To the railroad's delight, *Zephyr* 9900 replaced two heavyweight steam trains (due to its higher speed and the need for less servicing) and attracted so much new ridership that the train showed a profit.

Union Pacific's M-10000 did not enter public service until February 1935. Unlike the Burlington, UP's early intentions were to use the M-10000 in transcontinental mainline service and examined the feasibility of running it on a 24-hour Chicago–Los Angeles schedule (hence the sleeping car), in conjunction with Chicago & North Western, with sustained speeds of 100 MPH! When it finally did enter revenue service (being christened simply as *The Streamliner*), the M-10000 wound up with the considerably more mundane task of local service on the 187-mile Kansas City–Topeka–Salina, Kansas, route.

The impact these two diminutive trains made upon the public and the railroad industry was nothing short of phenomenal, in part because UP and CB&Q went all out in showcasing their new rolling stars. Both trains traveled beyond home rails, from coast to coast. The *Zephyr's* record-breaking Denver–Chicago run was a publicity coup, not to mention the train's starring role in the 1934 RKO movie, "Silver Streak." Although there had been several isolated efforts at streamlining since the turn of the century, credit goes to UP and CB&Q for refining

the concept of streamlining by combining lightweight construction, futuristic styling, internal-combustion power (especially diesel), high-speed operation, and much promotion. And so began a nationwide love affair with streamliners.

## PROLIFERATION

UP must have been confident of the M-10000's success, for the railroad ordered a second train while "Little Zip"—as the M-10000 affectionately would become known by crews—was still under construction. Sister M-10001 was a six-car train complete with full dining and sleeping cars and a power car equipped with a diesel-electric prime mover. It was delivered in October 1934, and UP (undoubtedly prompted by Burlington's dawn-to-dusk run of the *Zephyr*) sent the train on a high-speed demonstration run from coast to coast, running from Los Angeles to New York in just under 57 hours. In May 1935, after some modifications, this new trainset was placed into Chicago–Portland service as the *City of Portland*, America's first transcontinental streamliner. More new streamliners for UP came on line in quick succession:

•M-10002, *City of Los Angeles* (Chicago–Ogden–Los Angeles), May 15, 1936.

•M-10004, *City of San Francisco* (Chicago–Ogden–Oakland), June 4, 1936.

### ZEPHYR COUSIN

Burlington *Zephyr* 9900 was less than a year old when, in February 1935, the affiliated Maine Central and Boston & Maine took joint custody of a new diesel-electric streamliner nearly identical to the 9900. Originally christened as the *Flying Yankee* and placed into Boston–Portland service, the three-car train wound up performing in a variety of New England assignments over the years. It is shown in June 1952 departing Boston's North Station as B&M's *Cheshire* en route to White River Junction, Vermont. The train has since been returned to its *Flying Yankee* markings and is on display in New Hampshire. JIM SHAUGHNESSY

## GULF, MOBILE & OHIO *ANN RUTLEDGE*

Among the early band of lightweight streamliners were two American Car & Foundry trains built for the Baltimore & Ohio in 1935. These twin trains were of more or less conventional format (that is, non-articulated) but one was built of aluminum and the other of Cor-Ten steel. One entered service as B&O's *Royal Blue* between Washington and Jersey City; the other went to B&O subsidiary Alton Railroad to serve as the Chicago–St. Louis *Abraham Lincoln*. Shortly thereafter, B&O also sent the *Royal Blue* set to the Alton, which operated it as the *Ann Rutledge*, a companion train to the *Abe*. The "Annie" is shown northbound at Lincoln, Illinois, circa 1957. DAVE INGLES COLLECTION

## B&O STREAMLINER *ROYAL BLUE*, SECOND TIME

After B&O sent its new ACF *Royal Blue* streamliner trainset (above) to the Alton, it re-streamlined its *Royal Blue* service with heavyweight cars modernized at B&O's shops in Baltimore. The upgraded equipment, complete with full-width diaphragms, is shown at Washington Union Station. MIKE SCHAFER COLLECTION

• M-10005, *City of Denver* (Chicago–Omaha–Denver), June 14, 1936.

• M-10006, *City of Denver*, June 14, 1936.

• M-10003 (back-up power cars only for any of the above trains; no cars) June 14, 1936.

Two sets of equipment were purchased for the *City of Denver* so that UP could provide daily service in each direction. For the remaining new trains, though, initially there was but a single set of equipment, so daily departures from the home terminals were not possible, requiring the railroad to schedule "sailings" on specific dates.

Burlington likewise began ordering more *Zephyr*s. It introduced the Chicago–Minneapolis/St Paul *Twin Zephyr*s in 1935 and the Chicago-Denver *Denver Zephyr* in 1936. Many more *Zephyr*s were introduced throughout the Midwest during the 1930s.

While at first their fleets may not have rivaled those of the CB&Q and UP in terms of size, a raft of other railroads throughout the country also introduced lightweight trains, hoping to emulate the successes of the Burlington and UP. The designs of some of these trains mimicked those of the *Zephyr*s (e.g., Maine Central-Boston & Maine's *Flying Yankee*) and UP streamliners (Illinois Central's *Green Diamond*), and in other cases were based on completely radical new designs such as New Haven's low-slung *Comet* built by Goodyear-Zeppelin.

Others took a more traditional approach. Santa Fe created a streamlined version of its all-Pullman *Super Chief* in 1937, then quickly upgraded a fellow star on the Chicago–Los Angeles route, the *Chief*, with lightweight cars. A fast, streamlined, all-coach running mate to the *Super Chief*—the *El Capitan*—was added as well. With the addition of still more equipment and trains in 1938, including the *Kansas Cityan* and the *Chicagoan* between Chicago and Wichita, Kansas, and the *San Diegan* between L.A. and its namesake, Santa Fe suddenly found itself the operator of the largest fleet of streamliners in the nation.

### DESTINED FOR FAME: THE FIRST *SUPER CHIEF*

Santa Fe's reaction to UP's impending new *City of Los Angeles* streamliner launched on May 15, 1936, was a new luxury-service train comprised of upgraded heavyweight cars. Santa Fe called its new Chicago–Los Angeles runner the *Super Chief*, and it was inaugurated three days ahead of the *City of Los Angeles*. It is shown with its new Electro-Motive diesel-electric box-cab locomotive set Nos. 1 and 1A ripping eastbound through Winona, Arizona, during the train's first year of operation. SANTA FE

### SANTA FE'S *EL CAPITAN* OF 1938

Santa Fe streamlined its all-Pullman *Super Chief* in 1937, and in February the following year introduced a luxury all-coach companion streamliner, El Capitan. An Electro-Motive E1A leads an *El Cap* consist on display with another Santa Fe streamliner (possibly the *Golden Gate* or a *San Diegan*) at Los Angeles. SANTA FE, JOE WELSH COLLECTION

### FRED HARVEY DINING SERVICE

Santa Fe had the distinction of providing food service aboard its trains and hotels through the Fred Harvey Corporation. This Fred Harvey-issued postcard from the 1940s show the clean, modern surroundings of the dining car on *El Capitan*. DAVID P. OROSZI COLLECTION

H-4575 —DINING CAR OF THE SANTA FE'S EL CAPITAN

## STELLAR STREAMLINERS: SOUTHERN PACIFIC'S *DAYLIGHTS*

Not all new streamliners were diesel-powered. Southern Pacific's entry in the fast-growing legion of who's who in streamlining was a lightweight version of its San Francisco–Los Angeles *Daylight*. Powered by semi-shrouded 4-8-4s, the new streamlined *Daylight* made its first run on March 21,1937. The railroad unabashedly proclaimed it to be "The Most Beautiful Train in the World," and with its striking red, orange, and black paint scheme, there was probably little argument. The popularity of the new streamliner—by 1939, the *Daylight* was the most heavily patronized intercity train in the U.S.— prompted SP to expand the fleet, and in January 1940 introduced the *Noon Daylight*. Comprised of refurbished equipment from the original *Daylight* (which got the new cars in 1940 and was renamed *Morning Daylight*), the new *Noon Daylight* is shown storming out of San Francisco about that time, doubling *Daylight* service between the Bay Area and L.A.
UNION PACIFIC MUSEUM COLLECTION

## STILL THE *DAYLIGHT*

SP's vibrant *Daylight* color scheme survived into the 1960s, but in this scene of the *Coast Daylight* (the renamed *Morning Daylight* ) having just arrived in San Francisco on April 23, 1964, the cars ahead of the train's parlor-observation sport the new, simplified scheme of silver (or stainless steel) and red. By this time, the *Noon Daylight*s had vanished from the timetables. ALAN BRADLEY

Unlike UP's and CB&Q's new trains, Santa Fe's streamliners were comprised of cars of conventional (read, coupleable and non-articulated) design and hauled by true diesel-electric locomotives. This building-block approach to assembling a given train's consist made Santa Fe's streamliner fleet far more flexible in being able to respond to fluctuating market demands.

It was a design trend that harkened to pre-streamliner passenger operations. Indeed most new trains completed after 1937 were largely non-articulated, or had a combination of conventional and articulated cars. Proving the merit of Santa Fe's decision, some articulated lightweight trains—such as NH's *Comet*, with rigid consists that proved difficult to expand—were quickly demoted from mainline service when demand exceeded their supply of seats.

Up front, not all streamliners were hauled by new diesels. Some of the fastest, such as Milwaukee Road's new (1935) *Hiawatha* between Chicago, Milwaukee, and the Twin Cities, were pulled by sleek steam locomotives operating at speeds that rivaled their diesel-powered competitors. Both the New York Central and Pennsylvania Railroads' premier trains between New York and Chicago, the all-Pullman *20th Century Limited* and *Broadway Limited* respectively, were streamlined in 1938 with new, non-articulated equipment pulled by streamlined steam locomotives.

By and large, these streamliners were still minority members of their company's passenger fleet. In the pre-World War II period and for some of the postwar era, the streamliner was a relative rarity on a railroad's roster. Steam-powered heavyweight trains significantly outnumbered the lightweight trains before World War II and into the early 1950s. Indeed, in at least one case (B&O's *Royal Blue* of 1935) a railroad even replaced a new lightweight train with a redesigned "streamstyled" heavyweight train when it felt the lightweight's performance wasn't up to standards. But the long-range trend was still toward introducing more streamliners of one type or another to attract passengers.

## Economy Luxury Trains

In addition to the use of lightweight equipment, another trend that developed in the frugal 1930s was the "economy luxury train," catering to a market that could no longer afford sleeping-car travel. Union Pacific pioneered the concept beginning in 1935 with its wildly successful (and yet largely heavyweight) *Challenger* trains between Chicago and the West Coast. The idea was to provide a high level of service to passengers for a

THE FAMOUS "400" SHOWN LEAVING THE CHICAGO STATION OF THE CHICAGO & NORTH WESTERN RAILWAY

## HEAVYWEIGHT CONTENDER

More than one railroad attempted to go head-to-head with new streamliners by introducing "new" premium-service trains that utilized heavyweight equipment. The Chicago & North Western did just that in 1935 with its new Chicago–St. Paul/Minneapolis "400", shown leaving Chicago in a colorized postcard scene. High-speed steam locomotives sped consists of refurbished heavyweight rolling stock over the 400-or-so miles between Chicago and St. Paul in about as many minutes, hence the name. STEVE SMEDLEY COLLECTION

## EXECUTIVE CLASS

Almost always financially frail, the Chicago, Indianapolis & Louisville—the Monon Route—would have to wait until after World War II to introduce streamliners. Meanwhile, in 1939, Monon wooed Indianapolis business clientele with a new Indianapolis–Chicago train, using heavyweight equipment, called the *Executive*. MIKE SCHAFER COLLECTION

For the
Greater Convenience of
Indianapolis Business Men

*THE NEW*
"*Executive*"
TO CHICAGO

The luxurious, air-conditioned, radio-equipped club-lounge car, above. The restful, air-conditioned observation parlor car, to the right.
Modern railway travel at its very best.

**MONON ROUTE**

low fare. The trains offered comfortable coach seats (and sometimes tourist sleeper accommodations), complete yet thrifty meals, bonuses like train stewardesses to assist with children, and even entire cars set aside for women and children. In some cases, such as the early *Challenger*s, they were comprised almost entirely of upgraded heavyweight equipment. Other examples of the concept would eventually include Santa Fe's lightweight *El Capitan* (1938), Pennsylvania's highly successful streamstyled heavyweight *Trail Blazer* (1939), and New York Central's rival heavyweight *Pacemaker* (1939), the latter two between New York and Chicago.

To Florida went a host of lightweight coach trains. In February 1939, the Seaboard Air Line created the first of many Florida streamliners with its all-coach *Silver Meteor* between New York and Miami; competitor Atlantic Coast Line/Florida East Coast soon followed with their *Champion*. Midwest railroads also got into the Florida market with new streamliners. In 1940, Midwesterners welcomed Illinois Central's flashy *City of Miami*, PRR's romantically named *South Wind*, and the Chicago & Eastern Illinois' *Dixie Flagler*. Relying on an alphabet soup of connecting carriers, the three trains departed their home terminal of Chicago on alternating days, so as to provide daily service to Florida. For much of the rest of the century, Florida would remain one of the strongest rail markets in the nation. It was all part of trend which saw streamliners serving an increasing number of places.

## Not All Good News

Did all these improvements have a positive impact? While the introduction of streamlined trains clearly attracted attention and ridership, between 1930 and 1940 railroad passenger traffic actually decreased from 29 billion "passenger-miles" (a passenger carried one mile) operated in 1930 to 25 billion operated in 1940. Likewise, the railroads' share of the total percentage of travel dropped as well. In 1930 the railroads operated 74.6 percent of all passenger-miles in the U.S. By 1940 they operated 67.1 percent of U.S. passenger miles—both air carriers and intercity bus companies increased their market share during the same period. A more accurate viewpoint is that the early streamliner and the publicity and ridership it generated for itself and its heavyweight running mates, curbed the harsh slide precipitated by the Depression. It did not, however, completely reverse the trend of dropping market share—until 1941.

## World War II

The entrance of the U.S. into World War II in 1941 resulted in a quick, dramatic rise in rail passenger traffic. The demands of a two-front war (unlike World War I) resulted in significant mileage increases. Total rail passenger

Streamliners were immensely popular with the public before World War II. They caught on for reasons that appealed to both our emotional and practical sides. What was it that "sold" streamliners to often skeptical railroads? Beauty, efficiency, and peer pressure.

## BEAUTY

By the dawn of the streamliner, the Art Deco movement was gaining momentum, as was its closely aligned cousin, *Moderne* design. Popularized at the Exposition Internationale des Arts Decoratifs et Industriels Modernes at Paris in 1925, Art Deco styling was hallmarked by geometric motifs, paralleling elements or shapes, and exotic colors. Moderne styling brought boldness, simplicity, and curvilinear forms to a high level.

The smooth, curving forms of these styles were in part rooted in earlier aerodynamic principles that aimed to reduce air or water resistance in moveable objects, mainly boats and planes. However, by the end of the 1920s, aerodynamic styling was being applied to all sorts of things, whether they moved or not.

Peer pressure brought this train to Atlanta on a daily basis. Southern Railway's new *Southerner* is on exhibition at Washington Union Station in 1941. RON FLANARY COLLECTION

These design influences were brought to life on the rails by a new breed, the industrial designer—part artist, architect, and engineer. The industrial designers' skills lay in applying art to moving objects. The smooth, bullet shapes conceived by designers for the new trains said speed; the bold colors, shiny metals, and interior materials they used were designed to awe. But perhaps the designers' most important contribution was in blending the elements of the new trains into a unified concept. All who viewed New York Central's *20th Century Limited*'s cool, modern, two-tone gray exterior immediately recognized the elegance of Park Avenue. The bright green and yellow citrus colors of the Illinois Central's original *City of Miami* said "fun in the sun."

## EFFICIENCY

The use of lightweight metals and sometimes new propulsion in the form of the diesel locomotive meant the streamliner could typically operate faster than a conventional train. In 1930, prior to the streamlined era, American passenger trains operated at an average speed of 60 MPH for only 1,100 miles daily. In 1940, six years after the streamliner was born, American passenger trains operated at 60 MPH or better for 75,000 miles daily. By 1941 four major world speed records belonged to North American railroads.

The lighter weight of a streamliner's cars also meant that the railroads could haul more cars and passengers with the same number of locomotives—a significant increase in revenues for a similar operating expenditure. Finally, the speed of the new trains coupled with the reliability of their diesels meant that the trains could often be turned around much faster than a conventional train at terminals. With less maintenance required, the new *Zephyr*'s diesels accumulated 30,000 miles per month while their steam locomotive cousins only chalked up 20,000 miles. These "selling points" weren't lost on the railroads or the manufacturers.

The usually conservative Pennsylvania Railroad quickly embraced the concept of lightweight trains because it felt the cars would reduce operating expenses while attracting more passengers. Manufacturer Budd Company, whose exotic stainless-steel cars were expensive to buy, had a standard sales approach. The company would use the prospective buyer's own statistics to show how a diesel-hauled Budd-built train could be operated twice as often in one day on a medium-distance run than the carrier's current steam-drawn heavyweight train. It worked. The streamliner may have been attractive to the public, but its practicality endeared it to even hard-nosed railroader management.

## PEER PRESSURE

The least remarked reason the streamliner caught on was the very real concern for "keeping up with the Jones's." The mighty Pennsylvania Railroad bowed to the pressure of the Pittsburgh business community in 1938 when Steel Town civic leaders—some of whom served on Pennsy's board or directors—pressured the railroad to give Pittsburgh streamliner service like Chicago and St. Louis had. The railroad changed its plans, quickly adding two new streamlined trains directly tied to the Pittsburgh market.

The south Florida tourism industry wielded its considerable clout through an all-out press campaign to convince the conservative Atlantic Coast Line and ally Florida East Coast to add daily streamliner service to south Florida. The result? Sold-out streamliners operated to Miami for decades. Atlanta leaders too, used the press to pressure the foot-dragging Southern Railway to bring lightweight trains to Atlanta. A new lightweight coach train, the *Southerner*, began serving Atlanta in 1941.

Before World War II changed American priorities, the streamliner was the hottest new form of transportation in the country—and everybody wanted on board.

mileage in 1942 was 25 percent more than it was in the busiest previous war year of 1918. Mileage in 1943, 1944, and 1945 was more than double the mileage of 1918. Passenger traffic during the war years was six times as high as it had been at the low point of the Depression in 1932.

Those increases represented millions of people using the U.S. rail system. During the war, nearly 97 percent of all domestic troop movements occurred by rail. Between 1941 and 1945, over 113,000 troop trains carried 43.7 million troops—an average of nearly a million troops a month moved on the nation's railroads. Gas and tire rationing resulted in more civilians using passenger trains, too, and extra sections of schedule trains and "SRO" (standing-room-only) trains became the norm rather than the exception.

The increased demand had predictable results. The railroads were not prepared to handle the crush, and they pressed older motive power and equipment into service. For example, the Pennsylvania—the nation's largest railroad—pressed ancient steam locomotives back into mainline

passenger service and converted a motley assortment of 302 cars, including 112 boxcars reequipped with wooden slat seats, into intercity passenger cars to handle the demand.

To efficiently move people and goods, the Office of Defense Transportation (ODT) a federal agency, coordinated the activities of the railroads. In September 1942, an ODT order froze passenger service, requiring a permit for the operation of special trains or extra sections of existing scheduled trains. To a large degree this action curtailed the operation of seasonal, tourist-oriented passenger trains such as the fabled *Orange Blossom Special* between New York and Miami, but it made Pullman cars available to carry troops. Likewise, in July 1945, another ODT order prohibited the use of sleeping cars to destinations shorter than 450 miles from point of origin. The order resulted in freeing hundreds of Pullman cars for use to move troops as the war came to an end.

The war had other impacts. Production of new equipment virtually ceased during the conflagration. Manufacturers who had previously made railcars retooled for war. Some of their best workers heeded the call of Uncle Sam and shipped out for boot camp. Under the watchful eye of the War Production Board, exotic raw materials that distinguished the streamliner vanished overnight as

## GETTING THE PUBLIC INVOLVED

When it came time to name their first new joint streamliner, Atlantic Coast Line and Florida East Coast went public with a contest. Over 100,000 people submitted suggestions. Betty Creighton of Pittsburgh, came up the winner with *Champion*—a train name that would last into the Amtrak era. KEVIN HOLLAND COLLECTION

## CHAMPIONING THE *CHAMPION*

ACL and FEC spared no expense in promoting their new New York–Miami streamliner— they couldn't, because neighbor Seaboard Air Line already had made a major impact on the market with its tremendously popular *Silver Meteor*. Ads like this provided detailed information about the all-coach train's feature cars and emphasized Coast Line's main advantage over the single-track Seaboard: ACL had a 100 MPH double-track main line to Florida. Fortunately, the demand for Northeast-to-Florida service was so high, that SAL, ACL, and FEC would all be winners. JOE WELSH COLLECTION

## NYC *MERCURY*

LEFT: NYC's first streamliner, the *Mercury* of 1936, was created from surplus 1920s-era commuter coaches and a regular Pacific locomotive that was given a rather extreme shrouding, all the design work of Henry Dreyfuss. The train is shown during its exhibition tour as it pauses at Central's old Syracuse station only months before the facility closed. In June of that year, the *Mercury* went into Cleveland–Detroit service. CAL'S CLASSICS

## WAS THIS THE GREATEST TRAIN?

BELOW: Railroad historians will forever argue the merits of any of hundreds of trains that have come and gone over the decades, but few will argue that the *20th Century Limited*—in particular its 1938 first streamlined edition—was the finest ever. The 1938 train, shown departing Englewood station on Chicago's South Side on September 23 of that year, was again the work of Henry Dreyfuss—and arguably his finest ever. The rolling stock was built by Pullman-Standard, but Dreyfuss oversaw all aspects of the train's design and decor, from its two-tone gray paint scheme to its earthy but elegant menus (RIGHT). PHOTO: R. H. KENNEDY COURTESY WILLIAM A RAIA; MENU: AUTHOR'S COLLECTION

**MENU**

**The 20th Century Limited**
KNOWN THE WORLD OVER FOR
LUXURY AND DEPENDABILITY
**New York . . . . Chicago**

aluminum, stainless steel, and curved specialty glass became more precious than gold. In fact, UP's famed M-10000 streamliner was scrapped during the war for its aluminum content. (*Zephyr* 9900 was spared, thanks to stainless steel not being easily recycled.)

Tooling for unique parts was virtually impossible to do, and steel became hard to find as well. The number of newly built passenger cars increased only one percent during the war, while traffic increased 400 percent. The last complete prewar streamliner delivered was Illinois Central's *Panama Limited*. The train's new streamlined equipment was ordered in April 1941, but while it was under construction, the War Production Board nixed the completion. IC convinced the agency that the new equipment would put the railroad in a much better position to handle the influx of wartime travelers. The new *Panama* rolling stock was delivered in 1942.

A tiny number of other new cars for various carriers trickled in through 1942 and 1943, and the railroads continued to post orders with manufacturers in 1943, 1944, and 1945, but they had no idea when their new trains would be available.

Existing streamliners themselves changed in character. Many were diluted with heavyweight cars to accommodate demand. Extra sections of trains became the norm, food rationing impacted the dining-car experience, and the demand of heavy traffic took its toll on railroad operating departments. And casualties weren't just occurring overseas. Some of the worst American passenger train wrecks in the twentieth century took place during World War II. In 1943, PRR's *Congressional Limited* derailed at speed on a curve at Frankford Junction, Pennsylvania, killing 79. The same year, Atlantic Coast Line's northbound *Tamiami Champion* sideswiped its derailed southbound running mate in the middle of the night at Buie, North Carolina, and 72 people died. In November 1944, a CB&Q freight train smashed into the rear of *Zephyr* 9900 at Fairmont, Nebraska, with fatalities in the observation car. In December 1944, a Southern Pacific mail train disregarded warning signals and rear-ended the *Pacific Limited* at Bagley, Utah, taking the lives of 50 people.

As the war ground to an end, the railroads' job wasn't finished. All those troops had to be mustered out. Except for 1944, 1945 was the second highest year in history for American railroad passenger traffic. In 1945 alone, New York's Pennsylvania Station handled nearly as many people as resided in the entire United States. The profits of war, coupled with the havoc that war traffic wrought on equipment and facilities, led the railroads to plan massive reinvestment in the immediate postwar period. While the railroads put together long lists of the expensive new streamliners they would buy with private monies, the government was beginning to plan the country's transportation future. And railroads were not part of the plan.

## FRISCO'S *FIREFLY*

A number of railroads wanted to become members of the streamliner generation but didn't necessarily have the capital available to purchase brand-new equipment. The solution, of course, was to build their own streamliners, and that's just what the St. Louis–San Francisco Railroad did in 1940, creating *The Firefly*, a high-speed, steam-powered day run between Kansas City and Oklahoma City, Oklahoma. The westbound run is shown near Spencer, Oklahoma on March 17, 1946. The train was comprised of coaches and a diner-parlor car rebuilt from heavyweight equipment and painted blue and cream.
PRESTON GEORGE, COURTESY BERNICE ARGO AND TERRY LA FRANCE

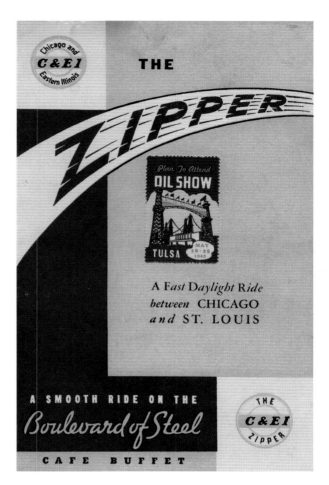

## CAFE-BUFFET MENU FROM 1943

America was in the depths of war when Chicago &
Eastern Illinois issued this menu for its *Zipper* between
Chicago and St. Louis in 1943. Regular items on the
menu included such delicacies as Tongue with Potato
Salad (75 cents) and Preserved Figs (a pricey 30 cents).
Edward J. Walker was the Head Waiter in Charge on
this day, and his recommended specials included Baked
Oysters with Macaroni au Gratin (60 cents) or Club
Sandwich "C&EI" (65 cents). MIKE SCHAFER COLLECTION

## WASHINGTON AT WAR

The banner hanging in the Great Hall at Washington
Union Station dates this scene to 1943. Countless
soldiers and civilians filed through this Beaux Arts depot
from 1941 to 1946—the peak of rail passenger travel in
America. KEVIN HOLLAND COLLECTION; BURLINGTON WAR-ERA
BAGGAGE TAG, OLIVER D. JOSEPH COLLECTION

### MOUNTAIN-CLIMBING
### *METROPOLITAN*

World War II has been over for two years, but Pennsylvania Railroad's westbound *Metropolitan* is doing battle with the Allegheny Mountains on this November day in 1947 near Cresson. For the rigorous climb up out of Altoona, Pennsylvania, through Horseshoe Curve to the summit at Gallitzin, a sturdy K4-class Pacific has been added ahead of the train's T-1-class 4-4-4-4. The *Metropolitan* was a New York–Pittsburgh day train, handling Washington cars west of Harrisburg, Pennsylvania, that fed connecting trains at Pittsburgh for St. Louis and Chicago. BRUCE D. FALES, COURTESY JAY WILLIAMS

## THE LAST CENTURY

The final edition of NYC's *20th Century Limited* was delivered by Pullman-Standard in 1948. Had the bottom not dropped out of the U.S. rail passenger market, there might have been a 1958 edition, but by that time, the NYC knew it was all over for the *Century* and its ilk. Shown speeding along the Hudson River on a late summer's eve in 1961, the 1948 *Century* wore a different variation of two-tone gray than its predecessor and lacks the Mercury blue pin-striping. Streamlined Hudsons had yielded to more efficient, if less inspiring, diesel-electric power. Nonetheless, it still held a star role in American passenger railroading—and on the silver screen. The '48 *Century* played a starring, if understated, role in the 1950s Alfred Hitchcock classic "North by Northwest." JOHN DZIOBKO

## CENTURY CLUB

Two feature cars built for the '48 *Century*—*Lake Shore* and *Atlantic Shore*, one for each of the two consists required to protect the *Century* schedules—contained a bar-lounge known as the Century Club. In addition, these cars also featured a barber shop and an office for the train secretary, who assisted business travelers with dictation, cable messaging, and other duties long before the era of the cell phone. Cutaway views of the bar-lounges were featured in the *Century*'s promotional brochures. JOE WELSH COLLECTION

## POSTWAR OPTIMISM AND SUDDEN FAILURE

An idea of the incredible hurry American railroads were in to reequip after the war can be gleaned from a look at the order books. From the small Bangor & Aroostook hoping to re-equip its *Aroostook Flyer* to the colossal Santa Fe looking to spruce up its mighty fleet, they came with checkbooks in hand. They'd need lots of patience. By 1946, the largest car manufacturer, Pullman-Standard, had nearly 1,200 cars on back order. Shortages of skilled labor and components were so bad that Pullman, which had partially completed cars scattered all over its Chicago and Worcester facilities, considered temporarily closing. These record orders would eventually be filled, but in many cases the new equipment would not be available until years later. In 1948, NYC's *20th Century Limited* was reequipped, and in 1949 its competitor, PRR's *Broadway Limited*, received new cars, too; the trains had been ordered in 1945 and 1946 respectively. Some railroads, like the Chicago, Indianapolis & Louisville—Monon—didn't want to wait for carbuilders to catch up and instead created their own streamliners.

The streamlined concept was back with a vengeance, and literally hundreds of other trains were streamlined after the war. Some of the most famous were in their second incarnation as lightweight trains, others were heavyweight stalwarts that were getting a facelift with new streamlined cars for the first time. And yet others were brand-new trains altogether.

Unfortunately, there were far more old names missing from the timetables than there were new faces. Despite the record ridership of World War II and the relative success of the streamliner in stemming the loss of traffic, the rail

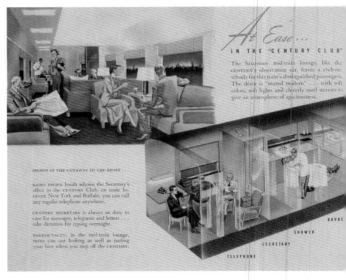

industry as a whole—and the passenger train in particular—remained in long-term decline. In 1929 there had been 20,000 passenger trains roaming the U.S. By 1946 there were 11,000 trains left. The survivors had to do everything in their power to stave off the growing competition of the airplane and government-sponsored highways, the latter increasingly populated with private autos and the buses of Greyhound, Trailways, and other carriers.

In the prewar era and in the wake of the Depression, much of the emphasis had been on giving passengers the best transportation value for their limited dollar. After the war, Americans, looking to forget the hardships of war, were anxious to roam the country in style, so the railroads gave them the "cruise train." Designed for sightseeing and chock full of amenities, some of these new trains represented the pinnacle of the streamliner era. The greatest of the lot was the new *California Zephyr*, inaugurated in 1949 between Chicago and San Francisco over CB&Q, Denver & Rio Grande Western, and Western Pacific. Scheduled to show passengers the most scenic parts of the West in daylight (versus providing the fastest schedule between Chicago and the West Coast by rail), the *CZ* featured a new design which would symbolize the postwar Western streamliner—dome cars.

Although a precursor "dome" car first appeared on the Canadian Pacific in 1900, the idea didn't truly blossom until 1945 when industry leader Burlington Route built the first true dome car and placed it in test service on its Chicago–Twin Cities route. General Motors/Pullman-Standard's demonstration domeliner, the *Train of Tomorrow*, toured the country in 1947. That same year, Burlington premiered the third edition (after that of 1935 and 1936) of its streamlined *Twin Zephyr*s, featuring new Budd-built dome cars. Within a decade, fourteen other

railroads were operating dome cars, and the nation's railroads rostered more than 200 domes (chapter 5). More than any other postwar innovation, the dome car boosted patronage, albeit temporarily.

Other spectacular car designs flowed from the drawing board to the coach yard: glass-enclosed marvels like Milwaukee Road's Skytop observation cars and triple-unit diners with glittering lounge and dining facilities for SP's *Cascade*, *Daylight* trains, and the *Lark*. Continuing a practice that had originated in UP's prewar streamliners with the likes of the Frontier Shack lounge on the *City of Denver*, cleverly themed lounge and food-service cars were back in style: the Ranch Car on Great Northern's 1950-edition of the *Empire Builder*; the "French Quarter Lounge" on SP's newly streamlined *Sunset Limited* of 1950; and the glass-roofed, driftwood table-lamped "Sun Lounge" of Seaboard's 1956 edition *Silver Meteor*.

Canada, too, moved into streamlining in a big way after the war. In 1954–55 the Canadian National placed 359 new streamlined passenger cars in service nationwide on a *continued on page 116*

## END OF THE *CENTURY*

As departure time nears for the *20th Century Limited* standing in Chicago's La Salle Street Station in 1965, passengers are already hob-nobbing in sleeper-observation car *Sandy Creek*. Although it was still a fine train in its own right, the *Century* by this time had been diluted with coaches and economy sleeping cars—"Sleepercoaches", NYC's version of the Budd Slumbercoach—handed down from the now-defunct Century running mate, the *Commodore Vanderbilt*. In two more years, the *Century* would be gone forever.

# Rest and Relaxation in the "Vista-Dome"

## THE FIRST DOMELINER

In 1947, Chicago, Burlington & Quincy's *Twin Zephyrs* became the first trains in America to feature Vista-Domes as their regularly assigned equipment (Burlington's home-built test dome had operated on these and other trains as early as 1945). The 1947 re-equipping gave each train four dome coaches and a dome parlor-observation car—perfect for the scenic 437-mile trip, with nearly 300 of those miles following the shore of the Mississippi. On an autumn morning in 1964, the westbound *Morning Zephyr* makes a brief passenger stop at Oregon, Illinois. Leading the train (which is minus two of its domes on this day) is an A-B set of Electro-Motive E5 passenger diesels clad in stainless-steel fluting. This was passenger train design at its finest. JIM BOYD

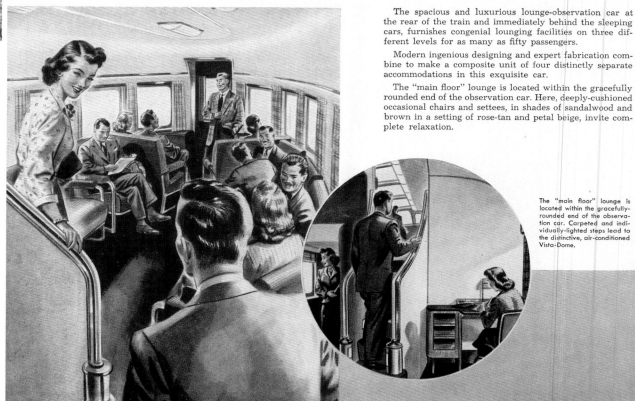

The spacious and luxurious lounge-observation car at the rear of the train and immediately behind the sleeping cars, furnishes congenial lounging facilities on three different levels for as many as fifty passengers.

Modern ingenious designing and expert fabrication combine to make a composite unit of four distinctly separate accommodations in this exquisite car.

The "main floor" lounge is located within the gracefully rounded end of the observation car. Here, deeply-cushioned occasional chairs and settees, in shades of sandalwood and brown in a setting of rose-tan and petal beige, invite complete relaxation.

The "main floor" lounge is located within the gracefully-rounded end of the observation car. Carpeted and individually-lighted steps lead to the distinctive, air-conditioned Vista-Dome.

## ROCKY MOUNTAIN HIGH

RIGHT: With Vista-Domes, the original *California Zephyr* and its foreshortened descendant of 1970, the *Rio Grande Zephyr*, provided the best way to tour the Colorado Rockies. The Vista-Dome sleeper-lounge-observation car of the westbound *RGZ* near Wonderview, Colorado, is about to duck into one of some 25 tunnels between Denver and Salt Lake.

## AMERICA'S MOST TALKED ABOUT TRAIN

To the *California Zephyr* goes the distinction of being the ultimate domeliner. The Chicago–Denver–Salt Lake City–Oakland train had as many domes as its little cousins, the *Twin Zephyr*s, but lots more in the way of spectacular scenery. The train was in fact scheduled for sightseeing more than as a fast way to the West Coast (take the Santa Fe for that). The first night out was spent covering the Great Plains between Chicago and Denver on the Burlington; almost the entire second day was spent winding along Denver & Rio Grande Western's main line through the ever-changing vistas of the Rocky Mountains of Colorado and Utah. On the second night, the train sprinted across the Utah and Nevada desert on the Western Pacific, and on the third day, before an afternoon arrival in the Bay Area, passengers were treated to the mystique of California's Feather River Canyon for more than 100 miles. Lavish promotional brochures were part of the *CZ* experience. This spread from a large brochure issued in January 1949, almost three months before the train began operation, explained the then-still-new dome-car concept with cutaway drawings, such as this of the Vista-Dome sleeper observation-lounge. MIKE SCHAFER COLLECTION

# LOUNGE · OBSERVATION CAR

Carpeted and individually-lighted steps from the lounge lead to the distinctive air-conditioned Vista-Dome—tastefully decorated in tones of sandalwood. Here, enclosed in shatter-proof, glare-resistant glass, are twenty-four deep-cushioned seats, where passengers may ride in comfort and enjoy a complete view in every direction.

Nestled beneath the Dome is a buffet. Tastefully decorated in rose and gray-green, it provides a delightful rendezvous in which to speed the miles and minutes. At one end of the buffet is a refreshment counter with carved linoleum base and back bar of stainless steel and etched mirrors. Electric refrigeration units assure an ample supply of cool, refreshing beverages at all times. The buffet has a telephone connection with the dining car, over which table reservations can be made.

Forward from the buffet are three bedrooms and a drawing-room, each having enclosed toilet facilities. Each room is attractively decorated in harmonious shades of rose-tan, petal beige, taupe and ashes of roses.

This car is completely carpeted and windows are equipped with Venetian blinds—those in the observation-lounge having drapes of gold and white.

Nestled beneath the Dome is a buffet—a delightful rendezvous in which to speed the miles and minutes.

## NANCY IN THREE-D

Even railroads of modest stature got onto the streamliner bandwagon. In 1947, the 1,800-mile Central of Georgia added two of its own lightweights to its passenger network (the railroad was already handling some Midwest-to-Florida through streamliners). The Atlanta–Columbus, Georgia, *Man O' War* and the *Nancy Hanks II*, between Atlanta and Savannah, Georgia, 294 miles. Named for a famous racehorse, Nancy became an institution on the CofG right up until Amtrak. This billboard near Terminal Station in Atlanta in 1963 was an institution, too, for several years. JOHN DZIOBKO

## GOLDEN-ERA RAILROADING IN THE AGE OF STREAMLINERS

This scene on the Pennsylvania Railroad near Philadelphia has all the look of pre-Depression railroading, but in fact was recorded in May 1955. Not everything was streamliners after World War II. Trains like this were still in abundance, but—shadowed by streamliners—their work in moving the masses went largely unnoticed. JOHN DZIOBKO

*continued from page 113*

number of trains, notably its Vancouver–Toronto/Montreal *Super Continental* (formerly the *Continental Limited*) and the Montreal–Halifax *Ocean Limited*. CN rival Canadian Pacific introduced a Budd-built domeliner as breathtaking as the Rocky Mountain scenery through which it passed. The *Canadian* began operation between Montreal, Toronto, and Vancouver in 1955, and its running mate, the *Dominion*, also received new cars.

As impressive as all these premier streamliners were, the majority of trains of the era were less glamorous. Intercity trains that were largely if not still totally heavyweight remained common, even on the Santa Fe, whose *Grand Canyon* would trudge back and forth between Chicago and the West Coast with a bevy of heavyweight cars right into the mid-1960s. Heavyweight equipment adorned all manner of secondary services on PRR routes such as Chicago–Cincinnati/Columbus, New York–Pittsburgh, Washington–Buffalo, and even New York–Chicago. Though a pioneer in the streamlining movement, Illinois Central fielded heavyweight trains almost to the end of the 1960s, among them the Chicago–Jacksonville, Florida, *Seminole* and the Chicago–New Orleans *Louisiane*. The New York–Washington–Florida routes likewise hosted a number of trains that were primarily heavyweight, including Atlantic Coast Line's *Everglades*, *Palmetto*, and *Gulf Coast Special*, and Seaboard's *Palmland* and *Sunland*.

A number of Midwestern and South Central carriers relied on heavyweight rolling stock well into the 1960s.

## CHESAPEAKE & OHIO'S F.F.V.

Bound for Union Terminal, C&O's *F.F.V.* (*Fast Flying Virginian*) cruises into Cincinnati on a sunny afternoon in the fall of 1964 following its overnight-and-half-day trek from Washington, D.C. Long a pro-passenger railroad, the C&O was among several carriers who were a bit too optimistic after World War II. The winds of change came all too soon. In 1948, C&O aborted its planned Budd-built Chessie streamliner between Washington, Newport News, Virginia, and Cincinnati and Louisville; then, in 1950, the railroad took delivery of part of a huge fleet of 287 new cars from Pullman-Standard that had been ordered in 1946, and several cars from that order can be seen in the rear half of the consist of this F.F.V. By this time, C&O realized that perilous times lay ahead for the passenger train, and thus cancelled many of the cars of this massive order before delivery. Other railroads acquired them from P-S at that time, including Rio Grande and Nickel Plate. Over the years, C&O sold some of these cars to other railroads, including Illinois Central (which removed the fluting). ALLEN BRADLEY

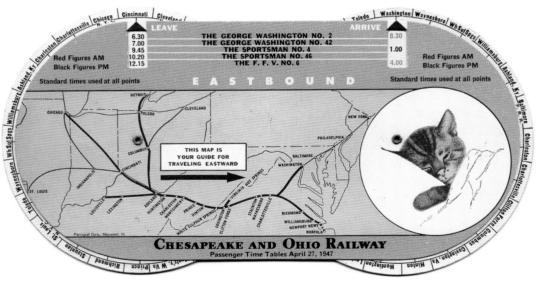

## DIAL-A-TRAIN

Although railroad timetables usually seem to read in a logical manner to railroad crews and historians, they often baffled the traveling public. To address this concern, the always-innovative C&O came up with this interesting easy-to-read timetable in which the passenger simply dialed in the towns of origin and destination and chose which of C&O's three principal trains was most suitable for his or her travel needs. Through a brilliantly executed device—this edition was issued on April 27, 1947—it had to be rather expensive to produce. KEVIN HOLLAND COLLECTION

## CORN BELT CONSERVATIVE

Chicago Great Western never went for streamlining in a big way. Rather, classic heavyweight trains like the southbound *Mill Cities Limited* departing St. Paul Union Depot in April 1948 was still a common sight on the Corn Belt Route after World War II. Behind its lanky 4-6-2 is an RPO-baggage car, combine ("smoker"), Pullman club–lounge sleeper, coach, and a motorcar apparently getting a free ride to the shops at Oelwein, Iowa. RAILFAN & RAILROAD COLLECTION

## NP'S GLENDIVE LOCAL

Hefty Northern Pacific 4-8-4 No. 2681 drifts away from its coaling stop at Beach, North Dakota, with train No. 3, the St. Paul–Glendive, Montana, local. It's July 14, 1956, and within a year, timetables will note that this train is "diesel powered." SANDY GOODRICK

Even Burlington—synonymous with streamlining since 1934—routinely operated heavyweight mail cars and reclining-seat coaches on overnight trains such as the *American Royal Zephyr* (Chicago–Kansas City) and *Black Hawk* (Chicago-Twin Cities) until 1968. On the Gulf, Mobile & Ohio, heavyweight diner-lounges, coaches, and occasionally parlor cars from the 1920s operated in Chicago–St. Louis service into the late 1960s (1971 for diner-lounges). Frisco passenger trains between St. Louis and Oklahoma and Kansas City and Birmingham, Alabama, were also a bastion for heavyweight rolling stock.

Similarly, steam locomotives lasted in regularly scheduled passenger service into the late 1950s in the U.S.—later in Canada and Mexico.

## Losses Worsen

Even new equipment and efficient motive power couldn't eliminate the losses. Between 1946 and 1958, Class I American Railroads and Pullman invested $1.3 billion in new passenger equipment and millions more in advertising. The result of this investment was record deficits as operating costs continued to rise, revenues remained flat, and ridership dropped thanks to the auto and the airplane. By 1948, the annual national passenger deficit was $500 million dollars—far more than it is today if adjusted for inflation. Many railroads, especially Eastern carriers, were hit hard. In one of the worst years, 1951, the nation's largest railroad, the Pennsylvania, lost $71 million on passenger service. The loss amounted to more than half the profit the railroad had earned in freight service. Nemesis New York Central lost $54 million the same year.

Getting out of the passenger business wasn't that easy. Passenger trains could only be discontinued through state commerce commission proceedings. Railroads were also hesitant to drop passenger service because of large, recent investments. PRR estimated, for example, that it had $863 million invested in passenger facilities (stations and yards).

Raising fares sufficiently to offset the losses proved impossible because operating costs (labor being the highest of those costs) increased rapidly and regulations hamstrung the railroads attempts to adjust fares to address market demand. From 1942 to 1953, the average hourly pay rate of passenger-service employees on Class I railroads increased 125 percent. During the same period, revenue per passenger mile rose only 39 percent.

The railroads did what they could to cut costs. Since 1944, PRR had eliminated 35 percent of its passenger-miles, NYC cut 28 percent, and B&O 23.5 percent. Those reductions meant reduced train service, and in some cases, the loss of all train service on a route. As the interlocking network of rail services disintegrated, it became harder to keep the survivors breathing. Connections dried up and fewer trains were transferring fewer passengers to each other, especially at the major terminals such as St. Louis. Many costs such as terminal charges remained fixed, but they were charged against fewer trains, so the bottom line of each surviving train became even more dismal.

## Competition Expands

Competition for rail was getting worse. By 1954, the country had spent $20 billion on highway construction in just eight years, responding to the growing demand that Americans had for the personal freedom and almost unlimited convenience offered by auto travel. Over 37 million autos had been sold since 1946, and bus companies like Greyhound and Trailways found themselves with ready made new "tracks." Impressed by

### GOLDEN STATE

Regional carrier Chicago, Rock Island & Pacific had strong ties with the Southern Pacific, with which it interchanged traffic at Tucumcari, New Mexico. Through this connection, Rock Island and SP operated the *Golden State*, a through streamliner between Chicago and Los Angeles via Phoenix, Arizona. A colorful brochure from 1957 lavished praise upon the train, but it was always the weakest of the big-name streamliners between Chicago and L.A. Little more than decade hence, the *Golden State* would be gone. MIKE SCHAFER COLLECTION

### CHOCTAW ROCKET

The Rock Island was best known for its fleet of *Rocket* streamliners, the Memphis–Amarillo *Choctaw Rocket* being one of the more obscure of the family. In 1947, the *Choctaw Rocket* is at Oklahoma City, Oklahoma, passing the city's street-railway storage yards. The "streamliner" today includes an express boxcar and two heavyweights. A pair of rare Electro-Motive TA units from 1937 lead the train. ED BIRCH

## THE MAINE LINE

Until the 1960s, passenger trains of the Bangor & Aroostook and Maine Central (MEC) reached into several remote corners of Maine, of which there are many in this largely uninhabited state. We're at one of those corners—Calais, on the New Brunswick border—on the afternoon of August 23, 1958, as MEC train 116 readies for its near-five-hour, 269-mile trip down to Bangor. A single Electro-Motive E7 powers the heavyweight train. JOHN DZIOBKO

## VEST-POCKET INTERURBAN STREAMLINER

Illinois Terminal Railroad bought three electric streamliners from St. Louis Car Company late in the 1940s. Midday on June 1, 1952, the streamliner *Mound City* trundles away from its stop in Lincoln, Illinois, while on its 171-mile journey from St. Louis to Peoria, Illinois. Though dogged with mechanical problems, the little trains—which initially featured cafe and parlor service, soldiered on to the end of IT intercity service (along with some heavyweights) in 1956. Their corroding hulks could be seen in a St. Louis scrapyard into the 1980s. SANDY GOODRICK

the amazing German Autobahn which had helped the Nazi's move troops efficiently in World War II (and prodded by the trucking industry), Congress legislated the creation of the Defense Highway System in 1956. It would create a tax-subsidized, 40,000-mile system of limited-access, high-speed roads linking the nation in the name of national defense. Suburban sprawl, high-speed highway access, and cheap gas would hit the rail commuter business and the short- and medium-distance rail business hard.

The airlines had been expanding rapidly, too, taking away much of the long-distance market. By 1957, airlines had eclipsed the railroad in total commercial passenger-miles and handled a higher percentage of total commercial passenger traffic. In 1958, with the advent of the commercial jet airliner, travel times were reduced significantly, air travel became more comfortable, and passengers abandoned trains in ever greater numbers. The airlines' amazing success story was made possible through extensive local and federal government support. New or expanded airports were sponsored largely by local (state or regional) governments, through taxing, while the federal government provided air-traffic controllers.

The railroads fought back with new designs for trains serving both the intercity and commuter market. Some were successful and some were a disaster. Budd Company's

self-propelled Rail Diesel Car (RDC), introduced in 1949, went a long way toward improving the economics of providing passenger service on lightly trafficked routes, particularly secondary or branch lines.

In 1950, the ever-pioneering Burlington introduced the first true bilevel passenger cars to its Chicago suburban services. With bilevel passenger cars came a significant improvement in economics through higher capacity at lower operating costs. The bilevel concept would have far-reaching implications, felt to this day, as the bilevel format spread to other commuter operators and, beginning in 1954, to intercity trains of the Santa Fe and, in 1958, Chicago & North Western. Today, the bilevel format has become the norm, not the exception, for commuter and long-distance intercity service.

Other passenger experiments of the mid 1950s were dismal failures. In an effort to cut costs and revive interest in the medium-distance market, a few railroads dabbled in radical experimentation that took the original streamliner format to extremes. Super lightweight, low-center-of-gravity trains such as the *Aerotrain*, *Train X*, and the original "Talgo" train failed to deliver comfortable, reliable service. Any operating savings yielded by the trains was offset by the high cost of the experimental equipment, repair bills,

*continued on page 124*

### BY MILWAUKEE ROAD TO THE NORTH WOODS

Two Milwaukee Road Ten-Wheelers— one streamlined, one not—grip the rails as they depart Woodruff, Wisconsin, with the southbound *Hiawatha–North Woods Service*. It's the summer of 1943, and the eleven-car consist seems to indicate that tourists abound in the Wisconsin north woods despite the limitations of a war-era America. The train will continue down the Valley Line to New Lisbon, Wisconsin, where it will turn eastward on to Milwaukee Road's Twin Cities main line to head for Chicago. From 1933 to 1948, the Milwaukee built nearly all of its streamlined cars in its famed Milwaukee Shops. RON MCDONALD

## BANNER BLUES (AND YELLOW)

Following Norfolk & Western's 1964 takeover of the Nickel Plate and Wabash, the N&W became responsible for the passenger trains of those two carriers. In 1967, the St. Louis-bound *Banner Blue* smokes its way of out Chicago with anything but a matching train: N&W ex-Wabash E-unit; an ex-Wabash baggage car; an ex-Nickel Plate coach; a former Wabash coach built for joint *City of St. Louis* service with Union Pacific; a second- (now third) hand Boston & Maine diner-lounge still painted Wabash; and an N&W ex-Wabash heavyweight parlor-observation car.

## SOO LINE'S *LAKER*

A head-end heavy *Laker* from Superior, Wisconsin, and the Twin Cities meets a northbound freight at Lake Villa, Illinois, during its morning trek into Chicago. It's August 1964, and the *Laker* will be history in just a few months. TERRY NORTON

### THE MORNING LINEUP

Morning sun floods the south end of Montreal's Central Station on the morning of August 27, 1958. At left, a Canadian National Fairbanks-Morse (Canadian Locomotive Company) will serve on a local passenger run. At center is the *La Salle*, about to depart for Toronto. The boxcab electric has rolled in with a suburban train from the north. JOHN DZIOBKO

### LAST PEEK AT PEKIN

Local trains like Peoria & Eastern's *Peorian*, shown at Rock Island's Peoria Terminal station at Pekin, Illinois, on October 14, 1957, were commonplace until the late 1950s. This was the last run of the P&E's train from Indianapolis, which by this time had been cut back from Peoria to nearby Pekin. PAUL STRINGHAM, WILLIAM A. RAIA COLLECTION

## THE ST. LOUIS GATEWAY

St. Louis, Missouri, was second only to Chicago as a gateway between East and West. Opened in 1894, the huge, rambling St. Louis Union Station was one of the best places in North America to watch passenger trains come and go. In this view looking eastward on August 4, 1966, most of the station throat is visible, with a portion of the landmark depot train shed visible at upper left. The station was a stub-ended affair, with tracks on a north-south alignment that swung off the east-west main line of the Terminal Railroad Association of St. Louis (TRRA). Normally, arriving trains pulled past the depot on the east-west main and then backed in. This scene illustrates the amount of activity that flourished at the station even during the waning years of the U.S. passenger train before Amtrak. As two red TRRA switchers shunt head-end cars about the station tracks, Illinois Central's *Creole* from New Orleans is starting its back-up move into the depot. In the distance, two Norfolk & Western Electro-Motive GP-series locomotives—one still in Nickel Plate colors—pull out from their storage track in preparation to taking that afternoon's *Banner Blue* up to Chicago.

*continued from page 121*

and their lack of reliability. Much of the equipment prematurely ended up on the scrap line—or in commuter service.

The late 1950s saw other milestones as the economics of the passenger train became an issue of national concern. In 1958 the Interstate Commerce Commission released the Hosmer Report, revealing that the annual intercity passenger train loss was now an amazing three quarters of a billion dollars. In response, the Transportation Act of 1958 made it easier for railroads to discontinue trains by taking the decision-making process away from the states and dropping it into the lap of the Interstate Commerce Commission.

For most American railroads, the late 1950s was a turning point. A national recession hit the railroads hard in 1958; that, coupled with the introduction of jet airliner service the same year hastened the demise of still more trains.

## Nearing the End

The industry's attitude changed from one of desperate cost control to abandonment of the long-distance passenger train and wholesale trimming of obscure branch or secondary services. Downgrades, train consolidations (two trains on similar schedules during a mutual segment of their trip combined into one over that segment), and outright eliminations picked up at a frightening pace. In 1958, New York Central permanently added coaches to what had been the greatest train in the country, its formerly all-Pullman *20th Century Limited*, while the great Pennsylvania eliminated a large number of its east-west "Blue Ribbon" trains. Other railroads abandoned entire markets. In April 1958, B&O conceded the New York (Jersey City)– Philadelphia–Washington market to rival PRR and retrenched passenger service from Jersey City to Baltimore. In 1961, Lehigh Valley's two surviving trains, the *Maple Leaf* and *John Wilkes,* made their final runs, and LV became America's first major freight-only railroad.

The list of great trains that were running their last miles was like reading like the obituary column of a retirement community newspaper. Every day a familiar face was gone. Then, during 1967 and 1968, a double-whammy caused the bottom to fall out. For decades, mail handled in storage

### BIG BRIDGE, LITTLE STREAMLINER

A few railroads such as the Kansas City Southern maintained a pro-passenger stance right up to the bitter end. KCS bought brand-new coaches as late as 1965 and assigned former-NYC observation-lounge cars to its trains, such as nameless No. 10 coming off the Mississippi River bridge near Baton Rouge, Louisiana, on January 17, 1966. The three-car train (baggage car, coach, snack-lounge observation car) is en route from New Orleans to Kansas City through territory that at the time was largely devoid of other travel options. Number 10, southbound counterpart No. 9, and their alter-ego train over the same route, the famous *Southern Belle*, did a respectable business until many of the connecting trains at Kansas City and New Orleans began to disappear. Number 10 will pick up a Shreveport–Kansas City sleeping car and additional coaches at Shreveport, Louisiana. BARRY A. CARLSON

### B&O'S WASHINGTON EXPRESS

Train 10, the *Washington Express*, was the late morning departure from Chicago of then-affiliated C&O-B&O. Overshadowed by its much more famous contemporary, the *Capitol Limited*, over the same route, train 10 provided local day service between Chicago and Pittsburgh, thence ran overnight to its namesake city. In the dog days of August 1966, No. 10 behind a single E-unit swings southward across the Pennsylvania Railroad's "Panhandle" line at Western Avenue interlocking with six cars in tow: three heavyweights (RPO-baggage, baggage, coach) and three streamlined cars (coach, food-bar coach, and Pullman-operated 10-roomette 6-double bedroom sleeper *Tuscarawas*). JIM BOYD

## PONTIFICATING *PANAMA* PASSENGERS

As Illinois Central's *Panama Limited* races toward Chicago on the morning of January 4, 1970, a passenger explains his views of the world while other lounge-car passengers listen, read, or nibble on Pecan Sandies. Frugal IC got the most out its rolling stock. This lounge car was built in 1916 as a coach. In its final upgrading, in 1952, it was rebuilt into a lounge car and here is being used on IC's premier train between New Orleans and Chicago. ROBERT P. SCHMIDT

## REDEFINING THE *EMPIRE BUILDER*

By the 1960s, passenger-train advertisements were rare indeed, but a few pro-passenger railroads still touted their trains. In this modernistic ad that appeared in a 1965 issue of *National Geographic*, Great Northern equates its *Empire Builder* to a "luxury hotel on wheels." MIKE MCBRIDE COLLECTION

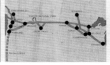

Rediscovered! The carefree way across America's great northern country. Travel relaxed aboard the incomparable Empire Builder and see for yourself what makes Great Northern really great !!!

cars or Railway Post Office cars on passenger trains significantly offset costs. But the post office had other ideas, and in 1953 systematically began moving mail from trains to trucks and planes. In 1967–68, prompted by its new ZIP mail-sorting procedures, the U.S. Postal Service did a wholesale slashing of nearly all RPO routes, a move that devastated the bottom line of remaining passenger trains that still carried RPOs. The move spelled the demise of even popular trains like Santa Fe's *Chief*.

The second blow occurred shortly after. When The Pullman Company lost New York Central—one of its largest customers—in 1958, the bottom line got tougher to meet. But when Pullman's greatest source of business, the Pennsylvania Railroad, pulled out in 1967 citing heavy losses, that was the final blow. On December 31, 1968, The Pullman Company stopped staffing its cars and collecting revenues, leaving that job to the railroads—if they chose to continue operating sleepers at all. At that point, trains that had heretofore survived the axes that had begun swinging as far back as the Depression vanished as well.

Late in 1967, the New York Central had begun a major restructuring of its passenger network that in some ways correctly forecast how, in the new millennium then still more than 30 years away, the passenger train might best fit into America's overall transportation scheme. The restructuring began on a somber note. In November 1967, NYC combined the *20th Century Limited* with the Chicago–Boston *New England States* west of Albany . . . and then on December 2, 1967, hastily discontinued the *Century*—the world's most famous train—with virtually no public notice. Shortly after, Central slashed through-train operations between East and Midwest, dropping all train names (except for the Chicago–Cincinnati *James Whitcomb Riley*, due to protests) and realigned schedules aimed at medium-distance markets, notably New York–Albany–Buffalo, which the railroad named its "Empire Corridor."

On the Pennsy side, things weren't much brighter. On December 12, 1967, the *Broadway Limited*—at this time carrying fewer passengers than crew members—departed New York and Chicago as an all-Pullman train for the last time. The *Broadway* name would be transferred to the coach-and-Pullman *General*, but the "real" *Broadway Limited* was gone forever.

In a sense, the culmination of all these draconian events can be symbolized by the passing of the nation's best cruise train, the *California Zephyr*, on March 22, 1970. Unlike the sudden, veiled discontinuance of the *20th Century Limited*, the *CZ*'s axing was a high-profile event that began in earnest several years earlier when the *CZ*'s smallest operator, Western Pacific, announced it could no longer afford to handle the train. Application was made with the ICC to discontinue WP's portion of the train (Salt Lake City–San Francisco), but it was met with so many protests—most of

## IT WAS A DARK AND STORMY NIGHT . . .

. . . for Chicago-area weather as well as the American passenger train. Passengers waiting under the scant protection of the platform canopies at Aurora, Illinois, on the night of April 12, 1970, are hoping Burlington Northern's *Black Hawk* will come to a stop and begin boarding before the storm hits full force. Tonight is the last run of the former-CB&Q overnighter between Chicago and Minneapolis, which for years also carried through cars for Northern Pacific's *Mainstreeter* and Great Northern's *Western Star*, both of them St. Paul–Seattle trains and all now operated by BN since the February 1, 1970, CB&Q-NP-GN merger. The loss of the *Black Hawk* would further erode traffic feeding the *Mainstreeter* and *Western Star*.

## CZ FAREWELL

On March 20, 1970, the *California Zephyr*s departed their home terminals for the last time, 21 years to the day after the *CZ* had been inaugurated. On March 22, 1970, and looking a mite grimy from its trek across the country, the Vista-Dome sleeper-lounge observation car of the final eastbound *CZ* is at Galesburg, Illinois, just moments before departing on the last leg of its run home to Chicago.

## ALL HAIL TO THE *CHIEF*

On March 13, 1968, the unthinkable happened. Santa Fe's *Chief*, since 1926 one of the most popular trains between Chicago and Los Angeles, began rolling out its last miles. On that day, the eastbound *Chief*, train 20, made its final departure from Los Angeles Union Passenger Terminal while its westbound counterpart, train 19, did likewise from Chicago's Dearborn Station. Had the Chiefs become skeletal remains of their former glory by this time, the loss may not have been so keenly felt, but—as this view of final 19 at Topeka reveals, the *Chief* was still a sizeable train. Alas, the loss of RPO contracts forced Santa Fe to downsize its entire fleet, and the railroad opted to retain the combined *Super Chief-El Capitan* and the *Grand Canyon* on its Chicago–L.A. route.
FORREST BECHT

them from the public sector, but also from co-operators Rio Grande and Burlington—that the ICC denied the request on more than one occasion. When it finally happened, the final months of complete *CZ* operation were rife with sold-out runs, newspaper and television stories, and public protests. The last runs in March 1970 made in front-page headlines in *CZ* locales from end to end. Burlington Northern and Rio Grande continued an ersatz "*California Zephyr Service*" between Chicago and Ogden, Utah, where passengers were transferred to the *City of San Francisco*.

## HIGH-SPEED, A SILVER LINING

If the long-distance train was dying, corridor-type intercity runs were still reasonably well-patronized, if unprofitable. The Northeast rail link between Boston, New York, Philadelphia, and Washington, D.C., had been a highly important passenger corridor for nearly a century with one of the highest riderships in the world. But, new highways and stiff competition from Eastern Airlines' aggressively promoted "Shuttle" beginning in 1961 had reduced Northeast Corridor ridership to less than half of the 1946 level of 130,000 riders a day. Yet, abandoning a rail passenger service which retained significant market share of some 60,000

riders still would have had disastrous consequences on regional highways and air carriers, where little air or highway capacity remained. So, in 1966, the federal government finally turned its attention to rail passenger, investing, with the Pennsylvania Railroad, in an order with Budd for new, experimental high-speed trains—the *Metroliners*.

Teething problems delayed their implementation until January 1969, and other technical glitches plagued their entire career. However, the all-electric *Metroliners*, which operated on city center-to-city center schedules competitive with the airlines, saved the Northeast Corridor (NEC), which today is the most important rail route in America.

## DESPERATE TIMES YIELD A NEW BEGINNING

By 1970, the passenger train had become a ward of desperately ill patients overseen by private sector railroads. There remained only 547 intercity passenger trains in the U.S.; in 1929 there had been *20,000*. It had now become abundantly clear that it would take government intervention to keep the passenger train alive—and that there were good reasons to do so. For some time, the railroads had been pressuring the federal government to help them get out from under the burden of providing passenger service.

They got help in an odd way in June 1970 when the Penn Central Railroad, born of the 1968 merger of the New York Central and the Pennsylvania, declared bankruptcy. Penn Central operated the Northeast Corridor and its branches as well as a significant number of trains between the East Coast and Midwest, so any sudden cessation of service would have had severe repercussions. PC's collapse spurred Congress to pass the Rail Passenger Service Act in October 1970, separating freight from passenger railroading and creating a federally subsidized passenger railroad (not an agency), the National Railroad Passenger Corporation, better known as Amtrak.

On April 30, 1971, the day before Amtrak was to start operations, all intercity passenger trains that were not to be included in the frugal new Amtrak-operated network—except for a few carriers that chose not to join NRPC (chapter 7)—began their final runs. The event unfolding that day made banner headlines across the U.S. and were ripe fodder for TV news broadcasts as the famous and not-so-famous began rolling out their final miles: the *City of Los Angeles*, the *Panama Limited*, the *City of Portland*, the *North Coast Limited*, the *Twin Zephyrs*, the *Pocahontas*, the *San Francisco Chief*, the *Capitol Limited*, the *San Joaquin*

*Daylight*, the *Manhattan Limited*, the *City of Miami*, the *Midnight Special*, the *Gulf Wind*, and the legendary *Wabash Cannonball*, among many other liners. Nearly all trains were packed with farewell wishers, and thousands of people stood trackside or at depots to greet final passings, arrivals, and departures.

All told, some 150 trains fell victim to the bloodbath—the largest single train axing in railroad history. For U.S. rail passenger transport, it was a day that would live in infamy.

### THE END OF ENDS

The beginning of Amtrak on May 1, 1971, spelled the end for legions of trains throughout the U.S. At Los Angeles Union Passenger Terminal on May 2, 1971, the public has flocked to the platforms to witness the final arrival of a tardy Union Pacific's combined *City of Los Angeles/Challenger/City of Kansas City*. The Santa Fe locomotives head up Amtrak's new (and at the time nameless) Seattle–San Diego train, the future *Coast Starlight*. JIM HEUER

### ADIOS

The special drumhead adorning the last car of the last westbound *City of Los Angeles/Challenger/City of Kansas City* at Salt Lake City on the night of May 1, 1971, says it all. JIM HEUER

R enaissance is a grand word that implies a new dawn of enlightenment and understanding—a rebirth, if you will. The American passenger train was in essence reborn on that fateful first day—a Saturday—of May 1971 when the newly formed National Railroad Passenger Corporation, under the still-often-misspelled marketing name of Amtrak (an acronym for American travel on track), began operating the bulk of intercity passenger trains that had survived the previous day's bloodbath (chapter 6).

This rebirth would have far-reaching effects that spread beyond the intercity passenger train to the lowly commuter train. And the effects did not stop at U.S. borders, either. Facing similar problems with its intercity rail passenger network, Canada would develop its own form of an Amtrak, with a much more stylish name (VIA), by the mid-1970s. But this renaissance, which is still under way, is not all shining rays of light beaming down on fleets of sparkling new passenger trains (all on time, of course), brimming with smiling passengers, and reaping all sorts of profit. In fact, this 30-year period of American passenger train history has been a checkerboard of triumphs (sparkling new trains) and tragedies (another bloodbath of train cuts in 1979 and 1981); amazing graces (trains reborn, such as the *Capitol Limited* and *California Zephyr*); and grueling wars (Amtrak

## BY WAY OF VIA

ABOVE: VIA Rail Canada F40s stand side by side at Toronto Union Station with the Toronto–Montreal *Meridien* (left) and the Toronto section of the *Canadian*. MIKE ABALOS

## *COAST STARLIGHT* ALONG THE COAST IN DAYLIGHT

LEFT: Shown northbound along the California Coast near Gaviota, California, in 1997, Amtrak's Los Angeles–Seattle *Coast Starlight* was, as of the new millennium, considered by many to be the finest long-distance passenger train in the U.S. because of a combination of high service quality and splendid scenery. Like some premier trains of the early twentieth century, the *Starlight* offered some interesting feature cars, including the Pacific Parlour Car with a library, games, and wine-tasting sessions. There was also a playroom for children with sponsored games, movies, and other activities. The train's primary nemesis in recent years has been timekeeping on host railroad Union Pacific. PHIL GOSNEY

## AMTRAK TURBOLINERS

For its first purchase of brand-new rolling stock, Amtrak went overseas to buy two turbine-powered trains of a type used on corridor runs on French National Railways (SCNF). The trains were already in production as part of an order for SCNF, allowing Amtrak to quickly introduce a new breed of flashy trains to Americans. The pair arrived in 1973 and were placed in Chicago–St. Louis service where they are shown meeting, north- and southbound, at the Bloomington, Illinois, station. The trains in general were well-received by the public, although in Chicago–St. Louis service they replaced dining, dome, and parlor-observation cars, causing complaints. The Turboliners, as they were dubbed, had only a modest, always crowded, cafe facility and no first-class seating. Operationally, the turbos had problems in that they were voracious fuel hogs and did not fare well in harsh winter weather. The original pair were joined by four more of the same style, and all saw various Chicago hub services, although they never strutted their 125 MPH capabilities.

## RAINBOW-ERA AMTRAK

Drifting into Kirkwood, Missouri, near St. Louis in January 1972, the New York/Washington–Kansas City *National Limited* illustrates how the infant Amtrak has begun pooling its car fleet inherited from member railroads. Two Missouri Pacific Electro-Motive E-units are pulling a former New York Central baggage car lettered for Penn Central, a Union Pacific dormitory car, UP coach, Seaboard Coast Line diner-lounge, UP sleeper, UP coach (from Washington), and a former NYC Penn Central sleeper (also from Washington). The Washington section of the train joined the New York section at Harrisburg, Pennsylvania, for the trip west. The *National* was one of the very few passenger trains to operate through St. Louis. JIM HEUER

versus host railroads, U.S. presidents, and general ignorance—both public and governmental—regarding transportation issues); commitment (will the passenger train continue to receive funding?); and—above all, perhaps—controversy (*should* the passenger train continue to receive funding?). In short, between 1971 and 2001, the American passenger train has been on an often-bumpy ride.

However one views the extent of this renaissance, Amtrak was and remains a key player. Amtrak's roots date from 1968 when Anthony Haswell founded the National Association of Railroad Passengers (NARP), a Washington-based lobby group with a daunting mission: convince political leaders to save America's rapidly unraveling intercity passenger-train system. NARP did in fact convince Congress that private U.S. railroads—then a mish-mash of corporate successes (Santa Fe, Seaboard Coast Line, Union Pacific) and tragedies (Penn Central, Rock Island)—were no longer in a position to capitalize and redevelop a world-class passenger system, regardless of their financial standing. It would be up to the government to act if it ever hoped to build a world-class rail passenger system like those boasted by other countries—nations like Japan, Switzerland, and France whose governments had long ago firmly committed to the passenger train when it became clear that public transport systems rarely make it entirely on their own—not even private-sector operators—without some help, direct or indirect, from governments.

Enough congressmen agreed with NARP lobbyists to sign a resolution on July 11, 1969: their vague goal to somehow save the passenger train. Five days later, the Interstate Commerce Commission, which for the previous 20 years or so had ruled on an alarming number of passenger-train discontinuances, announced its support of subsidies for rail passenger service.

Though long indifferent to rail transport in general, the U.S. Department of Transportation nonetheless teamed with the Federal Railroad Administration (FRA) to study the matter further. An FRA task force concluded that a "core system" passenger network coordinated by a single entity could work, and in January 1970 the DOT unveiled plans for the launching of a quasi-public passenger railroad.

On May 1, 1970, a bill called the Railroad Passenger Service Act of 1970 was presented to Congress. The Senate overwhelmingly approved it, as did the House of Representatives. This "Railpax" bill, as it became known for a time, then went to the White House. Although the idea of such a widespread, openly subsidized operation went against the very grain of Republican mandate, President Richard M. Nixon reluctantly signed it on October 30, 1970.

The bill's passage resulted in the formation of a new company, the National Railroad Passenger Corporation, which in a few months would become better known by its marketing name of Amtrak. Although much confusion

exists to this day as to what Amtrak really is—many still assume it's a government agency, like the U.S. Army—it is very much a real railroad company, but with an interesting (and enormously controversial) twist: any financial losses and some capitalization would be underwritten by the American taxpayer. All railroads then operating intercity passenger trains (i.e., runs of about 90 miles or more) had the option of joining Amtrak. In turn for being relieved of the burden of operating money-losing passenger services, each member railroad could either pay a fee—in the form of cash and/or locomotives and rolling stock—that was approximately equal to half the railroad's passenger-train losses during 1970, or they could buy shares of common stock.

The intent—some would say ruse—was that Amtrak would become profitable within a few years, even though its creators probably knew deep down that this would be a nearly impossible task, especially without full governmental support in terms of capitalization. After all, moving the public profitably on any mode is an iffy proposition (as evidenced by the frequency of U.S. airline bankruptcies), which is in part why all modes of transport in the U.S. are subsidized in some way, even if indirectly.

As the countdown to Amtrak's official takeover on May 1, 1971, began, the establishment of routes to be retained by the new carrier became of paramount concern. The White House proposal was bare bones: Washington–New York–Boston, Chicago–New York, Chicago–California, and New York–Miami. DOT's leader, John Volpe—a rare U.S. Secretary of Transportation who was adamantly pro-passenger rail—threatened to resign. After much input from various parties—including DOT, NARP, the ICC, and the railroads involved—a final, and considerably more logical, route system was announced on January 28, 1971. Although compared to the heyday of the American passenger train, this system was frighteningly skeletal, but it would serve as a foundation for some surprising growth (and some shrinkage) over the next 30 years.

Of the railroads eligible to join Amtrak, the following did: Atchison, Topeka & Santa Fe; Baltimore & Ohio; Burlington Northern; Central of Georgia; Chesapeake &

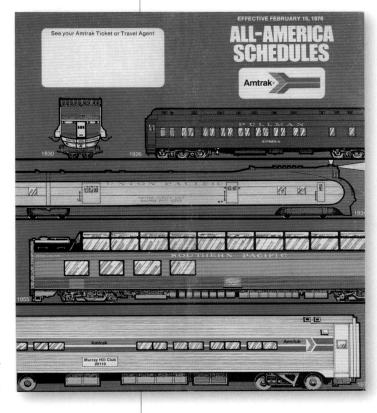

**AMTRAK TIMETABLE, 1976**

The February 15, 1976, edition of Amtrak's national timetable featured this clever artwork that illustrated the evolution of the American passenger car, beginning with an 1830 carriage-style coach, followed by a heavyweight Pullman car of the 1920s, Union Pacific's M-10000 streamliner of 1934, a home-built Southern Pacific dome-lounge car from 1955, and, finally, Amtrak's newest rolling stock, the Amfleet car. MIKE SCHAFER COLLECTION

## AMTRAK *BLACK HAWK*, WITH STYLE

Amtrak inherited a number of "feature"-type cars that had been in storage for years before Amtrak was even born, mostly observation cars, which many railroads had dispensed with by the late 1960s. In 1975, Amtrak's Dubuque, Iowa-to-Chicago *Black Hawk* sports a former New York Central observation lounge car wearing Amtrak markings—a classy conclusion to a short, three-car train!

## WELCOMING THE *MONTREALER*

New Amtrak runs were usually introduced with great fanfare—which is as it should be, to garner public awareness that "tracks were back." In the pre-dawn hours of September 30, 1972, high-school cheerleaders are on hand at White River Junction, Vermont, to greet the hours-late first run of the Washington–Montreal *Montrealer*. Celebratory new train startups had become a rarity by the early 1950s, but they were back in style in the Amtrak era, which saw the rebirth of dozens of new trains.

Ohio; Chicago & North Western; Chicago, Milwaukee, St. Paul & Pacific; Delaware & Hudson; Grand Trunk Western; Gulf, Mobile & Ohio; Illinois Central; Louisville & Nashville; Missouri Pacific; Norfolk & Western; Penn Central; Northwestern Pacific; Richmond, Fredericksburg & Potomac; Seaboard Coast Line; Southern Pacific; and Union Pacific. Those eligible to join who did not included: Chicago, Rock Island & Pacific; Chicago South Shore & South Bend; Denver & Rio Grande Western; Georgia Railroad; Long Island Rail Road; Reading Company; and Southern Railway. These railroads were obliged to continue their intercity passenger trains for at least five years, when they again were presented with the option to ante up.

The new railroad began operations with little fanfare on May 1, 1971, the previous day's carnage garnering much greater attention in newspapers, TV, and radio all across America. Whereas there had been close to 520 intercity schedules in effect the day before, by the end of May 2, when the last of the pre-Amtrak final runs arrived in their terminals, about half of those 520 schedules had been eliminated. Initially, the trains that remained under Amtrak appeared relatively unchanged from their pre-Amtrak days, as the member railroads were still providing

most operating employees, rolling stock, and locomotives and still called many of the operational shots. Most surviving trains remained on their pre-Amtrak schedules, as did the trains of non-Amtrak-member carriers.

Amtrak had been given a paltry $40 million for start-up costs, which didn't even come close to what would have been necessary to operate all the trains of the member railroads, hence the skeletal startup network and severely curtailed schedules frequencies between many city pairs. For example, prior to May 1, 1971, travelers had their choice of up to four schedules each way between Chicago and the twin cities of Minneapolis/St. Paul; three each way between Chicago and Los Angeles; and at least six each way between Chicago and New York. As of Amtrak's start, these frequencies were reduced to only one schedule each way between all these endpoints. Service between some city pairs, notably Chicago–San Francisco, was reduced to only three times a week each way. The new Amtrak was, at best, a token operation, and in its first few days the number of intercity rail passengers in the U.S. hit bottom.

Armed with its now-highly recognized (though recently discontinued) chevron-turned-arrow logo, $300 million in promised loans, and a handful of employees, Amtrak began the nearly impossible task of rebuilding the nation's rail passenger network and luring people back to the rails. One of the first orders of business addressed the equipment fleet. Amtrak had access to several hundred locomotives and some 3,000 passenger cars of its member railroads—far more equipment than it needed. The carrier selected the best of the crop (about 300 locomotives and 1,200 cars) and began re-deploying that equipment throughout the country. Within weeks, Amtrak trains began taking on a new "rainbow" look as cars from a multitude of pre-Amtrak owners and builders began mingling.

Another big order of business was to begin increasing the American public's "train awareness." Suddenly, Amtrak ads began appearing across the country, spreading the word that "We're Making the Trains Worth Traveling Again." Toward this goal, Amtrak also began establishing its own identity wherever possible through a new, unified paint scheme of red, white, blue, and silver/stainless steel along with the new Amtrak logo and lettering.

Some service improvements began almost immediately. Prior to Amtrak, for example, a passenger traveling between Seattle and San Diego had to change trains at Portland, Oregon, Oakland, California, and Los Angeles. On May 1, a new through train (then nameless, but destined to become today's *Coast Starlight*) between Seattle and San Diego eliminated all those inconvenient train changes. On the *South Wind* route between Chicago and Florida, passengers had to endure a miserable Penn Central coach train to Louisville where connection was made with the "real" *South Wind* (PC having terminated through-car operating agreements for the *South Wind*). On May 1, 1971, the new Amtrak had a shiny, clean *South Wind* in place at Chicago, complete with sleeping cars, domes, diner-lounge, and coaches, all operating through to Florida on a daily basis.

Early on, Amtrak also began expanding on its frail, basic route system. Route and service expansion were done at the behest of states, Congress, or Amtrak itself. Thanks to the 403(b) provision in the Amtrak bill, states had the option of adding service if they agreed to partial funding. The first addition to the basic system, added on May 10, 1971, was a 403(b) Chicago–New York train operating via Cleveland and Toledo, two of several major cities left high and dry by the April 30 slashing. On June 5, service was restored on the former Northern Pacific main line between Minneapolis and Spokane, Washington.

As 1971 wound down, Amtrak had begun refurbishing the equipment it had chosen for its permanent roster; famous color schemes and markings gave way to the new Amtrak image in the process. In November 1971, concurrent with the introduction of its first true, in-house public timetable, Amtrak made its initrial widespread introduction of new services, schedules, and train names. Radical (for U.S. rail service, anyway) new operations appeared, such as Milwaukee–St. Louis trains operating through Chicago. Washington–New York and New York–Boston schedules were dovetailed so that passengers could connect through at Pennsylvania Station in Manhattan; in addition, the number of through Boston–Washington sched-
*continued on page 138*

### RILEY ON THE ROLL AT RICHMOND

The Newport News, Virginia, section of the *James Whitcomb Riley* departs Main Street Station in Richmond, Virginia, in the spring of 1975. The E-unit, coach, and baggage-lounge wear the early Amtrak livery, including the carrier's famous chevron-turned-arrow logo. This stub connection off the Riley's main Chicago–Washington section at Charlottesville, Virginia, was discontinued in 1976 and replaced, in part with a Boston–Newport News train. It was just one example of how the new Amtrak was free to rearrange service to best fit customer demand, without going through regulatory bodies.

### BACK IN VOGUE: THE TRAIN FOLDER

With Amtrak came the return of the train folder, a once-popular form of promotion that railroads had largely abandoned by the 1960s. Unfortunately, the seasonal *Florida Special*—a name familiar to East Coast travelers since 1888—became a casualty of Amtrak economics. MIKE SCHAFER COLLECTION.

### RICKETY *ROCKETS*

The fabled Rock Island Lines once fielded a far-flung fleet of passenger trains, including numerous *Rocket* streamliners. But by the time Amtrak arrived, the beleaguered carrier had largely extricated itself from the intercity passenger business and had but two remaining trains, the *Peoria Rocket*—shown westbound at Joliet, Illinois, in 1975—and the *Quad City Rocket*.

### SOUTHERN'S "ASHEVILLE SPECIAL"

Southern's 139-mile, tri-weekly Salisbury–Asheville, North Carolina, run connected with the road's Washington–Atlanta day train, the *Piedmont*, at Salisbury. A remnant of Southern's once-famous *Asheville Special*, the Amtrak-era Asheville train, became a popular venue for local students learning about rail travel, as these youngsters are doing in 1975.

Overwhelmingly, Amtrak dominates America's rail passenger renaissance period. But initially it wasn't all Amtrak. There remained several intercity trains operated by the private sector in the U.S. after May 1, 1971. First and foremost was the Southern Railway, fielding three trains on its Washington–New Orleans main line and one on its Asheville line. With little confidence in the impending new Amtrak, SR said "thanks but no thanks" and continued to operate its quartet: the Washington–Atlanta *Piedmont*; the *Piedmont*'s delightful Salisbury–Asheville connection, a remnant of the old *Asheville Special*; a local between Washington and Lynchburg, Virginia; and the railroad's royalty run, the *Southern Crescent*—a Washington–Atlanta– New Orleans descendant of the streamliner era.

SR neighbor Georgia Railroad perhaps had the most unusual intercity operations as of Amtrak. Three of its four "intercity" runs were living anachronisms—mixed trains; that is, freight trains carrying limited accommodations for passengers. Georgia's Atlanta–Augusta train plying the railroad's 171-mile main line between those two points was the closest thing to a "regular" train, but even that soon became in essence a mixed train when the railroad began adding freight cars behind its single coach.

Things weren't quite as fortunate for the Rock Island, whose once-extensive *Rocket* fleet had been reduced to two trains by the time of Amtrak's start: a Chicago–Peoria run and a Chicago–Rock Island, Illinois, train.

With only two intercity trains (but a slew of Chicago-based suburban runs), the Rock calculated it to be more financially prudent to stay out of Amtrak. The twosome actually experienced modest comeback of sorts in the 1970s, thanks largely to the efforts of a Quad Cities tour operator who contracted with the Rock Island to provide first-class service and arrange group tours on both trains. As a result, the consists of both the *Peoria Rocket* and *Quad City Rocket* swelled appreciably on weekends as folks from central and northwestern Illinois flocked aboard the trains for day-long visits to Chicago. Properly promoted, people *will* ride trains.

Once the critical scenic link in operation of the world-famous *California Zephyr* of 1949–1970, Denver & Rio Grande Western was down to a single intercity train (and a seasonal ski train) as Amtrak day approached. Its

## DENVER & RIO GRANDE WESTERN'S *RIO GRANDE ZEPHYR*

Three times a week in each direction, D&RGW's celebrated *Rio Grande Zephyr* plied the gloriously scenic "Main Line Thru The Rockies" between Denver and Salt Lake, becoming a beloved, if relatively short-lived (1970–1983), Rocky Mountain institution. The westbound train is shown on the Front Range of the Rockies in 1979.

*Rio Grande Zephyr,* was linked with Burlington Northern's ambiguously named "*California Zephyr Service*" train (the ICC-mandated remains of the once-grand *CZ*) between Chicago and Denver and carried through cars from Chicago. Rio Grande backed out of joining Amtrak at the proverbial Eleventh Hour. (As proof of this, one only need to look at the map and schedules in Amtrak's first timetable, which shows an Amtrak-revived *California Zephyr* traveling across the Rio Grande between Denver and Ogden, Utah; Amtrak wound up rerouting Chicago–San Francisco service between Denver and Ogden via the Overland Route.)

Whether fueled by the increase in passenger-train awareness that Amtrak fostered on a widespread basis or simply by being "discovered" by hip travelers who knew the joy of travel for the sake of travel, the *Rio Grande Zephyr* became a much sought-after means of transport, particularly for Denver-area folks. What began as a four-car train in 1970 grew to eight or nine cars as the 1970s discoed on.

As for the remaining Amtrak-eligible carriers—South Shore Line, Reading Company, and the fabled Long Island Rail Road—all were primarily suburban-train operations and those of their trains that had been deemed "intercity" were nonetheless still closer to commuter than intercity. Consequently, the three carriers turned down the Amtrak offer and continued services to South Bend, Indiana; Philadelphia–New York; and eastern Long Island, respectively.

One of the most interesting carriers not to join Amtrak was Auto-Train Corporation, whose Washington, D.C.-to-Florida take-your-auto-with-you *Auto-Train* had only been in service a few months with refurbished streamliner-era rolling stock and a fresh, new outlook on how to pamper passengers. The instant success of the renegade operation vividly drove home the fact that innovation and marketing could lure passengers back into the coach seats and sleeping-car rooms of a passenger train. Within a short time, A-T would add a Midwest–Florida *Auto-Train*.

## BOSTON-BOUND

There's no snow on the ground at Boston's South Station on this January evening in 1982, but the air is frigid nonetheless as Amtrak's *Night Owl* awaits its late-evening departure for the overnight run to Washington. At right, the *Colonial* from Virginia has just arrived, and at far left stands an MBTA commuter train. With the 1976 acquisition of the Northeast Corridor from bankrupt Penn Central, Amtrak now had its own tracks from Washington to New York, Boston, Springfield, Massachusetts, and Harrisburg, Pennsylvania.

*continued from page 135*

ules were increased. Chicago–Cincinnati–Washington service was extended through to Boston, while Amtrak and Southern Railway coordinated operation of the latter's Washington–New Orleans *Southern Crescent* so that through cars could be handled to and from New York, including a new New York–Los Angeles sleeping car. Service was doubled between Chicago and the Twin Cities, and people in D.C., Maryland, and West Virginia welcomed the new *West Virginian* between Washington and Parkersburg, West Virginia. Whereas many trains had been operating since the start of Amtrak sans titles, classic old names—*National Limited, Hiawatha, Daylight, Yankee Clipper*—were revived to join new ones (some with twists on old names): *San Francisco Zephyr, Floridian, Saint Clair, Coast Starlight.*

On Amtrak's first birthday on May 1, 1972, the railroad unveiled a completely refurbished *Broadway Limited* between Chicago and New York/Washington. Wearing the red/white/blue/silver scheme developed by Lippincott & Marguiles, the *Broadway* sported a matching set of Electro-

Motive E-series passenger diesels pulling equipment—coaches, diner, lounge, sleepers, and observation car—originally built in the 1940s and 1950s. The streamliner era had returned!

However, the carrier was not satisfied making do with secondhand equipment. Management knew that the public wanted truly new trains and by the end of 1972 began ordering new motive power from Electro-Motive as well as two turbine-powered trains from France. In late 1973 Amtrak placed an order with the Budd Company for its first new locomotive-hauled rolling stock.

Were new routes, refurbished trains, improved services, and the promotion of all of these working? From the standpoint of ridership, yes. During the first half of fiscal 1972, ridership was up almost 13 percent over the same period a year earlier. Amtrak had managed to reverse an overall slide in rail ridership that had begun in the 1920s. More routes were added that year, including two international runs (Washington–Montreal via Vermont and Seattle–Vancouver, British Columbia), but there were some discontinuances, too.

Amtrak was growing in other ways, too. By the end of 1972, the fledgling carrier had 1,500 employees, though few, if any, actually operated or worked aboard the trains. Rather, most held clerical positions or managing positions that involved coordinating operations with the member railroads, which were providing locomotives, rolling stock, and employees—among them locomotive engineers, conductors, dining-car personnel, car attendants, and station staff—to Amtrak under contract.

If there is a key word describing a 1970s-era Amtrak, it might be "momentum." As 1973 closed out, Amtrak was on a roll that was fueled not only by the increase in ridership, but by a hyper publicized energy crisis resulting from an Arab oil embargo. Addicted to oil, panicked American drivers lined up at gas stations en masse, sometimes going as far as shooting others who tried to get in line ahead of them. The importance of alternative transportation in America suddenly became much clearer. Amtrak found itself with more passengers than it could accommodate, and itself in a frustrating position of not having enough capital to address demand. Nonetheless, several new trains and routes were inaugurated in 1974, and—prompted by the perceived energy crisis—Congress provided Amtrak with enough capital to eventually expand its locomotive and car orders. The initial 57-car order from Budd, for example, eventually rose to 500 cars.

Not everything was as rosy as the flowers in Amtrak dining cars. The increase in ridership did not translate to profitability, which Amtrak was supposed to have achieved early in the decade. In fact, costs were on the rise as Amtrak took greater control of its destiny by employing more people, buying more cars, setting up maintenance bases, building new stations, and running more trains. Amtrak critics have abounded since the railroad's formation, and the wisdom of the taxpayers funding a money-losing operation was often a target—one that wasn't easy for Amtrak to dodge, since its subsidies were out in the open. Never mind that Amtrak received but a fraction—less than 1 percent—of the total U.S. transportation budget. Further, and for a number of reasons, relationships between Amtrak and its host railroads were often tenuous. Though relieved of the financial burden of operating passenger trains, some member railroads now, ironically, regarded their obligation to host Amtrak trains as a nuisance. Timekeeping then, as now, often became an issue, and so did track maintenance. Although the Amtrak law required member railroads to maintain Amtrak routes to the standards that had existed before Amtrak, some companies—most notably the bankrupt Penn Central—simply could not. Considering the extent to which Amtrak relied on PC routes, the situation seriously affected Amtrak performance. In fact, track conditions on PC lines in Indiana deteriorated so drastically that the FRA shut them down,

forcing Amtrak to permanently reroute trains like the *Floridian* and *George Washington* in the Hoosier state.

On March 1, 1975, Amtrak got a new president, Paul Reistrup, who—unlike outgoing President Roger Lewis—was a longtime railroader who had worked in the passenger departments of affiliated C&O/B&O and IC. His railroad experience helped rectify the sometimes tenuous links between Amtrak and other involved railroads, including some of the non-member roads that were now handling passenger trains on newly established Amtrak routes.

The year 1975 was particularly significant for Amtrak in other ways as well. In April of that year, Amtrak placed its first order for Superliners—rolling stock that would revolutionize most of the carrier's fleet of long-distance trains. Then, in August, the first of hundreds of new Amfleet cars entered service, another breed of rolling stock that would define Amtrak in the years to come. Similarly, the first of what would become the signature passenger diesel of North America for the duration of the twentieth century—the F40PH—was ordered by Amtrak from the Electro-Motive Division of General Motors.

Appropriately, as America approached its 200th year of independence in 1976, Reistrup also led Amtrak toward ever greater independence. In April 1975, Amtrak acquired Penn Central's sprawling shop complex at Beech Grove, Indiana, near Indianapolis, and gained yet more control over its operations and maintenance. But one of Amtrak's most critical purchases of all came on April 1, 1976, concurrent with the birth of Conrail Corporation, another federally mandated railroad created from several

## TOASTIN' ALONG

As part of its Northeast Corridor upgrading program, Amtrak had to replace its elderly fleet of GG1 electric locomotives dating from the Depression era. It settled on a fleet of 54 brutish, boxy little electrics built by Electro-Motive under license from the Swedish firm that developed the locomotive. The powerful units—which have acquired the nickname of "toasters" (because of their shape and electric powering)—have provided reliable, high-speed service ever since. Wearing Amtrak's late-1990s blue-stripe livery, AEM7 No. 938 barrels along former New Haven Railroad trackage at Stratford, Connecticut, with Washington–Boston Acela Regional train No. 170 in February 2000. SCOTT HARTLEY

**A SEAT IN THE SIERRA**

Amtrak's westbound *California Zephyr* rounding Cape Horn in the California Sierra Range illustrates the typical look of a Western long-distance Superliner in the 1980s and early 1990s (except for the Southern Pacific business car at the end of this day's train). SP's route through the Sierra between Reno, Nevada, and Sacramento is one of the most spectacular rail crossings of any mountain range in North America.

bankrupt Northeastern railroads, chief among them Penn Central. On that day, Amtrak acquired PC's Northeast Corridor passenger routes: Boston–New York–Washington; Springfield, Massachusetts–New Haven, Connecticut; Philadelphia–Harrisburg, Pennsylvania. In addition, Amtrak took ownership of a portion of the Chicago–Detroit route. For the first time, Amtrak owned significant stretches of right-of-way (some 600 route-miles) as well as several significant terminals, including Penn Station in Manhattan.

By the time of the nation's Bicentennial, Amtrak had grown to 10,000 employees as the result of the carrier establishing direct control over station agents; coach, dining-, and sleeping-car attendants; shop forces; and station personnel. Amtrak's first five years were over, and its report

card from the public and government watchdogs was in. There was an A (mostly for effort), a couple of Bs (for improved on-board services, relative to those of the late pre-Amtrak era, and for expanded services), several Cs (on matters of convenience, comfort, and connectivity), more Ds than there should have been (mostly in the realm of equipment reliability and timekeeping), and a big F (for failure to make a profit).

## CLOSING OUT THE 1970S

With a significant chunk of real railroad infrastructure and anticipating deliveries of large numbers of new cars and locomotives and the construction of new station facilities at several locations, Amtrak continued to forge ahead. Of particular importance was the launching of the North-

**BOUND FOR SUNNIER CLIMES**
Amtrak's Chicago–Miami/St. Petersburg *Floridian* trundles slowly along Louisville & Nashville's former Monon Railroad main line down the middle of Fifth Street in Lafayette, Indiana, on a dismally damp morning in January 1977. Two years hence, the *Floridian* would be axed completely—a victim of the so-called "Carter cuts" of 1979. The discontinuance took Amtrak out of one of the biggest travel markets in the U.S.—Midwest–Florida—and left Louisville, Nashville, and Montgomery, Alabama, without rail passenger service. Since that time, Midwestern passengers bound for the Sunshine State have been required to change trains in Washington, D.C., except during a short period in the early 1990s when through coaches were offered via the *Capitol Limited* and *Silver Star*. Grass-roots attempts to revive Chicago–Florida service have been thwarted by financial considerations and an unwillingness of potential host railroads to handle the train.

east Corridor Improvement Project in 1977, a nine-year program to upgrade the Northeast Corridor for high-speed service and rebuild terminal facilities.

As new cars and locomotives came on line, they were deployed throughout the system, replacing much of the secondhand equipment—some of it dating from the 1940s—that Amtrak had inherited from its owner railroads. Nonetheless, in 1977 Amtrak had also begun a program of heavily rebuilding selected secondhanders into all-electric "Heritage Fleet" rolling stock. The conversion from archaic, steam-heated, alternator-generator/battery lighted cars to "HEP" (head-end power) electric climate control and lighting significantly improved reliability and passenger comfort.

The swearing in of U.S. President James Earl Carter in January 1977 was not-so-good news for Amtrak. Despite a written campaign platform that supported Amtrak and the fact that Democrats are usually sympathetic to Amtrak, Carter would not approve Amtrak's appropriations request for $534 million for fiscal 1978; Congress was even less understanding, authorizing but $488.5 million. The denial of full funding was a blow to the visionary Reistrup administration, which had just unveiled a five-year, $4.5 billion plan to revamp America's rail passenger network with high-speed corridor services outside the NEC; improved and expanded long-distance services; new station facilities; and new state-of-the-art locomotives and cars. A frustrated Reistrup resigned in 1978.

In Reistrup's place came Alan S. Boyd, whose main task seemingly was to save all the work that Amtrak's Reistrup administration had done. As 1979 got under way, the nation entered another energy crisis, and ridership hit an all-time high of 21-plus million while the U.S. Department of Transportation introduced a plan to cut Amtrak by 43 percent. The cuts indeed came, in October 1979. Fortunately, it was not 43 percent worth of cuts, but it was enough to send Chicago–Florida service to the crocodiles, terminate the New York–Kansas City *National Limited*, and end rail passenger service altogether in Oklahoma. On other lines, schedule frequencies were compromised.

The good news of 1979 was the arrival of the first of the Superliner fleet, which would be enormously important to the long-distance brigade. Like their Santa Fe Hi-Level ancestors of the 1950s, the Superliners were enthusiastically embraced by the general traveling public. Equally important, they vastly improved the reliability and bottom line of the always-vulnerable (to Amtrak critics) long-distance train. The first all-Superliner long-distance train was the *Empire Builder* departing Chicago for Seattle on October 28, 1979.

The 1979 cutbacks notwithstanding, a number of new services and new routes were introduced in 1979–80, most of them at the impetus of states taking advantage of the 403(b) clause in the Amtrak law. New and rebuilt locomotives and rolling stock were in place, including new high-speed (125 MPH) electric locomotives. As the end of its first decade approached, Amtrak had survived its chaotic infancy and painful adolescence and had come of age, although it still had woes and foes to face, the newest being Republican President Ronald Reagan.

The increasingly homogenized services offered by Amtrak as the 1970s wound down was relieved by the likes

## CP'S CELEBRATED *CANADIAN*

Still considered one of North America's finest trains—if not the finest—and a near perfect example of a classic from the streamliner era, the Canadian is a must-ride experience. The sleek domeliner is shown wending its way through the Canadian Rockies at Stoney Creek Viaduct in 1972. Under VIA, the original 1955 equipment is still used but has been tastefully refurbished and completely upgraded.

of D&RGW's *Rio Grande Zephyr* and Southern Railway's incomparable *Southern Crescent*. But with the end of the first decade came the death knell for some of these colorful anomalies. Already, Southern had discontinued all its secondary runs on account of dwindling patronage and increasing losses. However, patronage on the *Southern Crescent* had grown, thanks in part to promotion and a spirit of cooperation between SR and Amtrak. SR's Washington–New Orleans main line was seen as a critical link in a national rail passenger system, providing a useful travel option between the heavily populated Northeast and the swath of booming Southeastern cities like Charlotte and

Atlanta. Convinced that Amtrak could now maintain the high levels of service that *Southern Crescent* patrons had come to expect, SR conveyed operation of the train to Amtrak on February 1, 1979.

For the fabled Rock Island Lines, the news was not so good. A serious deterioration throughout the Rock's 14-state system had brought the carrier to its knees. With track speeds down to a crawl along much of the routes traversed by the two remaining *Rocket*s, which ran only in Illinois, patronage was nil. The now-bankrupt railroad simply discontinued the pair on December 31, 1978, and in 1980, the Chicago, Rock Island & Pacific folded altogether.

## Amtrak, Canadian Style

The story of passenger trains north of the U.S. border during the renaissance marked by Amtrak's birth was not remarkably different than what was happening in the U.S. The main difference was that, during the 1960s while the U.S. passenger-train network was unraveling, the Canadian National had proven that a cohesive marketing plan, new or refurbished trains, upgraded services, and aggressive promotion would indeed draw passengers back to the rails.

But CN was then in a good position to do this. It was (and remains) a sprawling transcontinental railroad; it was also (but not anymore) government run. What CN did not prove—because it didn't happen—was that passenger trains operated for the public could turn a profit. Canadian Pacific, CN's private-sector rival, had known this all along and was content to maintain the status quo as CN forged ahead with new vigor in the 1960s. By the mid-1970s and despite decent patronage on CN trains (relative to the times, at least), the lack of profitability rankled Canadian governmental leaders, and in 1976 Canada's Transport Minister called for a restructuring that included a cooperative rationalization of services between CN and CP.

Four months later, "VIA" (Latin for "by way of") emerged, a clever marketing concept borne of CN, which soon began working with less-than-enthusiastic CP to coordinate operations. Determined to relieve CN and CP of their money-losing passenger trains and enamored with the VIA image, Transport Minister Otto Lang announced on January 12, 1977, the formation of new Crown Corporation, VIA Rail Canada Inc. The new, federally funded VIA began assuming control over the operation of all CN and CP intercity trains on June 1, 1977. VIA's takeover of all CN and CP services and equipment—and 15,389 route-miles—was completed in late 1978.

From that point on, VIA proceeded on a path that was surprisingly parallel to Amtrak's. Duplicative routes and services were eliminated; the car and locomotive fleets of CN and CP were amassed into one large pool; rolling stock was refurbished complete with VIA markings; heavy promotion commenced; VIA and its host railroads squabbled over operational costs and accounting; and the politicians still argued over whether or not government should save the passenger train.

The period between 1976, when the VIA name first appeared, and 1981 saw limited service cuts, mostly with secondary trains or local routes. Meanwhile, ridership rose every one of those years: 10 percent (over the previous year) in 1977; 12 percent in 1978; 5.4 percent in 1979; 6 percent in 1980; and 5.5 percent in 1981.

### ON'S *NORTHLANDER*

The Ontario Northland Railway offered excellent service between Toronto and points north to James Bay. For mainline day service, ON purchased former *Trans Europe Express* equipment and ran it as the *Northlander*, shown at Washago, Ontario, in 1978.

### THE *RENAISSANCE*

An F40 rockets along Lake Ontario with a three-car LRC train running as VIA train 67, the *Renaissance*, near Newtonville, Ontario, in July 1993. JOHN LEOPARD

## MONON MEMORIES

As more and more older passenger equipment became surplus in the 1970s and 1980s, a number of museums, tourist operators, and even some regular railroads snapped up locomotives and cars for excursion service and other special duties. The Indiana Transportation Museum, for example, revamped a former Milwaukee Road F-unit, painting it in the colors of "Indiana's Own Railroad," the Monon Route. In this August 1992 scene, the locomotive is hauling fair-goers riding aboard a string of Budd coaches—originally built for Santa Fe's 1937 *El Capitan*—through downtown Noblesville en route to the Indiana State Fair at Indianapolis. JIM BOYD

### ALASKA RAILROAD
### *DENALI EXPRESS*

During the renaissance period of the American passenger train, leisure travel boomed, and passenger trains operating in tourist-heavy regions reaped the benefits. Alaska Railroad's regularly scheduled passenger service on the 356-mile line linking Anchorage and Fairbanks did a thriving business, as illustrated by the healthy consist (complete with dome car) of the *Denali Express*, leaving Denali Park Station in June 1985. PHIL GOSNEY

As with the Amtrak situation, a number of non-VIA intercity passenger trains survived VIA's official takeover of CN and CP passenger operations. Chief among them were trains of the provincially owned Ontario Northland, a railroad which reaches north from Toronto to James Bay. Linking the U.S. border at Sault Ste. Marie with Hearst, Ontario, was the Algoma Central whose intercity and excursion trains remained popular with tourists and sportsmen right into the 2000s. Farther west, the Northern Alberta Railway connected with CN's transcontinental route at Edmonton. In the far western reaches of Canada, nestled in the middle of beautiful British Columbia, is BC Rail, whose main route between Vancouver and Prince George provided yet another spectacular setting for intercity and excursion trains. Intercity trains survive on three of these railroads (folded into CN, NAR is the exception), separate from VIA, as the new millennium gets under way.

## On to the End of the Twentieth Century

For intercity passenger service in America, the decade spanning 1971–1981 was a frenetic, colorful, hopeful, frustrating period as toddling Amtrak and VIA struggled for identity and maturity. Having achieved this, more or less, by the early 1980s, both carriers focused on fine-tuning their systems for the ensuing 20 years that would lead to the new millennium, expanding their reach where possible and improving existing services.

As usual, though, the going was all too often a rough ride. Amtrak's out-in-front subsidies drew attention from the Reagan administration and axes were thrown Amtrak's way. Some of them hit.

Despite Amtrak's narrow slice of transportation monies (over its entire history less than 1 percent of the total U.S. transportation budget) compared to other forms of transportation, the high profile of Amtrak subsidies made them the perfect sacrificial lamb when it came time for budget-slashing. The FY1982 budget battle brought the end to several routes altogether and reduced frequencies on other lines. War-weary Amtrak President Alan Boyd called it quits.

A new era began for the beleaguered carrier when former Southern Railway chairman W. Graham Claytor was chosen as Amtrak's fourth president. As an exceptional statesman, politician, manager, and businessman, Claytor streamlined operations and improved the bottom line. He achieved marked improvements through a number of venues: leasing segments of Amtrak-owned property; increasing ticket sales through travel agencies; providing contract work for other carriers (Amtrak's Beech Grove Shops, for example, has assembled new cars for commuter-rail agencies); operating trains for commuter agencies; hiring its own engineers, conductors, and trainmen; improving labor contracts; and implementing a network of mail and express services. This last item remains an important legacy of the Claytor administration to this day.

One of the most significant route alterations in Amtrak history occurred as the result of Claytor's efforts: the rerouting of the Chicago–Oakland *San Francisco Zephyr* over the Denver & Rio Grande Western. D&RGW knew that the days of its well-loved *Rio Grande Zephyr* were numbered, mainly because of increasing costs and the looming need for equipment replacement. In July 1983, the *RGZ* made its swan-song run, effectively ending the era of private sector-operated, scheduled, public intercity passenger trains in America. In its place was Amtrak's daily Chicago–Oakland run, now re-christened *California Zephyr*. The spirit of one of America's most-cherished streamliner-era trains had been reborn as an Amtrak Superliner.

Another landmark of the Claytor years was the launching of Amtrak's own *Auto Train* between northern Virginia and central Florida. Due to a series of wrecks and management problems, the original Auto-Train Corporation had ceased operations in 1981, but in late 1983 Claytor took the concept and ran with it. Today, *Auto Train* is one of Amtrak's most successful operations, both in terms of patronage and financial performance.

The Claytor administration was also witness to one of the most successful terminal redevelopments in the whole Amtrak system. A leaking cavern of despair when Amtrak arrived in 1971, Washington Union Station faced a clouded future until Amtrak took possession of it in 1976. Working with a private developer and the City of Washington, D.C., Amtrak transformed the sprawling Beaux Arts station complex into a transportation jewel, complete with retail shops, restaurants, new ticketing and waiting areas, and a refurbished Grand Hall that often serves as the backdrop to high-brow political functions. Rededicated in 1988, Washington Union Station's success paved the way for similar developments, large and small, at other rail passenger stations throughout the U.S.

One of the most ambitious expansions in Amtrak history was unveiled in 1989 with the opening of Amtrak's 68-mile Philadelphia–Atlantic City corridor. Fed by local trains as well as through runs from outer points like Springfield, Massachusetts, and Richmond, Virginia, Amtrak hoped to capitalize on Atlantic City's rebirth as the East Coast's casino capital.

### AMERICAN ORIENT EXPRESS

Like their seaworthy counterparts, cruise trains catered to a growing leisure market who believed that getting there was indeed half the fun, especially if it could be done in style. During the 1980s and 1990s, a number of upstart companies purchased second- (or third-) hand passenger equipment for dedicated cruise-train service. Few of them survived, but one in particular stands out: the American Orient Express company, whose luxury, all-premium-class train wanders the continent on pre-advertised "sailings." In May 1999, the *AOE* skims the Pacific Ocean between San Diego and Los Angeles. The observation car on the rear was built in 1948 for New York Central's last edition of the *20th Century Limited*. PHIL GOSNEY

## ANACHRONISMS

The onset of the 1980s was a time to take last glimpses of railroading's past before new equipment and operating entities arrived. At South Amboy, New Jersey, in 1980, an elderly GG1 electric—born of the late, great Pennsylvania Railroad and now working for the New Jersey Department of Transportation—stood quietly at the head end of a New York & Long Branch suburban train, having just replaced E-units that had rolled the train in over the non-electrified portion of the line from Bay Head Junction, New Jersey. Immediately behind the soon-to-be retired locomotive is a coach that had originally been built for Louisville & Nashville's *Humming Bird* and *Georgian* streamliners in 1946. Protecting the train at the grade crossing were hand-cranked crossing gates (out of commission on this day). Today, shiny NJ Transit AEM7 electrics haul new coaches through South Amboy, and the gateman has been replaced by automatic gates.

A new boss came on board in 1993 when Tom Downs took the reins as Amtrak president. During Down's tenure, Amtrak began electrifying the Northeast corridor from New Haven to Boston. It ordered a new generation of high-speed trains designed to cut travel times in the Northeast Corridor and take a substantial portion of the short-haul market from the highways and airlines. If the concept worked, it was expected to draw 1.4 million annual passengers or 40 percent of the New York–Boston air market to the rails and 1.6 million passengers out of their autos—a 2 percent reduction in highway demand.

The model for the future—increased public/private investment and direct involvement in medium-distance passenger rail corridors—grew from the Claytor era to become a high point of the 1990s. Nowhere has this been so poignant as in California—a state once so steeped in automobile culture that it was thought the passenger train could never make a comeback there. But, in 1990 a voter-approved state investment in passenger rail in California resulted in sweeping new developments. Not only were frequencies increased on the Los Angeles–San Diego corridor (from almost the very start of Amtrak, service on this route had been growing), but some *San Diegan* runs—now called *Pacific Surfliners*—were extended through L.A. to Santa Barbara and San Luis Obispo. Where there had been four daily trains at the start of Amtrak in 1971,

almost 24 *Pacific Surfliners* plied the San Diego line each day as of 2001!

The success didn't stop there. In 1974, the state-supported *San Joaquin* had re-introduced passenger service on the 315-mile Oakland–Bakersfield corridor. The train was initially a weak performer, but the State did not give up, and, thanks to the 1990 rail initiative, today there are five well-patronized *San Joaquins* with one of them serving Sacramento. Through its bold leadership, the State also created a wildly successful new corridor—Oakland–Sacramento, 89 miles—from a route that, in the early years of Amtrak, had but one tri-weekly train, the Chicago–Oakland run. As of 2001, the Oakland–Sacramento "Capitol Corridor" featured nine weekday *Capitol* runs in each direction, plus the *California Zephyr* and *Coast Starlight*, with some *Capitol* runs extended south beyond Oakland to San Jose and east beyond the state capital, Sacramento, to Auburn. Supporting this cohesive intercity rail transportation network was a system of connecting "Amtrak Thruway" motorcoach connections that helped distribute train passengers to points not practical to serve directly by train.

All of these bolstered services required a large amount of new locomotives and rolling stock, which the State helped pay for and even design. It was a welcomed return to sanity for a state that had abandoned the passenger train in the 1950s and regretted it ever since.

Unfortunately, the Downs era was also characterized by less stellar accomplishments. Although its reliance on operating subsidies had by now dropped to about 20 percent (from almost 50 percent at startup)—making it more self-reliant than any other major public rail passenger carrier in the world—Amtrak was bullied into promising that it would achieve financial self-sufficiency in operations by October 2002, something no other public carrier in the world (in public or private ownership) has accomplished. Trains came off, most notably the *Pioneer,* whose termination severed the intercity connection between Seattle/Portland and Denver and left major parts of Oregon, Idaho, and all of Wyoming without passenger service. Its loss also hurt the ridership of other trains to which it had fed traffic. Also, Amtrak had been unable to penetrate the firmly established tour bus network that for years has flourished by feeding the East Coast gambling capital of Atlantic City, and Amtrak withdrew from the market.

While attempting to control costs, a critical concern, Downs butted heads hard with the unions and lost. Shortly thereafter he was gone, having lost support of the Amtrak board.

# A 21st Century Limited

**PACIFIC PARLOR CAR**

Passengers gather in the *Coast Starlight*'s Pacific Parlor Car (a remodeled ex-Santa Fe Hi-Level lounge car) for an afternoon wine-tasting session, with free wine, crackers, and cheese.
PHIL GOSNEY

For the better part of the twentieth century, a limited by the same name dominated the American railroad train scene. Conceived by a marketing genius named George Henry Daniels, it defeated its competitors and charmed its passengers with a simple formula: be the best train money could buy. From service to cuisine and accommodations to schedule, New York Central's *20th Century Limited* achieved that goal, earning a place in history as America's finest regularly scheduled luxury train.

Passenger trains aren't generally run that way anymore. The economics of the business tend to suppress quality. Today's typical long-distance train provides a service designed to satisfy the average passenger, but not to make him feel that he has had the experience of a lifetime. Of course, if you spend all that money to achieve mediocrity, the passenger may not remember you the next time he makes a travel choice—and if it's mediocrity he's seeking, there are plenty of other choices. They're called airlines.

But what if you could provide a train that offered truly luxurious first-class service, great food, a private glass-roofed lounge, beautiful scenery (and free wine) to those who could afford it. For the regular folks, there'd be an affordable, comfortable coach seat with room to roam and a lounge for the children, making them forget all about that nasty 20-hour bus trip they had planned. People would remember that—and most importantly, they'd come back. Well somebody's already beaten you to the idea, his name is Brian Rosenwald.

For much of the last decade of the twentieth century, Brian Rosenwald was the director of Amtrak's *Coast Starlight*—America's best regularly scheduled long-distance train. His formula was simple: give the passenger the best service for their dollar. Achieving that goal required innovation and a willingness to take risks. Rosenwald and his talented staff turned secondhand equipment into glamorous lounge cars, put together award-winning menus, trained crews in the art of real service, and virtually single-handedly re-educated America on what it feels like to ride a great name train. From this remarkable conveyance today it is possible to sip an outstanding wine, watch whales cavort in the blue Pacific, or take in the splendor of the Cascade Range.

If you want to learn what it feels like to relive the experience of the earlier great trains featured in this book, put down this volume and immediately book passage on the *Coast Starlight* between Seattle and Los Angeles. It's the closest thing the U.S. has to a *21st Century Limited*.

## THE TOUGHEST JOB IN RAILROADING

Taking over and managing Amtrak into the new millennium was George Warrington, who inherited what some say is the toughest railroad job in America. His funding and direction continued to come from the federal government, but without clear structure or policies in place for him to manage his company. As of 2001, Warrington's Amtrak was being overseen by an assortment of 535 congressional policy makers, each seemingly with his or her own personal agenda and views on how to make transportation work better—but with little or no new funding to do so.

The situation was further complicated by an array of Amtrak watchdogs: the Amtrak Reform Council (ARC)—a shadow board of directors keeping an eye on Amtrak for Congress; the U.S. Department of Transportation (DOT); the Government Accounting Office (GAO); the White House Office of Management and Budget (OMB); and the Federal Railroad Administration (FRA). Along with Congress, this alphabet soup of oversight agencies, each with its own goals and rules, turned what should be a straightforward transportation company into perhaps the biggest piece of taffy in the world, and Amtrak is constantly being pulled in ten different directions at once.

The issue of "performance" illustrates the paradox. To one policymaker or agency, performance may constitute how well you meet the bottom line. To another—a congressman perhaps—performance may mean how well you serve the isolated small communities back home which depend on your service. Both goals are diametrically opposed. In this politically charged environment Amtrak must follow the federal direction it receives, despite the lack of coordination of that direction. It must meet the bottom line, yet serve the nation with no guaranteed source of funding. With no secure capital, it has to maintain service levels, rejuvenate a passenger car fleet with an average age of 20 years, renew a locomotive fleet with an average age of 11 years, and implement a new generation of high-speed trains—each a daunting task in itself. Amtrak must also work with a diverse group of private railroads over whom it runs, while maintaining relationships with powerful unions that staff its system.

It all sounds eerily familiar to 1970, and if this were truly a private company, it would be lobbying Congress hard to get out of the business. But it's not and it can't. Amtrak belongs to American citizens, is government funded, and is by all accounts something the public values highly and wants. But how does one restructure rail passenger service to meet the demands of the future?

One option is privatization, which would bring the passenger train full circle in America. Proponents of this approach say that Amtrak and VIA should be abolished and their corridors turned into "for profit" agencies. But,

## WATER LEVEL ROUTE LEGACY: THE *LAKE SHORE LIMITED*

Skimming the banks of the Hudson River on a summer evening in 2000 is Amtrak's *Lake Shore Limited*, in the early hours of its overnight journey to Chicago. Were one to stand at this location—Cold Spring, New York—100 years earlier in early evening, you would still see the *Lake Shore Limited* heading out for Chicago. New York Central Lines launched the *Lake Shore* in 1897. It faded into history in the 1950s and was revived by Amtrak in 1975. At Albany-Rensselaer, New York, Amtrak No. 49 will be combined with the Boston section (train 449), pick up an extra locomotive, add a rake of mail and express cars, and head for the Windy City. JOE GREENSTEIN

for example, privately maintaining and revitalizing the expensive Northeast Corridor would result in service cuts and insupportable fare increases. The result? A mass exodus back to already overcrowded, publicly funded airports and "free" highways.

Although it can be improved by applying some of the principals of business, rail passenger service in this country is public; it's not a for-profit business. History proves it, and the public understands it. Referring to the collective wisdom of the common folk in a democracy, economist Frank Wilner put it eloquently, "The public is not going to permit the demise of Amtrak."

The public is right. And whether they know it yet or not, the national rail system they support may be the best hope for a solution to a growing problem which threatens the country's urbanized areas. It's a challenge that will require a shift in U.S. transportation priorities.

## THE AMERICAN PASSENGER TRAIN —ITS PRESENT AND FUTURE

Those opposed to the rail passenger option frequently cite an oft-repeated statistic that is quite alarming if viewed out of context: that Amtrak handles only about 1 percent of

U.S. travel. But it's a statistic that needs to be put in perspective on two counts. First, even the airlines, as busy and congested as they are, handle less than 20 percent of the travel market; buses handle another 1 percent or so. All the rest—about 85 percent—travel by auto.

Second, the 1 percent figure takes in all U.S. states, even those with no Amtrak service, like Wyoming and South Dakota, or very little (New Hampshire, Oklahoma, Kentucky), thus skewing the figure. The 1 percent figure goes to double digits in corridors where Amtrak has a strong presence. Between New York and Washington, for example, most travel on public transportation is by rail.

The imbalance between transportation modes is where the trouble starts. If there remains a "business as usual" approach to American transportation, the current system will eventually choke on the demand. America's shift to air and highway use, which began in earnest in the 1950s, came with astonishingly high hidden prices: pollution, traffic congestion, land loss, insurance costs, and reduction of natural resources (petroleum). By most accounts, America is fast running out of capacity on the nation's roads and airports. And it is no longer able to build its way out of the problem by adding more roads.

The U.S. spends $ 19 billion per year on aviation. Yet flight delays, attributable primarily to capacity problems at airports, grew by more than 33 percent between 1995 and 2001. It is estimated that 30 and 40 percent of all domestic flights travel less than 300 miles. Although speedy airplanes are marvelously productive over long distances, in markets under 500 miles, rail can be made competitive center to center with the airplane and relieve considerable congestion at airports, especially if direct links can be established between trains and planes, as is common throughout Europe.

Highway congestion has shifted the focus on rail transport. Despite an annual investment of $80 billion on highway construction and improvements, delays on highways serving the nation's 68 largest metro regions have nearly tripled since 1982. Some think the solution is to build new airports and highways, but the price tag might say otherwise: expanding a large metropolitan airport runs anywhere from $2.5 billion to $4 billion; building a new one costs significantly more. The amount of money needed to expand just one airport, one time, could fund an improved national rail system for half a decade.

And eventually, regardless of the desire to expand, there won't be any more room. Without change, the future goal of American transportation in more heavily populated regions won't be "how do I get there faster" but "how do I get there at all."

Rail is the obvious answer. Yet Amtrak's performance as of the new millennium has raised questions about its ability to carry the torch. Good on-time performance is a fundamental indicator of a well-run a transportation business. As of 2001, on-time statistics for Amtrak long-haul intercity trains hovered around 60 percent; corridor runs achieved 81 percent on time. Neither is remotely good enough. Between 1991 and 2001, intercity rail ridership dropped from 11.1 million passengers to 9.6 million passengers annually. Rail travel growth in the promising Northeast Corridor hasn't kept pace with the airlines. The high speed *Acela Express*, whose precious marketing budget was spent months before the trains debuted in 2000, saw a slow start in ridership and poor timekeeping. Hoped-for increases in mail-and-express revenues also have not materialized. All of these setbacks can be attributed largely to lack of dependability and convenience, not a disinterest in customers wanting to use rail. States like California and Washington that have provided strong leadership in rail passenger issues have proven otherwise.

Amtrak's dismal on-time statistics at the turn of the new century have had a great impact on business. Important mail-and-express contracts that would have underwritten costs on some long-distance trains such as the *Coast Starlight* went to the trucking industry. Amtrak's and VIA's power over the performance of their host railroads is limited.

Although a few railroads, such as the Burlington Northern Santa Fe, do an excellent job of operating Amtrak trains, others routinely hurt the system through delays resulting from questionable dispatching or through capacity problems brought on by the railroads themselves having wantonly abandoned alternative routes in the name of short-term financial gains.

It's a game of Catch 22. Amtrak's current fees to the railroads are inadequate in terms of paying for upgrading lines. Yet without infrastructure improvements, passenger traffic won't grow to justify a greater investment.

Future markets await long-overdue improvements, such as the corridor routes—existing and potential—hubbing at Chicago. Investing in those lines and routes is a policy decision, not an operating one. Already, several Midwestern states have formed a coalition to develop some Midwest routes into high-speed corridors, but they won't be successful

*continued on page 155*

## WASHINGTON UNION STATION

Amtrak's crown jewel property just might be Washington Union Station, thanks to a massive makeover of the grand depot in the late 1980s. Now filled with chic retail outlets, restaurants, and new passenger facilities, WUS turned a liability into a vibrant asset.

## AMTRAK MOVES THE MAIL (AND EXPRESS)

On more than one occasion, Amtrak has reinvented the wheel. Nowhere, perhaps, has this worked better than with the development of mail and express (M&E) business as a significant source of extra revenue. Though purists may scoff at the mail and express now being handled on even the big name trains—such as the *Southwest Chief*, whose M&E RoadRailers fly past the photographer at Model, Colorado, in September 1999—mail and express has long been an important revenue producer for passenger trains. TOM KLINE

# A Tribute to the Lowly Commuter Train

It is the passenger train that few people give much thought to—yet it's the passenger train that moves most Americans on any given week day. It is the lowly commuter train. Where does it hide out? Traditionally, large metropolitan areas like New York, Chicago, and Philadelphia. But their kind is spreading. And none too soon.

The commuter train—a.k.a. the suburban train—falls into the realm of this book in that it is a close cousin of the traditional passenger train: conventional-size coaches propelled by a locomotive (or self-propelled by traction motors) for the purpose of moving people from one city to another (usually from a central large city to surrounding suburbs or "satellite" cities). Contrast this with "light rail" (trolleys) or "heavy rail" rapid transit (subways), which primarily function to move people about *within* a metropolitan area.

Suburban-type train service dates back to the nineteenth century, and from then through most of the twentieth century, local railroads provided commuter service, and the general format was a glut of trains into the city in the morning and back out during the evening rush hour, with occasional service during non "peak" periods to accommodate casual travelers and shoppers or the relatively few workers then who abided by non-traditional workday hours.

New York City has by far the most extensive commuter-rail network, initially operated by numerous individual carries: Long Island Rail Road (still the number one busiest commuter railroad in America); New York Central; Pennsylvania; New York, New Haven & Hartford; Delaware, Lackawanna & Western; Erie; Central Railroad of New Jersey; New York & Long Branch (jointly operated by PRR and CNJ); and New York, Susquehanna & Western.

The Second City, Chicago, was next in line, with suburban service provided in varying degrees by Illinois Central; Chicago & North Western; The Milwaukee Road; Burlington; Rock Island; Wabash; Pennsylvania; New York Central; Gulf, Mobile & Ohio; North Shore Line; South Shore Line; Chicago Aurora & Elgin; and Chicago & Western Indiana.

Remaining large cities with extensive commuter-rail operations included Philadelphia (PRR, Reading) and Boston (Boston & Maine, New Haven,

## STAND BEHIND THE YELLOW LINE

ABOVE: A group of schools kids on a special weekend trip give the time-honored "blow the horn" signal to the engineer of Metro-North train No. 8723 out of Grand Central, as it enters the Dobbs Ferry, New York, station on November 4, 1995. JOE GREENSTEIN

## ROCK FEST

LEFT: As an F-unit-powered Rock Island commuter train backs in toward Chicago's La Salle Street Station from the storage yard on a late afternoon in 1965, another run heads out for Joliet behind an Alco road-switcher. Both trains sport 1920s-era "Al Capone" suburban coaches, many of which would remain in active duty well into the 1970s.

## NEW YORK CENTRAL SUBURBAN RUN

A New York Central Pacific lopes along the Brewster Line with a three-car commuter train circa 1950. There was a time when commuter operations were treated pretty much as a second-class operation, although timekeeping has always been of paramount importance to impatient commuters. But equipment usually was long outdated, and, when it was finally replaced, it often was with surplus lightweight streamlined equipment. JAY WILLIAMS COLLECTION

and New York Central). Beyond that, commuter operations were less comprehensive, but they could be found in Montreal, Baltimore-Washington, Cleveland, Pittsburgh, Newark, St. Louis, Milwaukee, and Detroit. On the West Coast, Los Angeles had extensive interurban service through the sprawling Pacific Electric until after World War II, but true commuter-rail service was almost non-existent. In the San Francisco Bay Area, however, Southern Pacific fielded a busy commuter-rail route between San Jose and San Francisco proper, while across the bay in Oakland, interurbans transported workers into both Oakland and San Francisco. Portland, Oregon, for a time also enjoyed suburban service offered through Southern Pacific.

Since travel was usually of short duration, commuter trains largely were and are a no-frills operation, and railroads were usually loathe to spend any more than absolutely necessary on suburban equipment. Well into the 1970s, it was possible to ride in 1920s-era non-air-conditioned, open-window suburban cars on a number of commuter lines.

The coming of the automobile in the early twentieth century curtailed many a commuter operation, and by the post-World War II period, railroads were getting restless about getting out of the commuter business. Had it not been for the tremendous amount of bad publicity and political ramifications that would have resulted from such action, more railroads probably would have left the suburban business years ago.

A few railroads went out of their way to upgrade their suburban offerings, and Chicago was witness to the first widely successful commuter

## ON THE (BI) LEVEL

TOP: Every weekday, hundreds of bilevel cars like these veterans of the Chicago, Burlington & Quincy and Burlington Northern at Metra's Hill Yard in Aurora, Illinois, carry thousands of people to work. The bilevel gallery car was instrumental in improving the ratio between cost and revenue on commuter operations throughout North America. The scene also illustrates a bane of commuter operation: commuter equipment sees most of its use only during two narrow periods of a workday—morning and evening rush hours—and the rest of the time lays idle. On weekends, CB&Q offset this problem by running its suburban equipment on special excursion trains, and some commuter cars were even pressed into intercity service. JOE MCMILLAN

## COLOR CODED TIMETABLES

ABOVE: As is common practice, commuter operators issue separate timetables for each line. Chicago's Metra did likewise, but also color-coded timetables for each line, based in part on colors used by the heritage railroads that make up today's Metra system. ANDOVER JUNCTION PUBLICATIONS

service innovation: the "gallery" commuter coach. Chicago, Burlington & Quincy was first to offer these high-capacity cars, in 1950, when it took delivery of new stainless-steel bilevels built by the Budd Company. Their upper-level gallery-style seating virtually doubled passenger capacity, allowed for shorter trains and faster schedules, and provided commuters with air-conditioned comfort. The gallery-car format caught on, and soon found its way to other commuter railroads, in Chicago and elsewhere.

Chicago-area railroads also popularized an operating format that has become nearly universal in commuter-rail operations where separate locomotives are employed: "push-pull." The locomotive, either diesel or electric, is positioned at one end of the train. It pulls in one direction (usually outbound from the main terminal) in the traditional manner, with engine crew in the locomotive, and pushes on the return trip, with the crew operating the locomotive from a control cab in the end of the car at the opposite end of the train. This scheme saves the time and expense of turning a locomotive at the end of every run, as was the case in the steam era.

As the postwar years rolled on, suburban service became almost as much of a financial burden for railroads as intercity service. Spurred by Amtrak's formation, perhaps, a number of new public agencies arose in the U.S., created to at least oversee funding for suburban-train operations if not outright assume operation of them. Among the earliest was Chicago's Regional Transportation Authority, a funding district created in 1974 in which a gas tax was levied for the improvement and operation of the area's public transportation. Under the RTA umbrella, Metra in the 1980s assumed the operation of most Chicago-area commuter-rail operations.

## PHILADELPHIA'S SEPTA SYSTEM

An m.u. train accelerates away from its station stop in Philadelphia's new City Center tunnel in 1986. Linking former Reading commuter lines with those of the former Pennsylvania Railroad, the new tunnel consolidated downtown suburban train access.

## PASSING THROUGH PASSAIC

An Erie Lackawanna commuter train pulled by an Alco road-switcher still wearing Erie Railroad markings (Erie and Delaware, Lackawanna & Western merged in 1960 to form EL) pauses in downtown Passaic, New Jersey, early in 1962. This line has since been abandoned, and today NJ Transit commuter trains use a bypass route around town. JOHN DZIOBKO

Similar new publicly sponsored entities began relieving private-sector railroads of their suburban operations all over the country. In the New York City area, suburban trains are now funded, governed, and/or operated by various agencies and operating companies: Metropolitan Transportation Authority (overseeing Metro North Railroad and the Long Island Rail Road), New Jersey Transit, and the Connecticut Department of Transportation. In Philadelphia, the Southeastern Pennsylvania Transportation Authority assumed area suburban operations; in Boston, the Massachusetts Bay Transportation Authority—the "T"—operates the commuter trains. On the San Francisco peninsula, Caltrans (California Department of Transportation) operates CalTrain service. In the Washington-Baltimore area, MARC (Maryland Rail Commuter) assumed the operation of commuter trains of Baltimore & Ohio and Pennsylvania Railroad heritage.

Whereas the coming of the automobile doomed many suburban operations earlier in the twentieth century, by the end of that same century, the auto was fast becoming responsible for the birth of all-new commuter-rail systems in cities that were experiencing rapid postwar growth. This had happened as early as 1967 when the Government of Ontario, with far more foresight than its U.S. peers, established a brand-new commuter-rail service, known as GO Transit, in Toronto. Not until the 1980s did U.S. city fathers begin turning to commuter rail as a very cost-effective solution to growing traffic problems. Suddenly, commuter-rail systems blossomed where none had been before, at least not in recent history.

Most notable among these newcomers was the second largest city in the U.S., Los Angeles, which for decades had no regional rail transport services. Now, the sprawling L.A. Basin is bound by a network of trolley, subway, and commuter-rail (known as Metrolink) lines. Metrolink operates over Union Pacific and former Southern Pacific and Santa Fe trackage, and its trains converge on Los Angeles Union Passenger Terminal where easy connections can be made with Amtrak and a new subway line. Other new systems are now serving Dallas-Fort Worth, Texas (Trinity

Express); Miami, Florida (Tri-Rail); San Diego and San Jose, California (Coaster and Altamont Commuter Express, respectively); Seattle, Washington (Sounder); Washington, D.C. (Virginia Railway Express); New Haven, Connecticut (Shore Line East); and Burlington, Vermont. Meanwhile, still other cities—among them Atlanta, St. Louis, and Madison, Wisconsin—have been considering adding commuter rail to address traffic concerns.

These new startups employed both brand-new and refurbished second-hand equipment—some of it converted long-distance cars and locomotives from the streamliner era or refurbished equipment purchased secondhand from other commuter-rail operators. Meanwhile, the long-established systems of Chicago, New York, Philadelphia, Boston, and other cities continue to take delivery of new locomotives and rolling stock—most of it of bilevel format—and at the same time implement new routes while planning for future expansion to meet growing demand.

The commuter train has finally come of age.

## TALGO TODAY

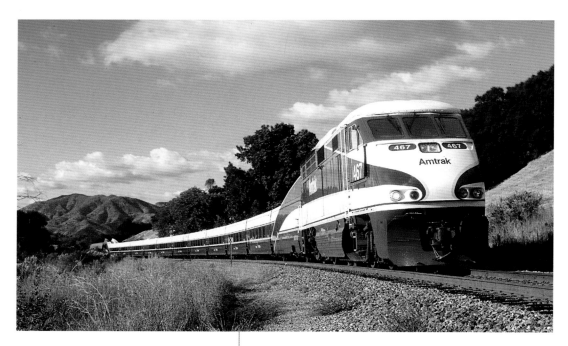

At the end of the 1990s, "Talgo"-style trains were the hottest new thing on North American rails—although they weren't really new at all. Talgo is an acronym: T = Train, A = Articulation, L = Lightweight, G = Goicoecha (the train's inventor), O = Oriol (the train's original financier). The technology was first tested on several U.S. lines in the 1950s but flopped. Since then, these speedsters have come of age and new Talgo trains—such as that shown during a special run in California in 1998—are drawing customers back to the rails in large numbers on Amtrak's Cascadia Corridor in the Pacific Northwest. The low-slung trains are pulled by conventional Electro-Motive FP59HI diesels outfitted with special shrouding to blend with the low-profile Talgo cars. PHIL GOSNEY

## A TASTE OF EUROPE IN AMERICA

In a scene that is reminiscent of Europe, one of Amtrak's all-electric, high-speed *Acela Express* trains glides across the Norwalk River at Norwalk, Connecticut, en route to Boston in July 2001. Will these sleek runners be the key to the future of the American passenger train?

*continued from page 149*

without clear direction, long-term commitment, and funding illustrated by California and Washington state.

Regardless of the past, there are a number of important reasons why passenger rail is the right investment for the future. The first is public support. As outlined above, the public has consistently supported increases in rail passenger service. A second reason is its available capacity. Adding capacity to some rail routes can be as simple as adding cars to existing trains or new trains to existing routes which have the capacity to handle them. In other words, unlike American highways and airports, excess capacity is readily available on many rail lines. Third, rail corridor expansion is already working where well managed. In the Pacific Northwest, on the 466-mile Vancouver (British Columbia)–Seattle–Portland–Eugene, Oregon, "Cascadia Corridor," European-style Talgo trains entered service beginning in 1993. Their astounding reliability rate of 99.9 percent convinced Amtrak and Washington State to invest in new trains in 1996. In 1998 three new custom-built Talgo trains entered service on the corridor. The trains' attractive looks coupled with incremental speed increases, schedule frequency increases, and excellent marketing resulted in a positive response similar to the streamliner phenomenon of the 1930s. Now citizens in the Northwest are supporting rail passenger service even more strongly. Ridership growth has been consistently rising in double digits annually. Between 1993 and 2001, ridership on the route grew an amazing 460 percent.

Rail is also the most cost-effective investment of tax dollars in corridors. Shifting medium-distance travelers from air to rail would free up gate space at existing airports to handle more-productive long-distance flights, thereby reducing costly investments in airport restructuring. Enhancing passenger rail in corridors is also much more cost effective than highway construction. Says Amtrak's Warrington, "We can move 450 people for every million dollars spent on track versus 45 people for every million dollars spent on highway lanes . . . We can add a third track for 125 MPH train travel along the Northeast Corridor for 8 million dollars a mile . . . yet another lane on I-95 would cost more than six times as much . . . The public policy choice should be obvious."

Finally, rail is the clear environmental choice. Railroads are more energy efficient than airlines using 2,441 BTU's per passenger-mile versus 3,999 BTU's. Since 1975, shortly after a major Middle East oil crisis proved the chilling reality of dependence on foreign oil, the airline industry has nearly doubled its consumption of fuel. Without a national policy shift to a wiser use of scarce resources, the problem will continue.

But what about the long-distance train—the *Empire Builder*s, the *Lake Shore Limited*s, the *Silver Meteor*s?

Opponents of rail passenger have labeled these as expendable "leisure" trains for the rich and retired. By their nature, long-distance trains are indeed the most expensive to operate, primarily because they are labor-intensive. A flight from Chicago to Seattle requires one plane, one crew, and about three hours. There is no need for an *Empire Builder*. (Or a *Southwest Chief*, or a *Sunset Limited*.)

Or is there? While the layman may assume that the Chicago–Seattle/Portland *Empire Builder* is designed to take people from Chicago to Seattle and Portland, a ride aboard the train between those points reveals otherwise. The daily train leaves Chicago with relatively few people going all the way through to the West Coast. Rather, it is used by passengers traveling from, say, Chicago to Havre, Montana; Milwaukee to La Crosse, Wisconsin; Minneapolis to Minot, North Dakota; and Glacier Park to Seattle—intermediate city pairs that do not necessarily have alternative public transportation. Besides, there are few better ways to learn about geography and culture, or to meet fellow travelers than a long-distance train.

Critics of the American passenger train state that its low-profile relativity in today's world signifies that it has outlived its usefulness. But the fact that some 22 million people still choose intercity rail passenger transport in America every year despite all of its (solvable) shortcomings—and there are many, from poor timekeeping to limited schedule choices—may indicate a potential waiting to be realized.

The passenger train will never again reign supreme as it did at the start of the twentieth century. But like all transportation modes, rail passenger has its place, and it has a future in a balanced transportation system. Whether that future is bright or dim remains to be seen.

### CALIFORNIA DREAMIN' BECOMES A REALITY

No state has addressed the development of rail passenger in recent years more effectively than California. Thanks to a very goal-oriented program and enthusiastic voter support, California's most heavily populated regions are now blanketed by a well-balanced, comprehensive network of medium-distance trains: the *Pacific Surfliner*s, the *Capitol*s, and the *San Joaquin*s, most of them featuring equipment of the latest design, including bilevel "California cars" whose design was spearheaded by Caltrans. An all-matching set of California equipment sweeps along San Pablo Bay as train 711, the first morning *San Joaquin* up from Bakersfield to Oakland, in March 2001. PHIL GOSNEY

# INDEX